ACCLAIM FOR NIGERIA REVISITED

Catherine Onyemelukwe embodies the best American attributes—a keen sense of adventure and curiosity, a can-do spirit, and a brave, ebullient heart. Going to Nigeria as a Peace Corps teacher in the early 1960s, she found the love of her life, mastered the Igbo language, and immersed herself in a moving, often complicated, relationship with Nigeria, especially with her husband's Igbo culture. Her memoir mines the rich vein of her experiences on two continents.

It's an absorbing account by a woman for whom the role of a passive bystander is always out of the question, filled with captivating anecdotes and told with the flair and narrative style of a consummate raconteur. This book, imbued with great laughter and humor as well as heartbreak moments, deserves—and is bound to find—a large, wide and enthusiastic readership.

> Okey Ndibe, Visiting Assistant Professor of Africana Studies,
> Brown University, author of *Foreign Gods, Inc.* and *Arrows of Rain*

Catherine Onyemelukwe's life story is a fascinating read. It's a brutally honest account of the intricacies of straddling two societies, of seeking to absorb the Igbo culture of her husband while trying to maintain her Midwest American sensibilities. And this while living in Nigeria during the politically tumultuous post-independence years of military coups and a civil war.

> Ebong Udoma, Senior Reporter, Connecticut
> State Capitol reporter, WSHU Public Radio Group

Courageous and candid, Onyemelukwe reports from the front-lines of tumultuous times--the New Frontier Peace Corps, Biafra, sexual and racial revolutions worldwide. Her fast-paced tale speeds from Cincinnati, New England, and Los Angeles to Lagos, Onitsha, and Enugu and back, with side-trips to Madeira, Madrid, and London. All the while a reader grows ever fonder of this daring author and the remarkable life and family she has crafted. Hold on tight!

> John Lemly, Professor of English and African Studies,
> Mount Holyoke College; Book Review Editor, African Studies Review

As my graduate student, Catherine displayed a firm grasp on the aspects of an emerging economy like that in Nigeria. Her years abroad expanded her perspective on both business overseas and life at large. Her book deftly captures her journey as an entrepreneur and beyond.

Sharon M. Oster, Frederic D. Wolfe Professor of Management
and Entrepreneurship, Yale School of Management

Nigeria Revisited is a lovingly written narrative of a fascinating people and nation that is little known and widely misunderstood. As a Peace Corps Volunteer, Onyemelukwe first fell in love with the country and its people and then with Clement who became her husband. Her perspective is unique, her insights are enlightening, and her story is delightful.

Charles F. "Chic" Dambach, Author, Speaker, Consultant,
Past President, National Peace Corps Association,
Author of *Exhaust the Limits*

For many baby boomers, the Peace Corps was the road not taken. This fascinating memoir gives us a glimpse of one woman's intrepid journey down that road.

Susan Boyar, Professional Book Group Facilitator, Weston, CT

Catherine Onyemelukwe is unique among my friends in her ability to balance what seems a normal, even prosaic, middle-class, comfortable American life with her almost unimaginable past and present life in Nigeria. She has brought her polished and accessible narrative skills to her memoir *Nigeria Revisited*, capturing her bifurcated life in a truly excellent read.

Denise Taft Davidoff, Senior Consultant for Development and
Alumni/ae Affairs Meadville Lombard Theological School,
Former Moderator, Unitarian Universalist Association

NIGERIA REVISITED

My Life and Loves Abroad

To Diana,
Thanks so much for
coming to hear my
story.
Catherine
May 2015

CATHERINE ONYEMELUKWE

A PEACE CORPS WRITERS BOOK

Nigeria Revisited: My Life and Loves Abroad
Catherine Onyemelukwe
A Peace Corps Writers Book
An imprint of Peace Corps Worldwide
Copyright © 2014 Catherine Onyemelukwe
Printed in the United States of America
by Peace Corps Writers of Oakland, California.
For more information, contact peacecorpsworldwide@gmail.com.

Peace Corps Writers and the Peace Corps Writers colophon are trademarks of
PeaceCorpsWorldwide.org.
Cover design by Miggs Burroughs
ISBN: 1935925474
ISBN-13: 9781935925477
Library of Congress Control Number: 2014953038
First Peace Corps Writers Edition, October 2014

With love to Clement,
without whom this story would not exist,
and to our amazing children, who are at home in both our worlds,
Nigeria and the United States,
Chinaku
Beth
Sam

Nwa nne di na mba.
Even in a strange land, a brother can be found.[1]
Oji luo uno okwuo ebe osi bia.
When the Kola nut reaches home, it will tell where it came from.[2]

1   http://nigeriavillagesquare.com/forum/lounge/21191-inu-igbo-sayings.html
2   http://www.igboguide.org/HT-chapter8.htm, Copyright © 2000-2011 Michael Widjaja

TABLE OF CONTENTS

PREFACE

NIGERIA'S PEOPLE FEEL strong ties to their country but also to family, clan, and tribe. The ties exist even for people from Nigeria who spend years away from the country, in the diaspora, as they say.

The country also creates a strong bond in foreign residents. Peace Corps volunteers in particular who spent time, often in close contact with colleagues, host families, students, and friends, feel connections to the country long after they leave.

I spent the usual two years as a Peace Corps volunteer. Because I fell in love and married, I stayed for another twenty-two years. Both our sons live in Nigeria today. I am pulled back to the country frequently.

I want to explain how Nigeria has such a hold on me.

I lecture frequently about Nigeria, its customs, and its culture. Those who have heard me ask if I have written a book. *Nigeria Revisited* is my answer.

Catherine Onyemelukwe
Westport, Connecticut
September 2014

ACKNOWLEDGMENTS

My MEMOIR AND essay writing class at Westport Writers Workshop in Westport, Connecticut, was an essential part of completing this memoir. Special thanks to our instructor, Marcelle Soviero, herself an accomplished writer, who was an invaluable guide and later my wise editor.

Several women were in the class with me for most of the two years and three months of my writing: Mary Ann Cooper, Daisy Florin, Ellyn Gelman, Christine Juneau, and Aline Weiller. They provided supportive, often brilliant, feedback and encouragement. Randi Olin, Michelle Turk, and Jennifer Smyth were there for less time but gave no less valuable critiques.

Thank you to Judy Hamer, Bill Buckley, Ann Kuehner, and Beth Hardy for reading and recommending changes to improve the manuscript.

Thanks to Gail Harris, my thorough copy editor, who had to cope with unfamiliar Igbo words, names, and phrases.

Doris Brenner, now deceased, was my friend at the Unitarian Church in Westport. She invited me to her home so she could listen to my stories and I could record my responses. After each session, she served tea and cakes to me and her husband Mel. Her interest and reassurance helped me understand that I actually could write my memoir.

Most of all, thank you to my husband, Clement, for his encouragement and for giving me the story, and to our children for providing much of the content in their experiences.

INTRODUCTION TO NIGERIA REVISITED: MY LIFE AND LOVES ABROAD

NIGERIA EXERTS A powerful hold on people. The ties to one's Nigerian home are strong and cannot be broken, even for Africans who live far away for dozens of years. Foreigners who live in Nigeria for any length of time feel the ties as well.

My own ties to Nigeria go back to the day in my senior year of college at Mount Holyoke when I received my acceptance letter from the Peace Corps. The Peace Corps was then in its infancy. I was given the assignment to teach German. I would be separating from good friends and family, going first to California for training, then on to Africa.

I had no idea then, but I was on my way to more than just two years as a Peace Corps volunteer in Nigeria. At that time, I knew nothing about the country where I was headed and little about how to teach the language I had learned during my years at college. Yet I was excited and eager to begin the next stage of my life.

I started my career in Nigeria as a Peace Corps volunteer and continued to teach after my Peace Corps service was over. But more importantly, I fell in love, married, became part of an extended family, raised three children, and learned my husband's customs and language. I helped start an organization for foreign wives of Nigerians that is thriving today. I created and ran a business. I became part of a country and culture completely different from mine.

During twenty-four years, I shared the difficulties of war and the joys of watching our children grow up with my family and friends in Nigeria. Twice, I spent extended periods away from Nigeria and my husband. And I learned about myself and developed my commitment to social justice along the way.

1

AFRICA UNVEILED

"WAKE UP. WE'RE in Africa." I nudged my companion Art and leaned over him to look through the plane's window. "Wake up. You have to see the sunrise." The vivid red, yellow, and orange were startling.

I descended the steps onto the tarmac. I felt like I'd walked into a wall of heat and humidity. I pulled off my sweater as I approached the shabby, single-story, cinder-block terminal—the Lagos International Airport.

"The American ambassador is here to welcome you," a man said, guiding me toward a tall, distinguished man standing at a podium on the tarmac.

The ambassador stepped forward, wiping his brow. "One of my proudest occasions as the representative of the United States is to greet Peace Corps volunteers and send you off for service to this great nation." He concluded with praise for the Peace Corps country director and staff.

I'd had enough of speeches. I wanted to see Africa and Africans.

Palm trees lined the road leading out of the airport. I could have been in Los Angeles, where I'd completed my Peace Corps training two weeks earlier. But when the bus turned onto a main thoroughfare and the trees were replaced by open gutters, which I saw and smelled at the same moment, I could no longer mistake the scene for Southern California.

Some men were in long white robes and skullcaps; others were in open shirts or dashikis. Women wore wrappers and head ties in bright blues, greens, and reds. Several had babies tied on their backs, a few had bundles on their heads, and some had both. It was just like I'd seen in pictures, but it was real, jubilant, and exciting.

And the noise matched the color, with loud voices in Yoruba, English, and other languages. I forgot my tiredness as I absorbed the shouts and laughter that poured into the bus.

I began noticing the ads, not just huge billboards but smaller signs—many handmade—that hung or stood outside houses and along the street, promoting the services of carpenters, dressmakers, tailors, and electricians. "Sew your wedding dress here," I saw. I spotted, "Consult the herbalist to solve your problem with gonorrhea!"

Then we were on Carter Bridge, the only link from the mainland to Lagos Island, the heart of the city. We were surrounded by bicycles, many battered and worn. Across the bridge, there were more people, more and larger buildings, and all more closely crowded together. Our Peace Corps handler pointed out the Lagos Central Mosque, an impressive concrete structure that dominated a stretch of the left side of the road, with Arabic designs painted on the reddish-brown walls. Its four minarets, tall spires with onion-shaped crowns, stood out.

In another few minutes, the bus stopped in front of a drab, three-story block of apartments. My training roommate, Mary, and I were given a minimally furnished room to share. The whole building smelled of wet cement.

A few hours later, the other volunteers and I were escorted to dinner at the nearby Federal Palace Hotel. Sitting in the lobby's plush armchair with a cool drink in my hand, I laughed at the absurdity. "This is Africa?" I said to Art.

We were ushered into the dining room and seated at tables for eight with white linen tablecloths and napkins, silverware, and glassware. The waiters, well-mannered and attentive in their white coats, didn't seem like real Africans. I could still have been in New York.

But the salad made me hesitate. Peace Corps trainers had stressed that I must not eat untreated vegetables. If not cooked, then all vegetables, including salad greens and tomatoes, should be soaked in Milton or another antiseptic solution to kill the bacteria. I glanced across to the Peace Corps director at the next table. He was eating it—it must be safe.

Then came the main course—steak and potatoes—with nothing African about it. I was disappointed but hungry. I had a few bites left when I paused to speak to Mary. The waiter was clearing others' plates when he leaned deferentially over me and said, "Are you all right?"

"Yes," I said, thinking how kind he was to be concerned about my health. He promptly took my plate away.

As I watched my last morsels of dinner disappear, I heard the Peace Corps director laughing. He'd seen my chagrin. "Didn't your training instructors tell you that 'Are you all right?' means 'Are you finished eating?'" he said.

I fell asleep thinking about the contrast between the boisterous crowds I'd seen on the streets and the sophisticated hotel dining room. I didn't yet know that this was a realistic foretaste of the two worlds of a developing country.

The next morning, we were welcomed again, this time at the American embassy. The Peace Corps doctor took all the men into a separate assembly room while we women waited. Forty-five minutes later, the men came out wearing crooked smiles. They avoided our questioning looks as we went in.

We were warned about engaging in unprotected sex, especially with Nigerian men, which could lead to sexually transmitted diseases. AIDS was not yet on the list, but gonorrhea and syphilis were—the sign I'd seen the day before flashed through my mind. If we were unlucky enough to get pregnant, we should come to him. Given my naiveté, I was sure I wouldn't need him.

That afternoon, we were entertained at a reception given by Nigeria's minister of education, Aja Nwachukwu. His home was on Queens Drive, an address that reflected the colonial era that had ended only two years earlier. The reception was outside, with tuxedoed waiters serving drinks and hors d'oeuvres. The minister, elegantly attired in a heavily embroidered turquoise-blue robe and dark-blue felt cap, assured us that we were eagerly awaited in our schools and would be able to influence the direction of education in his country. He had trained in the United States and was very happy to have Peace Corps in Nigeria.

A glimpse of my school, two hours each at the Nigerian Museum and the International Trade Fair, and a reception at the American ambassador's home filled the next day. In the evening, the Peace Corps country director pulled Roger and me aside. "Your assignments are here in Lagos, but your housing isn't ready, and your schools don't start for other week. So you can come with us tomorrow to take the volunteers going to the Eastern Region and the North. The bus will leave at six."

This was an unexpected treat! I packed eagerly before finding Art, who was posted to the Western Region, to tell him good-bye. He would be leaving on a separate bus the next morning with the other twenty volunteers headed for the same part of the country. With a casual, "See you sometime," and a quick hug, we parted.

Fifty of us boarded the bus together—Roger and I, the twenty-eight volunteers bound for the East, another eighteen headed for the North, and two Peace Corps staff. I was optimistic about the days ahead and knew I was in good company.

I looked around at my fellow passengers. Most were white, and about half were men and half women. A few already had master's degrees. The majority had just graduated from college. I was among the youngest at twenty-one.

Peace Corps training at the University of California Los Angeles had been intense. We had classes in the primary language of the region where we were headed and lectures in anthropology, political science, history, and African art. The men learned soccer and rugby, and the women were taught to play netball, similar to basketball. We had psychiatric evaluations, medical exams, and shots against tetanus, yellow fever, diphtheria, and hepatitis, and we were prescribed our malaria prophylactics.

The more I had learned, the more excited I had been to see the country for myself—to experience the political atmosphere of a newly independent country and see the mix of British colonialism and native culture.

Finally I was on my way to hear the languages and see people of different tribes.

Only a few miles from Lagos, we were surrounded by tropical rain forest, dense and lush, just as I'd seen in pictures and from the plane. "At last, here's the real Africa," I said to Roger.

"Can you identify the types of palm trees?" he said. I'd forgotten he was a science teacher! He helped me identify coconuts in their greenish-brown husks and oil palms with bunches of red palm fruits. Banana trees had leaves as big as umbrellas.

I was more interested in people than in trees. I stared wide-eyed at the masses of people on the streets of Ibadan, the largest city in Africa south of the Sahara. Two hours later, we pulled into a gas station in the ancient city of Benin. I heard attendants speaking the main language of the Eastern Region. Even though I'd studied Yoruba for my assignment in Lagos, I'd learned to say, *"Kedu ka ime,* how are you?" in Igbo, and I tried it out, getting big smiles and greetings in return. My language ability was a gift, and I knew it would serve me well for my two years. I didn't know then that speaking Igbo would help me convince future in-laws that I was a suitable wife.

The sun was dropping below the horizon at seven o'clock when we reached Enugu, the capital of the East. We bade farewell to our friends staying in the East before heading to bed and joined the staff and other volunteers going to the North early in the morning. This time, we went by train, and as we chugged along, I began to understand Nigeria's size. Almost a thousand miles at the widest section, east to west, and seven hundred miles south to north, it was 357,000 square miles. That's slightly more than twice the size of California.

I pulled my map out of my bag to see our route. We'd driven almost due east to reach Enugu, crossing the Niger River at Onitsha. Even though the equator wasn't marked on my map, I knew that Lagos was at about 7 degrees north. Today we would cross the major tributary of the Niger, the Benue River, at Makurdi on our way to Kaduna.

We left the tropical rain forest and dense growth behind as we entered the savannah—fewer trees and more shrubs. Roger pointed out the baobab trees, appearing to grow upside down.

We saw fewer people. Women were less flamboyant; several had their heads covered.

The city of Kaduna was completely different from the barely controlled chaos of Lagos, with newer buildings and streets laid out in a grid. The volunteers going to assignments in northern towns and cities were happy to use their language skills. Hausa seemed to be easier for Americans; it didn't have the three different tones or levels of Yoruba and Igbo.

My whirlwind Nigerian tour concluded two days later when Roger and I flew back to Lagos and were taken to the Peace Corps Rest House, or hostel, on the island of Ikoyi, less than half a mile from the ambassador's residence.

The following day, I met my principal, a tall Nigerian man dressed in an *agbada,* as I now knew to call the long robe. He greeted me formally in his slightly accented but excellent English. "You will meet the other staff when the session opens in another two days. Meanwhile, let me call someone to show you around."

An attractive young Nigerian woman in Western dress led me to the classroom block opposite the principal's office, where I would have my classroom. She was a student and hoped to study German. I was intrigued with her pleasantly accented English. She'd be fun to teach. Was I capable?

The principal gave me the address of the apartment that would be my home for the next two years, Twenty-Five Glover Road. I found Glover Road with no difficulty but couldn't see any number twenty-five. Since I couldn't move in for at least another month, I'd have time to find it. For now, I made myself at home at the Peace Corps Rest House. Roger too was waiting for his housing.

With a steward who shopped, cooked, cleaned, and did laundry, we could explore the area when our lesson plans were ready. "We should send our picture to our families and friends," I said to Roger on our second evening as we sat in our lounge chairs outside, sipping the drinks the steward had brought. I swatted away mosquitoes and said, "We could call this our tropical vacation." Was this really the Peace Corps?

2

ONE CAR, TWO SCHOOLS, AND THREE TRIPS

"*GUTEN MORGEN,*" I said as I stared out at the sea of black faces on my first morning as German teacher at the Federal Emergency Science School. The room was hushed, and the students looked at me curiously. "*Ich heisse Fraulein Zastrow, my name is Miss Zastrow.*" I continued, "Repeat after me: *Guten Morgen.*"

To my surprise, every seat was full, and more students were standing at the back of the large classroom. Were all two hundred Science School students in the room? I had planned a conversational beginning. But that would clearly not work. I had the whole group repeat greetings.

When class was over, I retreated to the staff room with a frown. "You look a little flustered," said Fred, the American botany teacher whom I'd met during the hour before entering my classroom. He was five feet ten, seven years older than my twenty-one, with dark hair, a thin face, and glasses.

"I didn't expect so many students. Surely they can't all want to learn German."

"They don't. They just want to get a look at you. They've never had a female American teacher, and one who speaks German! Word will get around, and anyone who wasn't there today will probably show up for your next class. But the numbers will drop."

By the end of the second week, about twenty students remained. When I returned to the staff room after class that day, I said to Fred, "Will the students keep dropping out 'til they're all gone?"

"No, you'll probably have those twenty for the term or even the whole year. You're no longer a tourist attraction!" he said. I laughed and mimicked the Statue of Liberty.

I'd been puzzling over the name of the school. Now I asked, "Why the name Emergency Science School?"

"We had to prepare for the day the British would depart," Dapo said, with a nod toward Keith, the one British teacher on the staff, "and we would need our own engineers, scientists, and mathematicians. Too few students were reading A-level science and maths, so the government created this school."

"But you kept the strange British phrases," Fred said. "Why not just say math instead of 'maths,' and how can 'reading' mean studying?" Dapo and Fred engaged in conversational jousting often, sometimes about language and other times about the relative importance of botany, Fred's subject, and math, Dapo's. I loved these lively conversations in the staff room and soon joined in.

Fred had been at the Science School for three years. He became my mentor on school issues and Nigerian life. He took me to the German Cultural Institute in downtown Lagos, which provided me with a couple of texts so I could photocopy exercises for my students. We started dating in October.

My twenty students were bright, eager, and fun to teach. German was a third or even fourth language for them—they spoke their own native language and excellent English, and some had studied French in secondary school. They taught me how to pronounce their names, while I taught them how to pronounce German words, conjugate verbs, and construct sentences.

I moved into my flat at Twenty-five Glover Road in mid-October. Peace Corps had told us to live as our Nigerian counterparts did, and no self-respecting Nigerian teacher would live without help, so I hired a steward named Aloysius. He didn't have a lot of work. I ate lunch at school and was often out for dinner. But he washed clothes by hand—no washing machine—ironed everything, dusted, and swept regularly—no vacuum cleaner—and shopped and cooked.

He lived in the boys' quarters, and I paid him eight pounds a month, less than a fifth of my monthly stipend from Peace Corps.

In early November, Peace Corps added teaching in Ojo village to my assignment. Although Ojo was only eighteen miles from Lagos, it was light-years away in development. There had only been a paved road for a few years. There was no regular transportation, so Peace Corps gave me a white Fiat 500 with an engine that sounded like a glorified lawnmower and a canvas top that opened. Months later, that car led me to meeting my husband.

The principal, Mr. Cardoso, welcomed me with a warm handshake on my first day. I was surprised to learn that he'd graduated with a degree in agriculture from Cornell in 1927. He'd trained in the United States at the same time as Nnamdi Azikiwe, who was now Nigeria's president. But unlike Zik, he'd met only frustration in his career. He took out his disappointment on the children, with frequent punishment and chastisement.

Twenty-two boys and ten girls made up the whole Awori-Ajeromi Secondary Grammar School. They were as different from the students at the Science School as the village was from Lagos. Emergency Science School students were sixth form—they had already completed secondary school, and some were my age or older—while those at the new Grammar School were in Form I, around twelve or thirteen years old. Nor were they well-prepared. Instruction was in English, but it was difficult for some of the children to understand and be understood.

The single classroom was in an abandoned cement-block church on the one road in town. It no longer had doors or windows. There were desks and a blackboard but nothing else. The occasional chicken wandered in.

Mr. Inyang, the only other teacher, lived in a rented room near the school. A soft-spoken man, he was near my height of five seven, with a wiry build. And like me, he was a novice Yoruba speaker. He taught math and science, while I taught English language, literature, and history. Though he and I spoke often, it was nothing like the camaraderie of the busy and cheerful staff room at the Science School in Lagos.

The men of Ojo were fishermen, plying their wooden craft along the coastline, or boatbuilders. A few were traders. I sometimes passed them on their way to Lagos markets, their bicycles loaded with baskets of the early morning's catch. Across the road from the school, women wove traditional multicolored raffia mats.

The village chief, the Olojo of Ojo, welcomed me when I visited him to pay my respects and thanked me for teaching his son. Rasaki was a pleasant but not very studious pupil. Like the other children, he barely spoke for the first few weeks. As I learned the children's names, they became less shy and responded to my casual manner, so different from Mr. Inyang's formal instruction and Mr. Cardoso's angry tirades.

My days were full, and my nights became ever more exciting. Fred introduced me to Kakadu, a lively nightclub where the trumpeter Victor Olaiya led his band in highlife. This music, popular all over West Africa, could be fast or slow. But it always had a strong beat that made me want to dance all night. I learned to copy the swaying hips of the Nigerian women. When other volunteers came to Lagos, I took them to Kakadu, where we danced with abandon to the sensual music.

By Thanksgiving, I had begun spending occasional nights with Fred at his flat. I didn't let on that he was my first sexual partner. I had the impression he didn't want to know, so I played along, staying lighthearted about our relationship. His attitude, I realized, was another one of the Nigerian customs he had adopted, and it suited me.

I spent my first Nigerian Christmas in Fred's apartment, sick with malaria. His steward prepared a lovely Christmas lunch, but it was all I could do to sit at the table for a few minutes before heading back to bed. Fred dosed me with Nivaquine, and I slept for most of Christmas afternoon.

He urged me to phone my parents. I called late in the afternoon, around noon in the United States, and assured them all was fine. I didn't mention the malaria or that I was sleeping with the man whose phone I was using.

A couple of days later, I boarded a train to Ibadan. Art and I had agreed in a letter exchange early in December to travel together after New Year's. I was thoroughly enjoying this experience, new to me, of dating more than one man. And I liked Art, with his often cynical approach to life. I looked forward to seeing him and Bob and Dave, who were also near Ibadan. We would all spend New Year's Eve together with other volunteers.

Art met me at the Peace Corps Rest House only to say he was not coming with me to the North. He didn't say why, nor did he urge me to spend a few days with him, though I wanted him to. I felt completely let down but recovered to enjoy the New Year's Eve celebrations, toasting the New Year with Bob. I danced with Dave and ended up spending the night with him, leading to frequent visits in the next few months.

The next day I continued the trip alone and disappointed. But it turned out to be a fortunate choice, for at the Government Rest House in Kaduna, I met an English woman and struck up a conversation. I must have seemed rather curious to her. I had just turned twenty-two, was casually dressed, and was on my own. I told her briefly that my friend had been unable to come at the last minute and that I wasn't sure of my next step, but I did want to see other cities in the North. She suggested that I join her, her husband, and their traveling companion to go to Zaria, a couple of hours north. I accepted her offer without hesitation.

John Harris, their traveling companion, was from New Zealand. He was the librarian at University College Ibadan and had made Nigeria his home for years; he had become an expert on the country's history and culture. I think the woman who invited me along may have been eager for female companionship or thought John would welcome another woman, especially a young and naïve one, to whom his stories would be new.

I spent a fascinating week with them. In Zaria, I was introduced to the old city walls and the dye pits where men embroidered the newly dark cotton fabric with intricate Arabic-style designs. We went on to Kano, an ancient Hausa city like Zaria but larger. More of its old city wall was standing. John told me it was started in the eleventh century and finished hundreds of years later.

The emir's palace was a sand-colored adobe building occupying a whole city block. The guards were striking in heavily embroidered dark robes and red turbans, mounted on richly decorated horses. John asked for an audience, and we were escorted to the throne room, where the emir sat on a heavy wooden throne, surrounded by courtiers and petitioners. John exchanged a few sentences with the emir and introduced us before we bowed our way out.

I marveled at the costumes, the people, and the traditional buildings. I liked best the impressive Kano Central Mosque with its four gold turrets. I took a photograph that I sent as a greeting card the following Christmas.

We started our return to the south but paused on the Jos Plateau in the Middle Belt region. John had his driver take us to two villages, not more than five miles apart, with two different languages. He wanted me to understand that Nigeria really did have more than two hundred languages, as I'd read. These spots in the hills had barely been touched by Western changes.

The men in the second village, where we stopped to take pictures, wore nothing but penis sheaths made of gourds fastened with raffia. The women had on loincloths, beads around their waists, and long earrings. The villagers didn't seem curious about us or mind our observing.

Our last night was in the Government Rest House in Jos, a comfortable colonial structure with wide verandas sheltered by deep thatched roofs with extending eaves. After dinner with wine, John came to my room. "I am so happy to have met you," he said as he stroked my face. "Will you come see me sometime?"

"I will. And thank you for bringing me along." I realized with a start that he wanted intimacy that I wasn't prepared to offer, and I moved his hand away. He quietly withdrew as he wished me good-night. Back in Ibadan, I boarded a train to Lagos with a much deeper knowledge of the North than I would have gained with my friend Art or other Peace Corps volunteers.

The spring of my first year was busy and exciting. I became more confident and a better teacher. The students at Ojo were progressing well, though the girls were still reluctant to speak. For the English and literature classes, there was a syllabus provided, so lesson preparation was fairly straightforward. African history was more challenging. I remembered some of what I'd learned in training, but to teach it, I had to study and decide what would be most interesting to the students.

I became ever more captivated as I read. Starting in the seventh century AD, just decades after Mohammed's death, newly converted Muslims from North Africa crossed the Sahara on trade and religious missions. They extended their influence southward into the semiarid lands of northern West Africa. But with forbidding tropical forests and mosquitoes barring their way, they never reached the coast.

There had been powerful Muslim kingdoms in West Africa—the Songhai Empire was a name I loved. Timbuktu had been a center of learning and trade in the 1500s. But by the seventeenth and eighteenth centuries, these empires had disappeared.

European explorers, then traders, approached the southern coast. Slaves were seized and shipped to Europe and the Americas. Catholic, Anglican, and soon other Protestant missionaries followed. The Middle Belt in Nigeria was largely untouched by explorers, traders, or missionaries from either the North or South, as I had seen for myself.

I wondered how my students at Ojo felt about the slave trade. I introduced the topic of Africans being taken as slaves to other countries, including the United States. They seemed surprised at first. Then Tunde, one of the more talkative boys, recalled seeing the old slave house at Badagry, just twenty miles east of Ojo. He knew that it had been a major shipping post. His description brought the history to life for his classmates.

I also came to understand better what the sophisticated students at the Science School wanted. The understanding in the early 1960's was that when they went to university they would need to read scientific papers in German. Though they enjoyed the conversational instruction, the language of science was more important. So I gave more instruction in grammar and scientific terms though I never relinquished my desire to have them comfortable with speaking the language.

Because of my contact with the German Cultural Institute, I was invited to a cocktail party to meet the famous mayor of West Berlin, Willy Brandt. I shook his hand with a sense of awe and told him I'd been in Berlin on the day the Berlin Wall, separating east from west, went up in 1961. I wrote to my father that Lagos had provided me the opportunity to meet this hero of his homeland.

During our spring break, I visited Dave, who was teaching at the University of Ife. "I have a proposal for you," he said as he handed me a gin and tonic. I sipped slowly. He'd become very fond of me and hoped for a long-term relationship, even marriage. I liked him very much but wasn't interested in any commitment, at least not at this point.

He saw me tense. "Don't worry. I respect what you told me, and though it's hard, I won't press you about marriage. But I know how much you love exploring Nigeria," he said. "I've been invited to accompany an Arab scholar here at the university on a summer research tour of Northern Nigeria. He says I can invite a guest. Would you come?"

We would go from Ibadan to Kano and other historic cities, then to Sokoto, the home of the supreme leader of the North, the sultan of Sokoto. "Of course I'll come. I'd love it," I said.

Roger had another trip to propose when I saw him at the Peace Corps Rest House in Lagos. "What about driving to Niger during vacation? You remember John, our friend who had been deselected from our Peace Corps training group?" I did, and I knew he had come to Nigeria to teach at a Catholic boys' school. He and Roger wanted to drive to Zinder in southern Niger, and if possible on to Agadez, a fabled stop on the Sahara trade route. The timing worked for me to take both trips. I was thrilled with the prospect of more exploring.

So my summer plans were complete. But I still had a couple of months before vacation. Mr. Cardoso held a rare staff meeting with me and Mr. Inyang one afternoon in May to tell us that the school was moving. He'd acquired a plot of land five miles closer to Lagos, and building had already started, so we could expect to move there in September for the next school year.

I hoped with being closer I would face fewer herds of the Fulani cattle that I often encountered on my drive. They were humped cattle, taller than my little Fiat, driven by their herders from the North to sell in Lagos. They filled the road, and I was terrified every time I had to drive through the middle of a herd. When their horns came near my windshield, I would cringe in fear.

But the day I had a car accident, the herders were helpful, and the cattle stayed away. Perhaps I was driving too fast on the road to Ojo one morning in late May. The rainy season had started, so the road was slippery. As I rounded a curve, the car tipped and then turned all the way over. I wasn't hurt—just stunned. I crawled out through the roof. A few hundred yards away, I saw a herd of cattle, and then I saw two boys in their grimy shirts and shorts running toward me. By the time they reached me, I was standing up. I showed them I was all right. They pushed the car right side up, smiled, and walked off.

My last adventure for the school year was another type of fright. A week after my car mishap, I said to Fred as we were driving to dinner, "I'm worried. My period is late; maybe I need to see the Peace Corps doctor."

"I'll take you to see him, and if he won't take care of this, I know someone who will." The next day, I knew it was a false alarm. I don't know who was more relieved, Fred or I.

And in a few more weeks, as soon as school was out and before I was leaving on my first summer trip with Roger, Fred left for his US vacation. He asked Johnny and me to drive him to the airport before leaving his car with Johnny for the summer. Just as I was getting out of the car at my flat, Johnny held up an envelope. "Look at this," he said. "I found this in the glove compartment. I think you should read it."

It was a letter to Fred from Alice, a name I had never heard him mention. It confirmed their plans to marry soon after Fred arrived home for vacation. Alice said she was ready now to come with him to Lagos. "Wow. That's news!" I said when I recovered enough to speak. "You'd think he might have told me."

But he had no obligation to do so. I thanked Johnny for letting me know. That evening as I thought about the letter, I guessed that Fred had actually wanted us to find it. Then in a flash of intuition I knew—Fred had asked Johnny to show it to me. He hadn't had the courage to tell me himself!

I was annoyed but not heartbroken. And, anyway, it was time to leave with Roger. We met John in Onitsha and packed the three of us and our luggage into his VW bug.

Roger and John were easy companions. In Kano, we found our way to the mosque and the emir's palace. This time I had no entry, but I described the interior to them, and we made the other tourist stops. I could have spent many more hours in this Arab-like city, so different from Lagos, but if we wanted to reach Agadez as we hoped, we had to keep moving.

The next day, we crossed into Niger. No one asked for passports, and we were only sure we had crossed the border when we saw the first signs in French. Soon after, we came across a camel driver leading several charges. With John's French and my sign language, I let him know I wanted to mount one of his camels. With a look of puzzlement, he agreed. He made the camel get down on its knees—an ungainly process—helped me mount, and had the camel rise and carry me for a few yards while my friends snapped my photo. It was one of the highlights of the trip for me.

We reached Zinder in the early evening. John's instincts led us a Catholic mission, where we were told about a hotel nearby. We took one room with three beds and its own bath, the only space available. There was a restaurant next door.

Zinder market had a whole section for camel traders. I didn't mount another camel, but I was able to take close-up photos. The goats I saw in another part of the market looked tiny by comparison.

I was intrigued by the native fabrics and bought a couple of yards of indigo-blue woven cotton. I had brought needles, thread, and a few buttons with me. That night in our hotel room, I sewed a skirt, which I wore the next day.

We were still hoping to go on to Agadez. But each person we asked said the same, "You'd be crazy to try in the VW bug. The rains have started, and the desert roads are not passable in that." Even though we didn't reach our goal, we had touched the southern edge of the Sahara.

Ten days later, I was back in Lagos with just a few days to prepare for my second summer adventure. I drove my Fiat to Dave's house, where the Sudanese professor, Ahmed, collected us early the next morning to head north.

I had thought the VW was not terribly comfortable for long-distance travel, though I hadn't minded, given the company, the scenery, and the excitement of new places. Now I thought the VW had been the height of comfort. Ahmed had a Land Rover for his research. He and Dave took turns driving. One passenger could sit in the cabin with the driver, while the other passenger had to sit in the open back. Either way, it was dusty, bumpy, and hot! Twice we ran into rainstorms, and then the passenger in the back had to shelter under a tarpaulin.

We stopped in Daura, north of Kano, where a guide led us to a wooden shelter. "Many centuries ago, this city was ruled by women," he said in his excellent English. Like other Hausa speakers, his pronunciation was more clipped than that of the southerners who spoke either Igbo or Yoruba as their native tongue. "A stranger from across the desert found that a snake was preventing the townspeople from drawing their water," he said, pointing to the well under the roof.

He lifted a heavy sword and held it out. "With this sword, the stranger killed the snake. The queen married him in gratitude. Their children became heads of the seven leading Hausa cities, with Daura as the spiritual home." A city ruled by women and the stranger crossing the Sahara captured my imagination. I would retell this story to my students at Awori-Ajeromi Grammar School.

Driving east in the Land Rover from Daura to Sokoto, I could believe we were actually in the desert. Apart from occasional baobab trees and plenty of scruffy shrubs, there was little vegetation or civilization.

Sokoto itself was impressive for its size and its monochromatic color— brown buildings, brown earth, and the few trees covered in brown dust. The sultan's palace, the same brown, was even larger than the emir of Kano's and had more attendants. All wore colorful garments and head covers similar to those we'd seen in Kano. I saw no women on the streets in Sokoto or in the sultan's palace.

I was accustomed to being the only white person in sight, but now I was also the only female. When Ahmed took us to meet dignitaries, he suggested I cover my head as a sign of respect. Otherwise I dressed in my usual casual skirt and blouse attire, and felt comfortable in my surroundings. I was proud to be allowed to move about easily in this male-dominated culture.

Over dinners and in the evenings in the rest houses where we stayed, I was fascinated by Ahmed's tales of Sudanese, Arabic, and Nigerian history.

After an amazing summer of sights, sounds, and smells unlike any I would ever see in the United States, I was back in Lagos and preparing for the next school year.

Johnny came to see me a day after I returned. He brought the *Daily Times*, the leading local newspaper, which I hadn't looked at before my first trip away.

"You will want to see this," he said, pointing to the announcement of Fred's marriage to Alice. I was over my annoyance. I had no inkling then, but by the next summer, I'd be planning my own wedding.

As soon as Fred arrived back in Nigeria, he came alone to see me. "Alice and I had been planning to marry for a long time," he said.

"And why did you not feel you should tell me?"

"Well, she'd changed her mind before, and I wasn't sure she'd go through with it," he said.

"So why give up a good thing if you don't have to? Was that it?" He apologized, agreed he should have told me, and asked if I would be willing to meet Alice. Of course I was. After all, he and I would be teaching together for another year. A day later, he brought Alice over, and we soon became good friends.

I continued with the same students into their second year of German at Emergency Science School, and I had a new class of first-year students. I also got drawn into activities, including playing the piano for two students who wanted to enter a national singing competition. They brought the nineteenth-century European songs they were to sing, and I urged them to choose African or at least contemporary music. They explained that they had to sing these—it wasn't a choice. Fortunately for us all, they found someone else who could accompany and guide them.

I also continued teaching at Awori-Ajeromi Secondary Grammar School in its new location. I missed seeing the fishing village, the raffia mats, and the old church building where we met. But having a shorter drive was an advantage.

Now that Fred was married, I spent more time with Panos, a Greek man I'd met. I also continued to see Art and Dave. I was most fond of Art with his self-deprecating humor. I hoped our relationship would grow. One evening, I was in his bedroom with him. Soon we were on the bed, and I was ready, indeed eager, to make love, but he wasn't having it. Instead, he told me a story to explain his hesitation: he had been engaged to a Swiss woman, but she had broken off their engagement to return to Switzerland, and he was not yet ready for another relationship. Years later, I visited him in the United States; he was with his male partner of many years.

I also saw Johnny and the other Nigerian men I had met through Fred. We would meet at my flat or one of their places. The customs that had seemed exotic at first, like dropping in on friends, were now familiar and natural. I had a hard time remembering my first couple of months, when being surrounded by Nigerians with their volubility and easy camaraderie had made me feel a little reticent. In fact, I now loved the way people behaved, and I began to feel less allegiance to the Western habit of rectitude.

Yet, now that I was in my second Peace Corps year, I had to think about what I'd do next. My Mount Holyoke friends Susie and Robin were married already, Joan was in medical school, and Darlene and Barbara were in grad school. I liked teaching and thought about graduate programs in education to prepare for a career. But I felt at home in Nigeria—did I really want to leave?

3

THE MEMORABLE MEMO

ONE AFTERNOON IN November 1963, I was surprised to find a memo from the chief electrical engineer of the Electricity Corporation of Nigeria, or ECN, under my door.

"ECN is conducting a survey of electricity usage in Ikoyi," it said. "You were not present when our inspectors came to your flat. You are asked to report to the chief electrical engineer's office at ECN headquarters."

My government-furnished apartment came with overhead lights, fridge, water heater, and ceiling fan. I had bought an iron, used by my steward, and a radio that was frequently on when I was home, but I wasn't home much. The stove—cooker, in British parlance—was gas.

I was annoyed but nervous. They might cut off my electricity if I didn't comply. The next day, after I finished teaching, I drove to ECN. I knew the building along Lagos' Marina Road, a main thoroughfare extending into downtown. I marched in. "The chief engineer is on the seventh floor," a re ceptionist told me. "I will tell his secretary you are coming."

I found the office and the secretary, a middle-aged Nigerian woman in a stiff, blue, satin head tie. "I received this notice." I held it out to her as if it held poison.

"Please wait here," she said. She returned quickly. "The chief engineer will see you now." She showed me into his office, and I saw a serious-looking Nigerian man dwarfed by the immensity of the space. He sat in a black leather chair behind a polished wood desk. He looked young, maybe around thirty, and had a roundish face that reminded me of a koala bear. He wore a dark wool business suit, white shirt, tie, and pocket handkerchief.

"Please sit down." He gestured to the chair in front of his desk. "Thank you for coming in."

"Why am I getting this notice?" I said. "I'm a Peace Corps volunteer. I have only the utilities that came with my flat, an iron I hardly use, and a radio I sometimes play—that's all my electricity usage!"

"We have no wish to make you angry," he said. "My staff is conducting this survey to check on unauthorized connections and the problem of overload. I'm sorry if you are upset."

I stayed only long enough to be assured that my electricity would not be cut off.

On the following Saturday afternoon, I was preparing the next week's lesson plans before getting dressed to go out when there was a knock at my door.

I opened it to see Grace, whom I'd met several times before. Beside her was a man wearing an open-neck sports shirt and dark trousers. "This is Clement Onyemelukwe, a friend of ours," she said. "I've been meaning to call, so I took advantage of his visit to ask him to bring me here."

"You don't remember me, do you?" he said. I shook my head. "You were in my office a few days ago, and you were not happy. In fact, you were actually a little rude!"

"Oh, you're the chief electrical engineer?" I was embarrassed. "Yes, I was annoyed. Was I really rude?" With his informal dress and away from his office, he looked different. I recalled the koala bear image that had struck me. I also noticed his smile. I thought he could be someone I'd like to know better.

"I'll take that as an apology," he said. I remembered that Grace didn't drive, so her explanation of their visit made sense.

"What would you like to drink?" I said after they were seated. "I have fresh palm wine."

"Where did you get that?" Clem said.

"Did you see the palm tree right outside my window? The tapper was here this morning. I usually buy when I see him." I brought glasses and the palm wine from the kitchen and poured them each a glassful.

We talked about Grace's son, who was a student at my school, the country's need for electricity, and Clem's life in Britain before he returned to Nigeria two years before.

"Would you like to come to my house next Saturday evening? I'm having a party," Clem said, looking from me to her. I liked the idea of spending time with him. I'd pick up Grace, who knew where his house was. I heard nothing more about the inspection of my electricity.

On Friday evening, the day before the party, I was visiting a former student of Fred's and now a friend of mine in his rented room near the Science School. I told him I'd met the chief electrical engineer at ECN and would be seeing him the next evening. Pius said, "I have heard of him. Isn't he an Igbo? I think he studied in the United Kingdom."

"Yes, he is, and yes, he did," I said. I was about to describe how we'd met when I heard the Nigerian radio announcer mention President Kennedy.

"What was that?" I said.

"I think he said President Kennedy was shot," Pius said, turning up the volume. In a few minutes, the news announcer interrupted the program again. "President Kennedy is dead," he said. "He was shot during a parade in Dallas, United States."

"It can't be," I said as my hand flew to my throat. Pius and I went into the hallway, where people were gathering. "I can't believe this," I said to a Nigerian woman who was crying loudly. "It's horrible."

"I'm sorry," a man who seemed to recognize me as an American said. Others followed his example.

I wanted to be with other Americans. I left Pius and drove to the Peace Corps Rest House, where I found a couple of volunteers who had also just heard the news. I shared my feelings of shock and sadness with them. At home, I turned on my radio and heard the BBC's announcement of the assassination. It seemed unreal.

Despite the shock of Kennedy's death, or maybe because of it, I wanted to go to the party the next night. I dressed carefully in a black, linen, embroidered dress and low heels. The conversation focused on Kennedy's death. Again, people told me how sorry they were, as if I'd lost a relative. And I felt I had.

Clem mixed with other guests but spent the majority of his time at my side. He was easy to be with, and I was pleased when he asked me to go out with him. We dated several times in the next few weeks, usually going to the cinema and sometimes to dinner as well. We visited a couple of his friends who were married to English women. I liked his friends and found myself liking him more and more.

Before Christmas, my school held an event for which I'd agreed to be in charge of the food. Clem suggested he drop me off and pick me up afterward.

"It was a disaster," I said as I got into his Ford Consul. "The food was delivered late, and there weren't enough large plates."

"Did everyone get something to eat?"

"Yes, but it took too long."

"Don't worry. You agreed to a difficult task, and everyone ate. That's all they will remember." He provided the comfort and reassurance I needed.

Later that evening, I told him I was going to Enugu right after Christmas to work at a day camp with other Peace Corps volunteers. "My cousin Isaiah lives in Enugu. I'll call him and tell him you are coming," Clem said. "He studied in the United States. He would be happy to meet an American. He can show you around."

On December 26, Clem drove me to the taxi park. "Ready to go! Board now! Best price!" shouted the touts rounding up passengers for the Peugeot 404 taxis and larger buses. Families with children, women carrying chickens, and men holding bundles of cloth were all bargaining for the lowest prices and the best seats. Clem helped me negotiate with one of the touts for a spot in the front seat of a Peugeot.

I was squeezed next to the driver and another passenger, with three passengers on each of the other two seats, as the car sped out of Lagos. The sour smell of so many sweaty bodies in the heat was intense.

I reached Enugu in one piece, despite the driver's speed and recklessness, and checked into the Peace Corps Rest House. Isaiah came for me on Saturday. He resembled Clem with the round face, but he was more outgoing. He wore a dashiki, a loose V-neck cotton shirt with a diamond pattern in red, white, green, blue, and yellow.

We drove up the five-mile Milliken Hill on a narrow, curving, two-lane road. It was in poor condition, and he was a nervous driver. His frequent gear shifting and haphazard control of the gas pedal imitated his slight stutter and frequent laughter and left me feeling carsick.

I wasn't reassured by having no guardrails at the side of the road. I could look down hundreds of feet through the trees. I saw one lorry that had missed the curve. I wondered what it would feel like to go over the edge.

"I'm taking you to Clem's family," he said. "They want to meet you. And you can see people of the region in their own home," he said. In my naïveté, I bought that story, as true as the survey of electricity use, I learned years later.

I looked forward to meeting an Igbo family. Knowing their son was a bonus that would make the meeting more fun.

We drove through Awka, with its famous carved wooden doors outside vendors' shops. In another half hour, we entered Onitsha, where there were none of the government buildings I'd seen in Enugu or Lagos. An impressive Anglican cathedral that would have looked at home in any large British city dominated a major intersection with its gray mass, stained-glass windows, and tall steeple. Across the street was the slightly rundown Dennis Memorial Grammar School, DMGS.

"I am sure Clement has told you about DMGS," Isaiah said. "Clement and our cousin Jonathan were there together; I was after them."

"Yes, he's very proud of the school," I said, wondering if it had looked better in its earlier days. Clem had told me he excelled in his secondary school; I knew he'd be pleased that I'd seen it.

We turned down a poorly maintained street with a church and stucco houses that all looked in need of paint. Many had market stalls in the front yards and businesses on the ground floor—vehicle repair shops, typing centers, tire sales, and sewing or tailoring establishments. The sounds of talking, laughter, and car horns mingled with shouts of small children playing. Older children carried goods for sale on their heads. After two more turns on streets that were getting progressively worse, we were at the house Clem had described. I was intrigued by the address, Five St. John's Cross.

The yard was bare of grass, but a flame tree and a few straggly bushes grew in the reddish-brown soil. The house was a single-story building of cement blocks covered with stucco, set back ten feet. The dimpled exterior had remnants of yellow paint from long ago. The windows had open wooden shutters.

As we got out of the car, children called out, "*Onye ocha!* White person!" We crossed the narrow board laid across the three-foot-wide gutter, mounted the two steps, and entered the living room, dim after the bright sun outside. There were dusty curtains at the windows, a smooth mud floor, and a low ceiling. Clem's mother met us. She had the same round face and shy smile as Clem. She wore a red and blue wrapper and matching *buba*, or cotton blouse, in a Dutch print. Isaiah hugged her warmly, calling her Mama.

Clem's father looked distinguished in a long, beige, embroidered top, cotton trousers, and leather sandals like those sold by the Hausa traders I saw in Lagos. Several young people peered at us from a back room. Isaiah addressed Clem's father as Papa, and they shook hands. He introduced me with a few words of English and continued in Igbo. Was he saying I was Clement's acquaintance, friend, or girlfriend? I had no idea.

"Welcome. How you be?" they said in hesitant English.

We sat in the wooden chairs, and Clem's parents took seats on the dilapidated sofa. Papa spoke to one of the children who came in a moment later with pinkish-gray kola nuts, green fruits that looked like tomatoes, and a large dab of peanut butter on a tray. "Guests are always given kola as a welcome," Isaiah said, as he took the tray from Papa to show to me before handing it back. Papa took one of the kola nuts and, holding it aloft, spoke a few sentences in Igbo. "He's praising God, thanking him for the kola and for our safe journey," Isaiah said. I nodded.

Then Papa broke the kola nuts into several pieces and held out the tray. "Take one, and dip it in the garnish," Isaiah said. I did as instructed. I bit into it and felt my mouth turn to fire. My eyes started to water as I swallowed.

"*Ndo.* Sorry," Mama said. "Is pepper too much?" I could only gasp. Mama called another child, who went out the door and returned a few moments later with soft drinks. I was grateful for the cold Coke.

"How be Clement?" Mama said.

"He's fine," I said, struggling to speak with my mouth still burning. "He sends his greetings." He hadn't, but then I hadn't known I would meet them.

"How be work?" Clem's mother said. With Isaiah translating, I explained my teaching jobs at the two schools, Clem's parents watching me intently.

"How is family?" I said to Mama. Her response was to call Clem's siblings and introduce them. They wore Western dress, the girls in colorful blouses and skirts and the boy in a sports shirt and khaki pants. Grace was in nursing school, she said, and Geoffrey was in secondary school. The youngest girl, Nebechi, had just finished primary school and was awaiting her common entrance exam results.

The children disappeared again, though I saw them watching from the back. Isaiah kept the conversation going, occasionally directing a question to me about Lagos. When we'd stayed for an hour and a half, Isaiah said, "We should leave so we have time to visit Nanka before night."

He turned to me. "You are going to see a real Igbo village, mud huts and all."

As we drove out of Onitsha, Isaiah described the town of Nanka and their family. "We Onyemelukwes are well known," he said. "The whole town is proud of Clement as the first Nigerian chief engineer in ECN."

He pointed out Agulu, the town Clem's mother was from. The buildings and trees that lined the road were covered by reddish-brown dust. Soon he announced that we'd entered Nanka. A large Anglican church anchored the corner where we turned. It was an anomaly among the ramshackle wooden structures and market stalls that bordered the other side of the road.

"This is the town shrine," Isaiah said as we rounded a bend, indicating an enclosure on our left. Bamboo poles held the thatch roof in place. I could see what must have been an altar at the center. "The missionaries chose to build the church opposite the shrine to diminish the importance of the traditional religion," he said as he pointed back at the church. "The church has won, but some of the elders still visit the shrine to communicate with ancestors."

We followed the dirt road downhill for two miles past thatch-roofed huts and occasional tin-covered houses, all of the same reddish-brown mud. There were banana and palm trees and fields of corn.

He parked by a six-foot-high mud wall. I followed him for about one hundred feet along a path beside the wall until we reached the entrance. Isaiah pushed open the carved wooden door. We had to step over a raised earthen step and crouch at the same time to go under a wooden beam. Children hung around outside the entrance watching.

I noticed a faint acrid odor. Then I saw the goats in their shed on the left. Just beyond them was an eight-foot-high open structure of bamboo poles holding what I later learned were yams. On the right, there was a deep hole about six feet in diameter, protected by a low mud wall.

A square thatch-roofed mud hut was at the center of the compound. "This is the *obi*, the spiritual center for the family and the house of the patriarch Ejike," Isaiah said as a man emerged. He was five feet ten, slender and muscular. As we approached him, I couldn't help staring at his facial markings, several horizontal striations on his forehead and others that started near his eyes and extended down to his chin. He wore khaki shorts, a loose shirt, and a striped wool cap, like a child's snow hat.

Isaiah introduced me. Again I didn't know what he said, but many years later he told me. He said, "This is the white woman that Clement wants to marry."

"*Kedu? Kedu maka ndi be gi?* How are you? How is your family?" I said. I had vaguely remembered that I'd once known a few Igbo greetings, and Isaiah had coached me on the way. Ejike exploded with laughter and shouts.

He invited us to enter his hut, with its rust-colored, four-foot-high mud walls. We sat on the mud bench built into the inside wall while he took the carved wooden chair. It was cooler inside, with a thatch roof at least sixteen feet high at the center, sloping down to hang over the walls. As my eyes adjusted to the darkness, I could identify cow horns and what looked like skulls of small mammals hanging from the rafters.

Ejike shouted, and a teenage boy appeared, listened, and disappeared again. He returned a moment later with kola nuts. I was relieved that there was no peanut butter-like substance.

Out of the corner of my eye, I saw that a group of children had gathered inside the compound, clearly afraid to approach closely. The kola ritual was repeated. Then I heard Isaiah say the name Clement a few times, but that was all I understood.

When Isaiah paused for a moment, Ejike reached down and lifted a calabash, a jug made from the hollowed-out shell of a gourd, of palm wine. He shouted again.

"He's calling his wife, Obele," Isaiah said. She came in with a couple of glasses, while Ejike took a cow's horn from a battered black briefcase. I wondered whether the palm wine he was pouring was safe to drink. When I bought it in Lagos, it came straight from the tapper to my fridge. But Isaiah and Ejike were drinking it, so why shouldn't I? I accepted a glass and sipped at it. The men downed theirs in one draught each.

A younger man resembling Ejike, but with fewer facial markings and with a slightly heavier build, arrived, and I was introduced to Obi, Clem's youngest uncle. Isaiah pointed out his wife, Mercy, who had followed him but didn't enter the obi. This was the real thing: a village, an extended family, the naked children, the goats, and the mud huts.

The wall that encircled the compound was broken by a gate that led into the adjoining compound. Isaiah took me through. "Clem sends money to his father as a dutiful son should. He doesn't know that his father is using the money to build this." I saw a partially completed, modern, two-story house with a veranda. "You can tell him," Isaiah said.

I would have looked more closely if I'd known that I would spend a year in this house during the civil war a few years later.

We made our farewells, and as we walked back to the car, still trailed by children, I offered to drive back. Isaiah accepted, so the ride itself was more pleasant. I thanked him for giving me this fascinating look at Onitsha, Nanka, and the people I'd met. The last thing on my mind was that this village, this family, and all the people would become part of my life.

When I got back to Lagos, I told Clem, "Isaiah was great. I loved meeting your parents. I met Grace, Geoffrey, and Nebechi, but they were shy and wouldn't talk to me."

"I hardly know them," Clem said. "They were so little when I left for England. I think Nebechi was only one or two."

"Did you know your father is building a house in Nanka?" I said.

Clem was surprised, so I filled him in as Isaiah had said.

That very week, my Fiat broke down on the way home from my village school. I abandoned it on Carter Bridge and took a taxi to Clem's house. He arranged for it to be picked up and repaired. For several days, he drove me the thirteen miles each way, which made him shorten his working day. This was an unexpected kindness. Our conversations became livelier and more intimate, and I began spending nights with him.

I was falling in love. I wanted to be with him whenever possible. I felt more complete around him. He was so mature and sure of himself. He clearly valued my company. But did he love me? He didn't talk of love, and I wasn't ready to initiate such a conversation.

Two months later, we were driving along Marina on our way to dinner at the Bristol Hotel. I said, "Why did you ask Isaiah to take me to your parents and not just to see the Onitsha market? And why to the village?"

"If you must know, it's because I want to marry you!"

I sat bolt upright. "You could have asked me first," I said.

"Forget it," he said angrily. "We don't have to talk about marriage again."

"I didn't say we shouldn't talk about it. I just said you should ask me, not assume."

We arrived at Bristol Hotel, parked, and made our way to the dining room in silence. Clem snapped at the waiter. I was relieved he was directing his anger at someone besides me, but sorry for the unsuspecting person in the line of fire. I had begun ordering for Clem at restaurants, but this night he chose and ordered for himself—no discussion of sharing an appetizer, no pondering which entrées to order.

Our conversation was limited to my asking, "How is your food?" I got a gruff, "Fine." I barely touched my lamb chops. We didn't order dessert. He paid the bill, and we departed as quietly as we'd come.

I wasn't sure I wanted to go home with him, but he didn't ask. Still not talking, he pulled into his driveway and got out, walked into the house barely waiting for me, and went straight upstairs. As we were getting into bed, his anger was palpable. "I'm sorry I took you unaware," I said. "I didn't mean to upset you."

"Well, you did." He rehashed the whole conversation, pointing out my error in asking him to explain why Isaiah had taken me to see his parents. What error? I had asked an innocent question. If he had felt attacked, wasn't that his problem?

As I listened, I realized that it was my problem too. I'd known him barely five months. Yet I loved him and hated to see him unhappy.

Gradually he calmed down. "I didn't mean to say what I did," he said. "It just popped out of my mouth. It won't happen again."

"That's not what I want. I just said you should ask me, not take me for granted."

"Well, I'll have to think about it," he said, taking my hand.

"When you're sure, let me know," I said, turning to kiss him.

We touched the subject gingerly again a week later, and I could tell he wanted to ask me. But he didn't seem ready to make a proper proposal, so I waited. I needed time to think too. I did love him, and I was sure I'd say yes when he finally asked, but was I being too naïve?

The obvious question—could an interracial, intercultural marriage work?—had been answered by Clem's friends. Of course it could. I would learn Igbo like Jean. I would get to know Clem's family, and he would meet and get to know mine. We would visit his village often but not live there. I would continue teaching.

I talked to Lucy, a friend from Cameroon, who said, "If you're going to marry a Nigerian, an Igbo is the best choice. They are more likely to be faithful." I knew the reputation of Nigerian men as philanderers, so her comment gave me somewhat backhanded relief.

One evening in late March, Clem was seated on the bed as I started to get in. He cleared his throat and said, "There's something I want to discuss with you." Not a very romantic opening, but I could tell what was coming. "You have shown me that you respect my culture and my people," he said. "You are adaptable and appear to be content living here. Is that true?"

"Yes, that's all true. I do respect your culture and your people." For good measure and in anticipation of his question, I said, "I am very happy living here."

Then he said it. "I love you, and I want you to be my wife."

"Are you sure?" I teased. "I'm not just forcing you to say this?"

"Don't joke," he said. "I'm very sure. I mean every word."

"Then I accept," I said, as I snuggled close to him. "I love you, too."

We'd spoken the words I'd been waiting to hear and say. I wanted to make my life with him. Nigeria felt like home.

The next day, we began to make plans. My Peace Corps service would finish in June, and Peace Corps would send me home to the United States. I would come back on my own and marry Clem in December.

4

MEET THE PARENTS

"*Nno*. WELCOME," I said to Clem's parents as they got out of the taxi that had brought them from the lorry park to his house on an April evening. "Come in. Clement is coming," I continued in Igbo. "Gabriel, please call Master," I said to the steward who came out from the kitchen.

I'd become accustomed to having servants, a necessary aspect of life in Nigeria, and was now comfortable using the terms "master" and "madam."

Clem and I had agreed on this approach—I would wait for his parents downstairs, greet them at the door, and send Gabriel to call him from his bedroom. I'd laughed when he suggested it. "Are you so important that you can't sit with me to wait?"

Then I got the point—it would let them know I was a visitor. I was spending most nights at his house, but we didn't want that to be obvious. So we carried out our charade, and he appeared on cue, embraced his mother, then his father, and led them into the parlor. This room to the left of the front door was long and well-lit by the setting sun and the lights I'd just turned on. Its modern Danish-style chairs, one long sofa, wood side tables, and matching coffee table were rarely used and still looked new.

Clem told the watch-day, another regular servant in a Nigerian home, to carry their luggage upstairs. When we were all seated, I rang the bell for

Gabriel. "Please bring drinks for us," I said. I'd made sure to have Guinness Stout on hand for Clem's mother and Star beer for his dad. And I remembered that the drinks had to be chosen by and then opened in front of the guests. So even though I knew what they'd want, I played my part. Gabriel returned and placed the drinks in front of me on the low coffee table. "*Kedu ife ichoro*? What do you want?" I said. My Igbo was rudimentary, and I said each word carefully.

I'd been studying seriously since Clem and I had decided to marry, using the Igbo book from Peace Corps training. But for a tonal language, hearing words and phrases is critical. I had asked one of my female Igbo students who excelled in German to make recordings of phrases from the book. Clem also tried, less successfully, to teach me common phrases. Eager as he was for me to learn, he wasn't always patient enough to be helpful.

Meeting future in-laws is cause for nerves at best. I was doing it in a foreign language and one I'd just started to learn. All I could do was try my best to convince them I would be a good wife for their son. Speaking their language, even haltingly, was a start.

With the drinks served, I went to the kitchen to oversee the final preparations for the meal. Gabriel's okra soup simmered on the gas stove. The strong aroma of palm oil, chicken, and stock fish filled the kitchen and even spread through the swinging door to the other rooms. I'd instructed him earlier to start boiling the yam, cut into two-inch pieces, when Clem's parents arrived. Now it was nearly ready.

He'd set the table earlier. I made sure the pan with water for washing hands was in place, with soap and a towel next to it, on the sideboard.

I went back to the parlor while Gabriel started pounding the yam, which would become smooth with a slightly sticky consistency, similar to mashed potatoes. My heart was pounding just like the thump, thump, thump of the heavy wood pestle in the mortar. How would these people—so important to my husband and to my future—react to me?

They were deep in conversation. I wondered what they were saying. Just be patient, I said to myself. If Clem thinks I need to be included, he'll translate for me.

I heard Gabriel put the yam and soup on the table. "*Bia, lie ife.* Come and eat," I said, leading the way across to the dining room.

Clem indicated the water for hand washing. When they'd scrubbed and dried their hands, I indicated the chair on the right of Clem's seat for his mother. Clem showed his father to the chair on his left. I took the chair beside his father. I began to cut into the mound of yam when Clem's father said, "*Chelu, k'ayi kpe ekpele.* Wait, let us pray."

After his brief prayer, most of which I didn't understand, I joined Clem and his mother with "amen" and went back to slicing the yam. I placed a large portion with several spoons of soup on each plate, including good-sized pieces of chicken and fish in each serving. We began eating silently. I used my fingers to take a ball of yam and dip it in the soup, as I'd learned. Clem's mother watched how I ate. Was I doing it correctly?

I gave them more. Clem and his parents ate their fish and chicken last, and then chewed the chicken bones. I was used to Clem's doing this, though it still made me cringe. I called Gabriel to replace the water so we could wash our hands again.

I could see they were getting tired. I turned to Mama. "*Agam ana. Agam abia echi.* I am going home. I will come tomorrow." She looked puzzled, and I knew I hadn't made my meaning clear.

Clem explained in Igbo. "Cathy is going home. She will come in the morning, and when I leave for work, she'll be here. When you are ready, she will take you to see Lagos."

We said good-night, and I went back to my flat. I tried to imagine what his parents were saying to Clem and then to each other as they went to bed. I recalled what Clem had told me. "My parents were relieved when I returned from England without a foreign wife three years ago."

"Why were they so happy that you came home unmarried?"

"Well, they'd heard stories about English women who married Igbo men, stayed in the country for a few years, and then went back to England, taking their children with them." He continued, "Now that I'm thirty-one, they are very worried that I am not yet married. You know, they even told my sister Monica to find a wife for me."

She'd sent several attractive and well-educated women to "visit" him in Lagos. "But I didn't like any of them and sent them home again," he said. "She even sent her best friend, Rose. I sent her packing like all the others. You're different from those women."

"But I'm still a foreign woman."

"They already saw you once. I'm sure they will like you," he said with a kiss.

"Great!" I said. "No pressure."

With that conversation in mind, I was determined to overcome any resistance they might have. I'd have the opportunity to try out my Igbo and show them I cared about them when I drove them around town. I finally fell asleep, with Igbo phrases running through my mind.

As I dressed the next morning, I kept practicing. *"Ebaa bu uno uka.* Here is the church. *Anyi ge je Kingsway.* We'll go to Kingsway." At half past eight, I drove to Clem's. He wished us well, said good-bye, and left for work.

I used every word of my limited vocabulary as I drove, pointing out the church we attended, the American Embassy, and Lagos Race Course. They, in turn, told me in English that they'd been to Lagos when Clem left for England twelve years earlier before there were so many tall buildings.

We parked across from Kingsway, the British department store at the center of the Lagos business district. Clem had thought they'd like to see this symbol of modernity. They liked the revolving door—a new experience. They seemed impressed by the orderly displays of Revlon lipsticks, Sony transistor radios, and kitchen utensils, all with prices clearly marked.

I led them to the escalator so we could visit the second floor. I said casually, *"Bia.* Come," and took Mama's hand. She stepped on by my side. *"Eeh, o gini?* What is happening?" she cried out loudly. She gripped me so hard I almost lost my balance. Customers and salespeople looked around to watch our ascent. I hoped there wasn't anyone I knew.

I held her tight. When we reached the top, I pulled her with me onto the steady floor and kept an arm around her. I turned to see if Papa was all right. He stepped off with a show of confidence. Then he realized he'd stopped moving and nearly lost his balance.

A rapid exchange in Igbo followed with no effort to make me understand. I was sure they were saying I was crazy, and they would never trust me to take them anywhere again. But gradually they recovered, and I led them through the women's dresses, skirts, and blouses, to men's wear. I avoided the women's lingerie.

When I suggested we go back down, Mama held back. Then, seeing no alternative, she gripped my hand and stepped on. She drew in her breath sharply and shut her eyes tight. But she didn't scream on the way down. This was a relief. Papa made a good job of pretending nonchalance, but I could tell he was a little uneasy too.

Our last stop was the food section on the first floor. "Na watt-in be this?" Mama said, pointing to a can of Heinz vegetable soup with its picture of carrots, potatoes, and lima beans.

"*Ofe Oyinbo*. European soup."

She stopped at the meat counter, where packets of steaks, pork chops, and hamburger were covered with plastic wrap. "This be for sick peoples?" she said, pointing to the ground meat.

"No, Europeans eat meat like this," was the most I could explain. I realized that having a chunk of meat, sometimes just one, in a stew was valued. Why would anyone grind it up to be nearly unrecognizable?

Most of their usual foods were not for sale in Kingsway. "We no like live here," Papa said. "They no sell yam, no pepper, no proper meat." I assured them as best I could that there were plenty of markets where we shopped, in addition to the department store that expatriates counted on.

We left Kingsway and strolled in the downtown area, where they marveled at the wide sidewalks and the number of cars and buses. They were accustomed to seeing Hausa men in Onitsha but were less accustomed to Yoruba men with their flowing agbadas and women in their blue, red, and yellow printed bubas, wrappers, and head ties. Nor had they seen so many European men and women in business suits or shirt-sleeves and summery dresses.

We went to Clem's office as he'd asked. In the lobby, we stepped into the elevator. When the door closed and we started our ascent, I realized I hadn't warned them. Mama cried out again. "E-wa, Jesus!"

"We'll get out very soon," I said. She was shaking when we reached Clem's floor. But she calmed down when she saw his secretary, his huge office, and his polished wood desk. They beamed with pride at his exalted position.

The next day was Saturday. Clem worked in the morning. So we repeated the scene with his departure and my taking over their entertainment for the morning. This time, I drove them around the residential area where we lived. "Why they leave grass grow like that?" Papa said.

I remembered the bare dirt in the compound I'd seen in Nanka and in Ojo village. The least attempt by a plant to take root was quickly thwarted. "Europeans and even many Nigerians like grass," seemed like a somewhat feeble explanation. "Clem has grass growing around his house. Didn't you see it?"

"Yes, I see um. I think his gardener, he be lazy, he no like work." My Igbo was not up to asking why they did not let grass grow in their compound. My best guess was that it would die in the dry season and there was no water for irrigation. Besides, land was for use, not beauty. Mama's next remark confirmed my suspicion.

"Why they no plant yam or corn?" she asked.

"They aren't farmers. They're people like Clem who work in offices."

Our last stop was Victoria Island. I showed them the federal government flats where legislators stayed when they were meeting. I also wanted them to know that was where I'd stayed on my first two nights in the country. I wasn't sure I conveyed this.

It didn't matter. I knew how far I'd come in those nineteen months. I'd arrived as a stranger in a land completely different from my own. In the months since, I'd fallen in love with the country, its complexity, and its diversity. I'd found a place where I felt at home, even though I looked so different. And I'd fallen in love with their son.

We drove on to Bar Beach, left our shoes in the car, and walked beside the ocean.

"Where the other side be?" Papa wanted to know.

"Very far away," was the best explanation I could provide. Pointing into the distance beyond the waves, I said, "My home is over there."

Gabriel had made Clem's regular Saturday lunch of yam and beans. I was already fond of this dish, though I found it was improved with the addition of completely un-Nigerian catsup. When we finished, Clem suggested a visit to his good friend Johnson, whom I'd met several times.

"You remember him, don't you?" he said to his parents. "He married a woman from England, and they have a daughter." Clem had been in primary school with Johnson. I liked him and his wife, Jean, and I was even a little jealous of Clem's having a friend he'd known for so long.

Jean and Johnson lived in southwest Ikoyi, where the houses were closer together, without large lawns like Clem's, and looked a little more like Onitsha. Jean already spoke some Igbo and welcomed them in their own language. To me, her Igbo was as difficult to understand as her English with her strong Lancashire accent. But to them, here was a foreign wife who had no intention of leaving.

The next day, we took them to the morning service at St. Saviour's Church. We returned to Clem's home for a leisurely typical Sunday lunch with rice, chicken stew, and plantain. Late in the afternoon, his parents asked Clem and me to sit down for a formal meeting. They were leaving the next morning early, they said, and wanted to address us.

"We came to visit you because you asked us to come," Papa said to Clement, who translated for me. "When Isaiah brought Cathy to see us in Onitsha, he said you wanted us to meet her. Do you now intend to marry her?"

"I do, but I wanted you to get to know her before I told you formally," Clem said.

Papa turned to me. "We have seen how you care for Clement. You took us around during our visit and showed us the city. You are learning Igbo. You are not proud like other white people."

He turned again to his son. "Clement, you must be good to Cathy. Continue to teach her Igbo and proper Igbo customs."

He then addressed both of us. "When you have children, you must make them know that they belong to Nanka." He glanced at Mama before saying, "If you have arguments, you should settle them well."

"Missus," he said to Mama, *"je'e wete ife anye ge nye fa.* Go fetch the thing we will give them." I wasn't sure I understood, but I thought he was referring to a gift for us. She came back with a common straw broom, nearly three feet long, bound near the top with brown strips of raffia. I'd seen these brooms used but had never seen a new one. It smelled like fresh-cut hay.

He directed her to hand it to Clem and me and told us to grasp it together by its rough handle. "The broom is a way to honor our ancestors," he said. "It is also a sign that you should sweep away anything evil between you and keep your marriage and home spotless." His final comment was, "We expect you to bear children for us, especially sons, and make us proud." Their wish would be fulfilled sooner than any of us knew at the time.

After Clem's parents had given us their blessing and returned home, I could no longer put off telling my own parents. I wrote every two weeks, and Mother responded with the same frequency. Once in a while there would be a note from my father.

By early spring of 1964, when I should have been making plans for my return to the United States, they did ask about my next steps. I ignored the question. Now I wrote to tell them about Clement, his background and professional life, how long we'd been dating, and our decision to marry. I said Nigeria would become my permanent home. I wanted them to meet him during the summer and come to our wedding in December.

I imagined my father saying something like, "Good for you. You'll give the people in Fort Thomas something to talk about." I didn't know what Mother would say. In ten days, I found out. "Is he a Christian?" was her most pressing question. She'd taken a course in Nigerian politics and culture at the University of Cincinnati during my first year as a Peace Corps volunteer. She knew the country was about half Muslim and that Muslims could have three wives and many concubines.

"Yes, he is a Christian. His parents brought him up as an Anglican, and he attended Anglican schools," I wrote back. "I go to St. Saviour's Anglican Church with him every Sunday. He's the chaplain's warden, like a senior deacon in the Presbyterian Church. That's where the wedding will be. The chaplain, Reverend Payne, will marry us."

My mother's next letter said they'd been considering a trip to Germany that summer with my sister and brother and suggested meeting Clem there so they wouldn't be strangers at the wedding.

"I should meet them in the United States first," Clem suggested as we ate *akamu*, a custard made from cornstarch and a little like grits, and fried bean cakes called *akara* one Sunday morning. "I don't want them to think I'm afraid of them."

"Aren't you, at least a little? I was certainly nervous about meeting your parents when they came to visit."

"You can prepare them," he said. "Tell them how wonderful I am when you get home." He held his arms out to his side in a familiar gesture to show he was ready to challenge anyone. "And then I can visit a couple of weeks later. I would just stay for two or three days." I agreed that it was a good plan.

But I needed something first. "I can't go home without an engagement ring," I said. The next Saturday afternoon, we headed downtown to the jewelry store I'd noticed on the corner of Broad and Nnamdi Azikiwe streets, across from Kingsway. I was surprised by the wide selection and the price range. So many rings, and I hadn't even thought about what I wanted, nor had Clem considered what they cost. He doesn't part with money easily and purposely doesn't carry much cash.

The Lebanese salesman kept a close eye on us as he offered first one, then another, ring for me to try. He talked about carats, gold, silver, and platinum, and a variety of settings. Clem didn't notice his slightly patronizing attitude and was surprisingly patient as I finally decided on a simple gold setting with a small diamond for twenty-five pounds. That was as much as Clem had. "You have to get the wedding band later," I told him, trusting that his best man would make sure he had the ring. I confirmed that the store would keep a record to make sure the band he chose would match the engagement ring.

With the parents now informed and on board, the engagement ring on my finger, and the wedding date set, I turned to the question of where I would teach in the fall.

The Science School didn't respond to my letter asking if they would hire me; maybe the principal was still miffed that I'd been uncooperative on our one date. But Mr. Cardoso at Awori-Ajeromi Grammar School offered me a contract right away and even said he would take over paying for my little Fiat, which Peace Corps had provided. I accepted.

In my wrap-up interview with the Nigeria Peace Corps representative, I told him about my plans.

"Have you considered what a major decision you are making?" he said.

"Yes, I have. I've come to feel like I belong here. I've told my parents, who will be coming for the wedding. I'll send you an invitation."

"You understand that the Peace Corps does not sanction marriage to host-country nationals, but you will not be a volunteer then. So I wish you happiness."

My Peace Corps friends would be gone by December, since our whole group concluded assignments in June. Besides, I'd hardly seen them in the past few months. Art had gone home early. I hadn't seen Dave or Bob, whom I'd also dated, since Christmas. I did see Roger at a Lagos Peace Corps gathering.

We were close; after all, we'd traveled to Niger together, and we'd shared accommodations at the Peace Corps Rest House in Lagos for six weeks at the start of our assignments.

"You look so happy," he said when I shared my news. "Why couldn't you get married sooner so I could come?" I couldn't do that, but he did give me an idea.

"Let's have an engagement party," I said to Clem as we talked about friends of his and people I'd introduced him to. He already knew the Hedglins. He'd met the Butlers, and through them, we'd met other Americans. Carol Obianwu, an American woman whose husband, Walter, worked at ECN, was a good friend. We invited other teachers from the Science School and a German couple we'd met through Carol. Clem's friends came with their wives. And I invited Roger.

I was determined to demonstrate my ability to prepare Nigerian food for our party guests, so I decided to make *moi-moi*, steamed ground beans. The traditional way was to make cones of banana leaves, pour the bean mixture in, tie it with a string of raffia, and steam it over a platform of sticks in a big pot. I had the steward buy the beans, what I'd call black-eyed peas, and get them ground in the market. He also bought the banana leaves and other ingredients and gathered the sticks I would use.

On the afternoon of the party, I poured the ground beans into a mixing bowl, added ground crayfish and pepper, chopped onions, and corned beef. Then I had Gabriel hold the cones while I poured the mixture in. He placed the wrapped packets in the bottom of the pot. An hour later, he brought them out, unwrapped them, and placed them on a platter.

They looked great—each serving had the right shape and even showed the characteristic creases from the banana leaves. When it was served and I took a bite, I realized I had forgotten the salt! I felt foolish and apologized, but of course our guests were kind, added salt, and ate it mixed with the tasty stew Gabriel had prepared.

On June 20, Clem drove me to the airport, where I boarded Pan Am with the ticket Peace Corps had provided and headed back to Cincinnati. My high school friends Ann, Ruth, and Carolyn were full of congratulations, although Ruth and Carolyn showed some doubt about my choice. Carolyn's mother was clear in her opinion.

"I don't know how you can marry a colored person," she said when I phoned one day to speak to Carolyn. "I don't mind if one is in a room with me, but to be with many of them at once, how can you stand it?"

"I can not only stand it," I said, "but I'm very comfortable. They don't show the prejudice against me that some white people have against them."

"Well, I just can't understand it," she concluded, before putting Carolyn on the phone.

As Clem and I had planned, I suggested to my parents that he visit briefly before we all met in Germany. As the time for Clem's visit approached, I wondered how he would feel in this all-white town. I shouldn't have worried; he'd spent nine years in England.

I went alone to pick him up from the airport. I ignored the covert looks that followed us as we embraced and walked through the airport. I led him to the black Pontiac in the parking lot. When we were in the car and away from others' eyes, I turned to him. "I'm so glad we're going to live in Nigeria."

We talked about his flight, my visit so far, and his work. In no time, we were in Fort Thomas. I drove up the steep driveway. Turning off the engine, I gave Clem a quick kiss. "Well, here goes. At least you don't have a language problem to overcome."

"Don't worry," he said. "I'll be on my best behavior." He got his battered suitcase from the trunk and followed me up the porch steps and in the front door, where Mother and Father were waiting for us.

"Welcome to the United States." It sounded so mundane, but what else could they say? They asked about his flight, and after a few moments of rather stilted conversation, I took him to his room upstairs. Over dinner, Clem told them about his own parents and their visit to Lagos four months earlier. "Cathy won them over in a couple of days," he said. "I hope I can win your trust as well."

"I hope so too," my father said.

I'd referred briefly in a letter to how Clem and I met but now gave them the full story. "I'd been practically ordered to show up at his office," I said. "Something about my electricity use."

"She was actually rather rude," Clem said.

"But when I saw him the second time, I was friendlier. And after the third, we started going out."

"Did you like England?" my mother asked.

"The first winter, I hated it. Once I got used to the cold, yes, I did."

Clem does not warm up easily, but my mother gradually drew him out. "Who will we meet at the wedding?" she said.

"My parents will be there. They are eager to meet you." Good for you, Clem, I thought.

"At least one sister, Monica, will be there. I'm planning to ask her to be my bridesmaid. And I think Geoffrey will come. He's in medical school," I said.

The next day, my parents presented Clem with a new suitcase. "We thought you could use this," they said as they handed it to him. "The one you brought looked a little the worse for wear." That was an understatement—it was so old Clem had to hold it together with a strap. He parted with it reluctantly. I was glad Father took it straight to the garbage where it belonged.

"You like throwing things away too much. I took that suitcase to England with me. I could have given it to someone in Nigeria," he said. I knew no one in Nigeria would want it. It was the first of many times we differed over what to keep and what to throw away.

Father took Clem to his office on the third day. I was envious—I'd never seen his office. "He introduced me to his colleagues and showed me all around the building. He told his friends I was a real-life Horatio Alger. He seemed proud of me," Clem told me that evening. "I like him very much. You said he might make nasty remarks, but he hasn't."

"I'm glad he's held his sarcasm in check. He likes you too, and so does Mother."

On the day of Clem's departure, my parents didn't present us with a broom or any other sign of acceptance as Clem's parents had. But Clem exchanged warm hugs with my mother and a solid handshake with my dad, and I felt sure that they'd started a relationship that could grow over the years. When I returned Clem to the airport for his flight back, I was relieved and grateful. I'd see him again in three weeks in Germany. He'd meet my siblings who would accompany my parents. I hoped that meeting would go as well.

5

PREPARATION, A SURPRISE, AND THE WEDDING

"LET'S GO SHOPPING," my mother said the day after I dropped Clem at the Cincinnati airport. "We can at least buy your dress, since we're apparently not paying for the wedding."

I had last shopped for clothes with Mother when I was getting ready for college six years earlier. I still remembered the tweed skirt and lamb's wool sweater set we'd bought at Peck & Peck.

When we walked into the large bridal shop in Cincinnati, I was astounded at the variety of dresses, fabrics, sleeve lengths, and bodice styles. I tried on three or four dresses. Each change brought me a little closer to feeling like a bride. With Mother's encouragement, I chose a white, silk-blend dress with a six-foot train, a low, beaded bodice, and three-quarter-length sleeves. I added a delicate veil, white satin pumps, and white stockings. The dress had to be altered, so Mother would pick it up and bring it with her in December.

"Maybe I should place an announcement of my engagement in the *Cincinnati Enquirer*," I said as we finished dinner that evening. My parents agreed.

I called and explained that I had just returned from the Peace Corps and was going back to Nigeria to marry. The editor was interested in my story and sent a reporter and photographer. I put on a Dutch print Nigerian blouse and wrapper with a head tie, and I held an ostrich feather fan for the photo while I answered questions about Peace Corps, Nigeria, and my fiancé. I was gone by the time the article came out, but Mother sent me the clipping. What she didn't tell me was that they received hate calls from people who found the idea of a white woman marrying an African offensive.

I left for Europe ahead of my parents and siblings to meet my friend Ann so we could travel together. She'd just finished graduate school and would be starting a job soon. I was enjoying my last free summer before returning to Nigeria and marriage. We visited the Rijksmuseum and the Ann Frank House in Amsterdam, and Copenhagen's Tivoli Gardens. I left her in Denmark and flew to Frankfurt to wait for Clem and my family.

"I'm here, just the way we planned." I grabbed Clem's hand when he was walking toward the reception desk in the hotel lobby. He turned and gave me a quick hug before putting his suitcase—the new one my father had bought him—down to embrace me properly. I had already checked in, so I waited for him to get his room and followed him upstairs.

We had a couple of hours to ourselves before meeting my family. He pulled me to him, but I held back. I felt we couldn't make love in his hotel room when we weren't yet married and my parents were coming soon. He was a little puzzled as I tried to explain why his house in Lagos was completely different in my mind. He went along with my prudishness—he had no choice.

Two hours later, we were in the lobby again to see my family arrive. Mother and Clem embraced warmly, Father shook Clem's hand, and then I introduced Peter and Beth.

"I've heard so much about you," Clem said with the shy smile I loved.

"Likewise," Peter said. Beth stared for several seconds, shook Clem's hand, and, turning away from Clem to Father, said softly enough that Clem wouldn't hear: "He's so short! I almost need to kneel down to talk to him!" She's taller than I am. Clem is a couple of inches shorter than I, though he wore lifts in his shoes then, so we were nearly the same height. At least she wasn't commenting on his race.

At dinner together, Peter asked Clem from across the table, "Have you been to Germany before?"

"No. When I was in the UK, I rented a car one summer and drove around France," Clem said, "but I didn't come here. I ran out of money and had to return to Leeds." The conversation was easy.

I had a moment of embarrassment over lunch on our second day, when my mother was speaking about an opera she'd recently seen. "Do you like opera?" she asked Clem.

"Yes, I saw *My Fair Lady* in London. It was excellent." I winced, waiting for a biting comment from my father or brother to point out that *My Fair Lady* was musical theater, not real opera. But the moment passed.

Clem only stayed in Frankfurt for two days. When he left, he was better acquainted with my parents, whom we would see again in December. And he now knew my siblings, so I could talk about them more easily.

I stayed on with my family for another few days. We drove to Lübeck to see Father's sister-in-law Lena, whom I'd met three years earlier when I'd spent a summer in Germany. I was delighted to show off my German now, after two years of teaching.

The next day, I learned that Father was planning a visit to Rostock, his birthplace, with my brother. How could he? I was the one who'd learned German, and he should have taken me. Yet I didn't speak up. At the age of twenty-three, I still had a lot to learn about expressing my feelings.

Neither parent had given me a good model. Mother was usually silent when challenged. She didn't stand up to Father's sarcasm, often at her expense, and avoided confronting him. Father would voice his opinions in a manner that didn't invite challenge. Six months later, I would shock myself and my family when I did speak up during our December wedding rehearsal in the church in Lagos. But that summer in Germany, I didn't yet have the courage.

Back in Lagos, the wedding planning picked up. We met with our planning committee—George Butler, Anthony Obelagu, and Simon Mkparu—and drew up our list of tasks. We decided to ask a leading Lagos businessman, Sir Mobolaji Bank-Anthony, to be the chairman of the event and rejoiced when he agreed.

Clem and I drew up our guest list, ordered five hundred invitations, and sent out almost all. We decided to have the reception in the large yard at Clem's house. Since December is the dry season, we didn't worry about rain. Clem hired the Police Band to play. I asked his sister Monica to be my bridesmaid and the Butlers' six-year-old daughter, Lizzie, to be my flower girl. They would wear pink.

My new school year started. Now I was full-time at Awori-Ajeromi Secondary Grammar School, and I drove there every day through the slums of Ajegunle. I loved the feeling of familiarity, of knowing the students I'd taught for two years. This year, I taught African history, religious knowledge, and English.

Clem and I decided to visit his parents and fill them in on the wedding plans. We took advantage of the October 1 Independence Day long weekend and drove to Onitsha. Clem took me for a closer look at Dennis Memorial Grammar School—his school. He showed me the field where Jonathan had told him about his intention to be a priest. I learned that there was a church, St. John's, at the far end of the street where his parents lived—at last I knew the source of the street name St. John's Cross.

How different this was from my first visit with Clem's parents. Now I was to be married to their son, and I was on display as friends and neighbors came by. Clem hovered a little nervously as I met visitors, but I took it all in stride. I'd always enjoyed meeting new people. My Igbo was tested, but everyone I met was so pleased with my effort that I was encouraged to continue.

After the meal was cleared on our final evening, Clem's father said he wanted to meet with us. I was surprised and a little worried. Was there some new difficulty? "What's happening?" I said to Clem.

"No idea," he said. Papa did look stern, but that was his normal expression. "Missus," he called, summoning Mama from her outdoor kitchen. She came, drying her hands on her wrapper. Her expression was cheerful. No sign of upset. That was good.

Papa opened by welcoming me. "You have made our son happy. Thank you." He continued with a discourse about Igbo marriage. "Usually there is a lengthy process involving both families," he said. Clem had already told me about traditional marriage customs, so I didn't need a lot of translation.

"My father chose this woman for me," he said, indicating his wife. "She has been a good wife and mother. You," he continued, pointing to his son, "have made your own choice. I know that men are doing this today."

Now he turned to face me. "For us, marriage is a bond between families. You should know what we would have done if Clement had come to us to tell us about an Igbo woman he wanted to marry. As his father, I would have consulted others before our family accepted you. It is our responsibility to ascertain the fitness of the family and the woman."

Papa continued, and I thought of Johnny, my Igbo friend who'd told me about Fred's marriage many months earlier. Johnny had fallen in love with an Igbo woman. When his family had checked her background, they found she was *Osu*, meaning from a slave family. Slavery is no longer practiced among the Igbos, but the stigma stays with a family for generations, and he couldn't marry her.

If an Igbo woman and her family prove acceptable, then an emissary from the man's family visits to see if there is interest. Gifts are presented. The families eventually negotiate the bride price, a payment from the man's family to repay the woman's family for raising her. The bride price is also a guarantee— if the woman leaves her husband without a major transgression on the man's part, the bride price must be returned.

As Papa finished his explanation, he said, "I am sorry I cannot visit your father and your family. I would like to ask them to let you marry my son. But we will have to wait until December."

I thought our meeting was over, but he was not done. "Missus, bring the palm wine," he said. He poured a glass of the white liquid. "Take this to Clement," he said, handing it to me, "and kneel in front of him. Take a drink, and give him the wine to finish."

I hesitated for a few seconds. Kneeling in front of my husband-to-be felt like the wrong message. I didn't intend to be subservient. But I liked the symbolic affirmation and the approval of Clem's parents, so I complied. Clem looked a little sheepish as I sipped and handed him the glass.

In Lagos, the weeks before the wedding sped past. One of our planners was responsible for the main food, but I had to get the cake. I ordered a four-tiered wedding cake from the Lagos YWCA to be delivered on the day.

Responses to the wedding invitations poured in, and we began receiving wedding presents. Mr. Sun, the CEO of the Electricity Corporation and Clem's boss, sent a lovely set of china.

Two months before the date, I missed my period. Was I just nervous? Or was it something else? In the busyness of wedding planning and teaching, I ignored it. Then I missed again. This time I went to my doctor, who did a pregnancy test. A week later, I learned that I was pregnant! This wasn't part of our planning, or at least not mine. This was for real.

I was half elated and half dismayed. Then I was embarrassed. I wanted to share the news, but I didn't want to tell anyone. In the sixties, getting pregnant before the wedding wasn't accepted. Of course, people did and kept it quiet. Then I had a sudden fear—would my wedding dress fit?

Clem, on the other hand, wasn't worried at all. "That's the best news I could get," Clem said on hearing the confirmation. He hugged me hard, and then pulled back. "Maybe I shouldn't do that. Are you all right?"

"You can hug me all you want. I'm fine. Being pregnant is normal," I said, as if I knew all about it. We walked upstairs so he could change after his day at work.

"How long before you have the baby?" he said as he took off his business suit and put on his wrapper. "Do you think it will be a boy?"

"The doctor said probably July, a long way off. And no way to tell if it's a boy. Does it matter?"

"If you have a boy first, you establish your credibility with the village, not to mention with my parents."

We agreed that we'd tell our parents right after the wedding.

On December 22, the *New York Times* ran the story, "Peace Corps Worker to Wed Nigerian Engineer," from United Press International's Lloyd Garrison. My parents heard from people in Fort Thomas who thought the wedding should be stopped right away since Kentucky still had a law against interracial marriage. But they didn't tell me this when we met them at the airport on December 23.

They commented on the blast of tropical heat that I remembered from my first arrival, even though it was less humid and cooler now that it was the season of Harmattan, the dry, dusty wind that blows south from the Sahara.

My mother had the wedding dress. I kept the news of my pregnancy to myself. We drove them to the home of Ruth and George Butler, their hosts for the week they were in the country. Clem's family arrived the same day and stayed with him. For propriety's sake, I moved out of Clem's house to stay with Anne and Ben.

On the twenty-fourth, as we all sat together in Clem's parlor, my parents surprised me when they said, "We would like to get you a piano for your wedding present."

I was touched and thrilled. They had already asked the Butlers and knew where to go, so the three of us drove downtown. We found an upright in a maple frame, with a good sound and a touch I liked, and a bench with a top that opened, just like the one we had in Fort Thomas. We arranged delivery for the Monday after the wedding. "This is a wonderful present. I didn't expect anything like this," I said as I dropped them off for their lunch and a siesta. "Just your coming was a present in itself."

Our wedding rehearsal was in the afternoon. The Butlers brought my father and their daughter, my flower girl. Clem and I came with Monica, my maid of honor.

Reverend Payne met us in the sanctuary. He had us line up at the back of the sanctuary, process up the aisle, and start through the vows for practice.

"I don't want to say 'obey' as part of my vow," I said, with a sudden assertion of my independence, surprising even myself.

"What's wrong with 'obey?'" Clement said.

"Why should I promise that? Are you promising to obey me? I think it's outdated, and I don't want to say it."

"How would it be if we change it to 'cherish?'" Reverend Payne said. Crisis averted. Clem wasn't too happy, but I was pleased with my victory. The rehearsal proceeded without another hitch. As we were leaving, Reverend Payne shook Father's hand, saying, "I think your daughter made a good choice."

Among the items Clem's parents had brought from the East to cook for the family was a goat. Gabriel had butchered it and used most of it in the meals he'd cooked. But the head was still intact. Mama planned to make a spicy stew called *ngwo-ngwo*, made from the head of the goat, to go with our Christmas lunch.

As we sat down for drinks at Clem's, Father said, "I'll get the ice."

"I can call Gabriel," I said. But Father disliked asking the steward to get things for him, so he headed into the kitchen himself.

A moment later, we heard a strange shriek from the kitchen. My father emerged without ice.

"There's a head in the freezer!" he said. "It was looking right at me." Goats are ugly even when alive, and this head had its mouth open and teeth bared. Father didn't enter the kitchen again and reconciled himself to sending the steward whenever he wanted something.

Our wedding was at 3:00 p.m. the day after Christmas, on the holiday I had come to know as Boxing Day. I'd taken my wedding gown to Anne's, and she helped me dress—it fit fine. She made a lovely bouquet of fragrant white and peach frangipani flowers for me and white boutonnières for the men. At 2:40 p.m., Father collected me to drive to the church. He was never one to show his emotions, but I could tell he was moved as he said, "I hope you will be happy with Clement. He seems like a good man." We were a few minutes early, and St. Saviour's had no waiting area. We circled the Race Course a couple of times so we would arrive on the dot!

The church was full when Father and I got out of the car. Monica was waiting to help me arrange the train, and Clem was already at the altar with his best man. "I was very, very nervous that you wouldn't come," he said later.

Lizzie led the procession as I walked up the aisle on my father's arm. My mother was waiting in her seat, and I smiled at her as my father stepped back to join her. She had tears in her eyes but a smile on her face. Clem's parents were across the aisle from them. Geoffrey, Clem's brother, was in the chancel at the front with a tape recorder.

"Do you take this man to be your wedded husband?" Reverend Payne asked. "Do you promise to love, honor, and cherish him, as long as ye both shall live?"

"I do." We concluded our vows, and Reverend Payne said, "You may kiss the bride." Monica lifted my veil for Clem's kiss. I couldn't stop smiling as we came out of the church, walked through the shower of rice, and let the photographer arrange and rearrange us. I was in a haze of happiness.

Soon Clem left to get back to the reception, while I was taken in another car for a brief stop at Mkparu's house to freshen up. I was very relieved someone had thought of this.

"Wait here," Monica said, leaving me in the car at Clem's house. She ran off to get Clem so we could walk in together as the Police Band played a livelier version of "Wedding March." I was overwhelmed by the crowd—the *New York Times* stated there were more than five hundred people[1]—the lavishly decorated "high table," and the music. Our guests applauded as we walked under the palm trees to our seats. I spotted Peace Corps Representative William Saltonstall and his wife in the crowd, along with Clem's colleagues and Mr. Inyang from my school.

Sir Mobolaji Bank-Anthony was a hit as chairman of the occasion. He loved being in the spotlight, extemporized easily, and had the crowd captivated. Clem's good friend Dozie gave the toast to the groom. He spoke of their long friendship and concluded with, "Thank goodness, the most eligible bachelor in Lagos, indeed in Nigeria, has finally been conquered. So the field is open for me at last!"

My father offered the toast to the bride. "I am honored to be here. Thank you to Clement for choosing Catherine as his wife. Otherwise, we would not have seen this lovely country and met his wonderful parents." He lifted his glass for a toast. "To the bride and groom and to all of you who have been so kind to us."

In the heat, the cake didn't fare well. The top two tiers began leaning dangerously and would have fallen if we hadn't cut it when we did.

After our wedding, we were celebrities. The creation of Peace Corps was still recent enough that the wedding of a volunteer to a "host-country national," especially when the marriage was interracial, was newsworthy. The *New York Times'* story, "Nigerian Marries Peace Corps Girl," ran with the subheading, "Bride's Grandfather Headed Land Bank under Wilson."[2] Our photo appeared in *Life* magazine a week later.[3] There was an article and photo in *Jet* magazine a week after that.[4] I was stunned—I didn't realize our wedding was news to anyone but us and our families.

We received dozens of congratulatory telegrams from people who knew Clem or me and wished us well, and even from people who simply read about our wedding and sent good wishes. But my parents returned to a barrage of hate calls. And I didn't know until years later, when my brother told me, that they finally had to delist their phone number.

We said farewell to his parents and then mine and a day later left for our delayed honeymoon. We went to neighboring Dahomey, a former French colony with a decidedly French flavor.

"Try the French onion soup," I said to Clem on our first evening. He loved it.

I thought this would help him overcome his aversion to cheese, which he swore was spoiled milk. I was sure there had been a mistranslation on someone's part when teachers at DMGS had told their students that cheese was made from "fermented" milk. So I said, "You know it had cheese on top."

He was horrified and was sick all night but got little sympathy as I was sure it was feigned illness, or at the least psychosomatic.

The next day, he'd recovered. As we walked around the city, we paused to chat with a stranger who smiled a greeting. He turned to my husband and said in Yoruba, "Where are you coming from?" Clem looked at him blankly while I responded, also in Yoruba, "We're from Lagos." Seeing his look of amazement at the language coming from me instead of Clem was pure delight.

Two weeks later, we were visiting the Hedglins. Alice found life in Lagos hard. She told me they were returning to the United States as soon as the school year ended. Their first son, Nils, had been ill frequently during his early months. I was sorry, as was Clem. He didn't make friends easily but had become comfortable with them. "So you won't be here in July. I'm expecting a baby then," I said, finally able to tell a close friend.

"I'm so happy for you," she said, getting up to embrace me.

"You didn't waste any time," Fred said. I wondered if he was remembering the pregnancy scare I'd given him a year and a half earlier. I couldn't help thinking about it as the two men exchanged a congratulatory handshake.

"I'm so sorry I won't be here," Alice said. "I wish I could be, but I can't keep subjecting my baby to this climate."

I was eager for any advice. She told me about her challenges with breastfeeding, the necessity of sterilizing the bottles, and how hard it was to keep everything clean. She promised to leave her copy of Dr. Spock's *Baby and Child Care* for me.

The next few months, as my waistline expanded, I bought maternity clothes. When I couldn't find what I wanted, I visited the cloth market for fabric and made my own. The Singer sewing machine Clem had bought as part of his wedding gift to me got good use. I also made a couple of little baby kimonos in pastel prints that would work for a boy or girl. I was full of enthusiasm with preparations for my first child.

Dozie, Clem's friend, was now my obstetrician. He gave me iron pills and vitamins, weighed me regularly, and told me all was normal. He gave us the delivery date of July 10. "I can finish the school year," I said.

That's what I thought. But babies don't wait for school years to end. Or even for their fathers to be home.

6

GOD IS THE ONE WHO CREATES KINGS

"I NEED TO HIRE a nanny," I said to Clem two months before the baby was due. "Does she need to be Igbo?"

"Of course," he said. "But you don't need to hire anyone here. My mother can help us find someone." He told her we would come in early June and that she should have some prospects.

I knew nothing about caring for a baby. I was only four when my little sister was born. When I babysat as a teenager, it was for older children. I hoped for someone who had experience and would live with us to be available round-the-clock. I would have to trust her to look after the baby during the day when I returned to teaching.

Mama told her younger sister Mmafo to bring her daughters to Onitsha for our visit. She had cared for Clem when he was a baby. The symmetry was appealing, and I could see the advantage of a family member.

We approached the fourteen-year-old, Nwakaego. My Igbo was still not enough for this conversation. Mama and Clement told her what we wanted.

"*Mba, Mama, achoram ije. Achorom ino ebaa.* No, Mama, I don't want to go. I want to stay home," Nwakaego said. Even I understood her answer. Now what? I wondered.

Immediately Mama called the younger sister, Rosa. Her hair, like her sister's, was tied in neat, shiny, inch-long plaits that stuck out all over her head. She was pretty but shy. I couldn't tell if she was always so quiet or just nervous. The invitation was repeated, and Rosa agreed.

I pulled Clem from the room to the veranda to be out of earshot of Mama and the others. "Why did Mama ask her before consulting me?"

"She knows you need someone. What is the problem?" he said.

"She's only twelve. How can she take care of a baby? I'll go back to work when the baby is little. And did she even want to come? I couldn't tell if her mother was forcing her." I wanted to scream, not talk softly so we wouldn't be overheard.

"She wants to come."

"She doesn't speak English. How will I talk to her?" I said.

"She knows a little English. She will help you learn Igbo," Clem replied.

Still unsure, I followed Clem back inside. He asked his mother to explain Rosa's experience with child care. "She's been taking care of her younger siblings and cousins. Lots of older children watch over younger ones. They expect to," Mama said in Igbo, with Clem translating. "Many girls not much older than Rosa have babies themselves."

"All right," I said to them. "We will bring her back if this doesn't work." She and I would be teaching each other. She probably did know more than I did about child care, and certainly I would improve my Igbo.

Rosa packed her few belongings, said good-bye to the life she had known, and departed with us to Lagos. I could only imagine how she must have felt leaving her family behind. She hardly spoke on the trip.

Back home, I took her to the bedroom she would share with the baby and, in my poor Igbo, explained the crib and her own bed. She marveled at all the white fixtures and chrome fittings in the bathroom. So much was new for her. I realized she'd never had a bed of her own. She'd seen running water but had not had it in her home. The toilet that flushed was a surprise.

I took her with me to the dining room, calling Clem from our bedroom on the way. As I walked carefully down the stairs, aware of my swollen body,

I kept thinking that I had brought a child into our home just as I was gearing up for my own baby. What was I thinking?

"Sit down," I said to her. Clem took his usual seat, but I could see he wasn't pleased.

"What's wrong?" I said as I served our plates with the rice, stew, and plantain. No answer.

Rosa looked even less relaxed than Clem as she picked at her food. "Eat!" Clem said to her. She did but not with much enthusiasm. We finished our meal, and I sent Rosa to bed.

"What was bothering you?" I said to Clem when we were getting undressed in our own room.

"Rosa should not eat with us. You could see she was not comfortable."

"She's your cousin. Doesn't that qualify her for a place at our table?"

"No, it does not. She is here as a servant, and that's how we should treat her."

I frowned. "So when and where should she eat?"

"In the kitchen after we are finished. That should be obvious."

It wasn't obvious to me. Didn't we expect her to be part of the household? Did that not include eating with us?

"Do you want Gabriel to sit with us while we eat?" Clem said.

"No, of course not."

"You need to get over your egalitarian American ideas," he said. "I love the fact that you are kind. But sometimes you're too kind. You have to let servants know their place."

The next evening when Clem and I went to our upstairs parlor to watch TV, I called Rosa to join us. "What are you doing?" Clem said.

"I'm asking her to watch TV with us. What do you think I'm doing?"

I wasn't going to negotiate again. "It will help her learn English, and she won't be alone all the time." Clem saw my determination and didn't argue.

I would start a new job, teaching fourth grade at the American International School, in September. But now I was finishing the year at Awori-Ajeromi Secondary School. I left early in the morning and returned in the late afternoon. When I was home, I conversed as best I could with Rosa. She was patient and helpful with my efforts at Igbo and as eager to learn English as I was to learn Igbo. I found out that her father had married a second wife and deserted his first family. Mmafo struggled with a small farm and petty trading. The children attended school sporadically.

Now Rosa was eager to make up for the education she had missed. Her English improved daily as we talked. TV helped too. She watched news and *Village Headmaster*, a popular TV drama, with us or on her own. The very proper English used by the newscaster was mostly beyond her, but *Village Headmaster* was in Pidgin English, easier for her to understand. She was a little puzzled at first by the ads for Lux Beauty Soap, Omo Washing Powder, and Star beer but caught on quickly. They gave her added vocabulary.

While I did not particularly like the role of mistress to her servant, I loved the role of teacher. I dug into the stack of paperbacks I had left from the Peace Corps book locker I had received when I first arrived in the country. I found the Ladder Editions with their simplified language and read them with her.[5]

I asked Gabriel to give her tasks and told him to take her along to the market. I took her with me to Kingsway to buy diapers, or nappies in the British parlance of Nigeria, baby powder, and baby cream.

"Will you be very unhappy if the baby is a girl?" I said to Clem on June 21, the night before he was to leave for Taiwan. He would be hiring senior engineers for ECN.

"I just want a healthy baby. A boy would be a bonus."

He departed, planning to return well before the baby's due date of July 6.

But the baby wasn't waiting. After dinner a few days later, I began to feel pain. By 11:00 p.m., I knew I was in labor and needed to go to the hospital. George and Ruth Butler had assured me they would help if needed while Clem was away. I roused Clem's brother Geoffrey, who was staying in our servants' quarters, and sent him on his bicycle to their house. In ten minutes, Ruth was at our door. "How frequent are your contractions?" she asked.

"Five minutes apart, I think."

"Let's go," she said. She tossed my suitcase into the backseat, helped me into the front, and sped through Ikoyi to Lagos Island Maternity Hospital. Ruth pulled into a parking spot right in front and helped me out. The four-story building, extending over half a city block, was new and modern. But it was hot. We found the receptionist asleep, slumped over her desk. Ruth woke her, and with grudging, heavy steps, she took us down a long hallway of offices to a bench in the waiting room. The smell of too many sweaty bodies was mixed with too little disinfectant. She said a nursing sister, as nurses are called in Nigeria, would see us soon. When no one appeared, Ruth went searching. We waited another fifteen minutes before a nursing sister arrived. "Has your water broken?"

"I don't know." I had no idea what she was talking about. But I discovered in the next few minutes what she meant. She seemed to regard it as a good sign, but that didn't lessen my discomfort at being in pain and now wet. She said she would call Dozie, my obstetrician.

As my contractions became more frequent, Ruth encouraged me with stories of her own children's births. "My first took almost a whole day. I thought she would never come," she said. "It's painful, but you'll forget the worst."

The nursing sister returned. "I can't reach the doctor, but the midwife is in the hospital. She will assist if the baby comes before I can reach him." I was taken to a room, and Ruth went home at 3 a.m., promising to return later in the day. The nursing sisters gave me a hospital gown to put on, told me to lie down, and left me alone. There were other beds, but no other people—it was too lonely, and I was frightened.

Half an hour later they returned to place me on a gurney and wheel me into the delivery room. "What's happening?" I asked. They must have done this hundreds of time, but this was my first, and I wanted information.

"Just relax and breathe." They seemed tired and reluctant to give me updates. To my relief, the midwife finally walked in at 4:30 a.m. and took charge.

"Tell me when you feel the next contraction," she said.

I couldn't have hidden it if I wanted, and I didn't. "Now bear down," she said. For three more hours, the contractions became longer and more painful. When I thought I couldn't bear down once more, I felt the baby emerge. I saw the midwife pull and lift the infant.

"You have a baby boy," the midwife said as she held him up for me to see. He looked wrinkled and wet, not what I'd imagined. But he looked whole. I watched her clip the cord and carry him to a table at the side of the room.

Two minutes later, she placed a pillow behind me and put my baby in my arms. His skin was a lovely light tan color. He had a mass of curly black hair. I ran my fingers through it, savoring the feel.

The midwife told me I had a tear that had to be repaired. A nursing sister stitched me up, every one of the needle pricks a new assault. What else would I have to endure?

I was wheeled into a small, private room, spare but clean. It held a single bed, a small table, a chair, and a crib. One nursing sister helped me get off the gurney, into a clean gown, and into bed. Another brought my baby, now swaddled in a soft layette blanket. She placed him in my arms. I cradled him, stroking his hair and admiring his eyes. The nurse encouraged me to hold him to my breast but he barely took hold. When I felt sleep coming, I put him gently in his crib, took out the photo of Clem I had packed in my suitcase at the last minute, and placed it on the bedside table.

My delight with the baby was bittersweet since I couldn't share it with my husband. I felt terribly alone. Even my obstetrician had disappointed me! He had given me a due date but hadn't warned me that the baby could be early. I fell asleep feeling sorry for myself.

I woke at noon and ate the hospital lunch. It tasted delicious and I felt restored. The nurses helped me with my next attempt to breastfeed. The baby had a hard time latching on. When he finally did, I was startled by the unexpected pain. But I loved holding him in my arms; I also hadn't expected the feeling of total adoration.

George came with Ruth shortly after, I was my usual self and happy to show off my baby.

"I've never seen such a head of hair on a baby," Ruth said. "He's so handsome, and he looks so alert." I was thrilled to hear her confirming what I already thought.

"We've sent a telegram to Clem," George said, admiring the baby Ruth was holding. "We phoned your parents. They send their love and wish they could be here."

Soon after they left, Dozie did come. "The midwife did a great job. My presence wouldn't have made any difference," he said on looking me over. "What a gorgeous baby. Clem must be very happy."

"Clem isn't here! He won't be back for days. You could have told me that the baby might come early."

He apologized for his oversight. "Babies don't obey rules very well. You'll have a lovely surprise for him."

Dozie came back the next day to perform the circumcision. He took the baby away and brought him back twenty minutes later. "Tomorrow you need to remove the bandage," he said. "I'll put a new one on if it needs it when I come. But today don't touch it."

After breakfast the next morning, I sat on the metal chair at the edge of the bed for twenty minutes, only daring to gingerly touch the bandage and try to remove it bit by bit. I was transfixed by the tiny penis and by the four inches of umbilical cord that were still attached. I was so intent on the task and my baby that I didn't notice the buzzing. Suddenly I realized my exposed legs were covered with mosquito bites. I couldn't undo the assault, but it reminded me to be careful with the mosquito nets for my bed and the baby's.

My closest friend, Carol Obianwu, came on Wednesday after school. She picked up the baby and echoed Ruth's comment. "What a head of hair. Neither of mine had this much when they were born. What does Clem say?"

"Clem is in Taiwan for ECN; he hasn't seen him yet." I was suddenly embarrassed, as if it were my fault for not having my husband with me. I choked up as I said, "I'm really upset that he isn't here. I suppose it isn't fair to be angry, but I'm angry too."

"You probably want to get over that before he comes back. You know he had to make the trip." I didn't care for her advice, but I knew she was right.

The Butlers came again on Wednesday. They brought Rosa and Geoffrey to see the baby, and they brought the cable from Clem that said he loved me and would return on Saturday. Geoffrey reported that he had called his parents to announce the birth. Clem's friends Ben and Johnson came with their wives. Clem's colleagues from ECN came. I couldn't miss their voices when they were still far down the corridor, and I had to smile at their boisterousness. The four men, all fairly large, filled the room while I held the baby for them to admire.

I sent word to the school that I had delivered the baby and would not be back for the rest of the term.

Nearly every time the baby woke, I tried to breastfeed, but it was challenging and painful. The nursing sisters tried to help and occasionally provided bottles.

By Saturday, five days after rushing to the hospital, I was more than ready to leave. I was again overwhelmed by sadness and anger that Clem wasn't going

— 59 —

to accompany me as I took our first child home. I tried to be reasonable—it wasn't really his fault. "He will be so sorry that he wasn't here," George said when he noticed my glum face as he and Ruth helped me pack up my belongings, the baby's nappies and layette blankets, and the photo.

"I know he will, but it doesn't make up for not coming in time."

Still, I carried the baby proudly while we drove back to the house.

I was alighting from the car when a taxi pulled up. Clem! He had come back and could walk in the door with me and our baby! I was so happy to see him that we nearly squashed the baby between us as we embraced. He took a tentative first look at his new child. I held the baby out for him to hold, but he stepped back. "Don't you want to hold your baby?" I said.

"Not yet. I need to adjust my thinking, and I'm dirty from traveling."

"Adjust your thinking? You've known for seven months that this baby was coming."

"But I didn't expect him to come before I returned."

"Neither did I! But here he is." I let the subject drop and kept the baby in my arms. He apologized profusely for his absence at this critical time but assured me that he had come as soon as possible. Ruth and George got back in their car as we thanked them for being lifesavers and a source of comfort while Clem was away.

I showed the baby happily to the cook, the gardener, and the watch-day. Rosa was eager to hold him. I was ready to spend a few minutes with my husband and gladly gave her the baby.

He held me again. "Tell me what happened."

I related the last week's experience. Then he told me his.

"When I got the cable on Tuesday, I was at a dinner," he said. "I read it aloud, and my hosts erupted with congratulations and many toasts. I got a little drunk." He smiled at the memory. "I booked the flight home the next morning."

"The Butlers called my parents. Geoffrey called yours."

"You could have waited for me to tell them. This is their first grandchild, and a boy."

"You weren't here, remember?" I realized I still wanted to rub in his absence, despite his apology. And I was also harboring some annoyance at his refusal to hold his son. But I recovered quickly. "Why don't you call them now?"

He did. Of course, they were excited all over again. Papa promised to send the name soon. I had agreed with Clem to follow Igbo culture, giving the responsibility of naming the child to the baby's paternal grandfather and family elders. My only stipulation was that I could supply a middle name.

Within a week, we received a cable from Clem's father. There were two names—Chinakueze Iwenofu.

"I know that *Chi* means God, *ku* is to grow, and *eze* is king," I said, handing Clem the telegram. "But God grows kings?"

"A name sometimes has a meaning that isn't necessarily a literal translation," Clem said. I could tell that he was grappling with his father's intention. "I see what it is," he said suddenly. "God is the one who creates kings. I like it."

Clem looked again at the telegram in his hand. "Iwenofu—it means that anger, or *iwe*, should be thrown away."

"So what is the significance?"

"I don't know," he said. I was pretty sure it was chosen because there had been a quarrel going on between Papa and his brothers, and they wanted to end it. I suggested this to Clem, and he agreed that could be the meaning.

"This is a mouthful," I said to Clem. "Whatever are we going to call him?"

"Why not use the whole first name?"

"Five syllables for the first name and another five for his surname? I think that's a heavy burden for a small boy."

Within two days, we had shortened it to Chinaku. I added the name Danforth, my mother's maiden name and my middle one. "He can use Dan as a nickname when he's older if he wants," I said.

I loved watching him move his fingers, curl his toes, and focus his eyes. Clem was equally enraptured. I began to feel like a real mother with my little family. I wrote a long, glowing letter to my parents to describe their grandchild. Rosa loved him too. I was as pleased as she was that she now had an important role in the household.

Clem's parents called a few days after we'd received the cable. "When are you coming for the naming ceremony?" Mama said to Clem. "The usual time is two weeks. It's already been five."

"No, I just came home from the hospital two weeks ago," I said when Clem told me what his mother said.

"The Igbo week," Clem said. "Remember?" I did—four days to a week.

"What happens in a naming ceremony? Is it like a christening?" I said, looking up from the baby in my arms to watch Clem.

"You'll see," Clem said. Turning back to the phone, he said, "I think we can come next weekend?" He looked to see me nod my head in agreement. I was being pulled deeper and deeper into Clem's Igbo culture, and I loved it.

As if a new baby were not enough, I had the Igbo language, a different calendar, and new customs to adjust to. Was I in over my head?

I had been to his village, three hundred miles from the capital, Lagos, where we lived, only once, and just for a couple of hours. Now we would spend two nights there, with no electricity and no running water. Although I was thrilled with the traditions, I wasn't sure how I would manage with a tiny baby.

I couldn't believe how much there was to pack. We had the baby's formula, nappies, baby clothes, and the little yellow carry-cot. We took a water filter, linens, and pillows.

We set out early on a Friday morning. Near Benin, the halfway mark, we ate the *jollof* rice we'd brought, and I nursed Chinaku. I was already tired of traveling, but we still hadn't crossed the Niger. The new bridge was under construction but wouldn't be open for another few months. I dreaded the wait for the ferry.

Clem saved us from the long wait. He explained to the men blocking access that, as chief electrical engineer, he was the one in charge of the cables carrying electric power across the bridge. He needed to drive across to be sure the installation was in order.

Still, I was exhausted when we arrived that night. It was already dark. Mama had Tilley lamps, the best type of kerosene lamp available, lit for us and dinner of pounded yam and *egusi* soup, my favorite, ready.

The house I had seen under construction nineteen months earlier was now completed. There were three rooms upstairs and a room over the gate at the front of the compound. Downstairs, there was a parlor with a few wooden chairs. Another two rooms were off a small hallway.

The kitchen was a shed to the left as one faced the house. The outhouse was near the kitchen, also on the left.

Papa had furnished the house with a double bed for us, his own bed in the gatehouse, and Mama's in another upstairs bedroom. I kept the baby beside us. Rosa slept on a mat in the third upstairs bedroom. The cook slept in one of the downstairs rooms.

I asked Clem about his parents' sleeping arrangements.

"When a man marries in our tradition, he has to build a house for his wife, and if he marries a second wife, he has to provide another. A wife's children stay with her," he said. I thought of Ejike, Clem's uncle next door, and his wife, Obele, who each had their own thatched huts. But they were just a few feet apart.

"I think Papa likes his privacy too. He can entertain men in his room and just shout for Mama or someone else to bring his food and drink," Clem added.

I remembered learning in Peace Corps training that couples practiced birth control by staying apart as long as the woman was nursing, usually about two years. Perhaps their arrangement was an extra dimension now that Mama was no longer of child-bearing age.

Mama had organized the water supply, sending children from the next compound to the spring. I had Gabriel boil the water and run it through the filter, as we did in Lagos. Mama found this very amusing.

The ceremony would take place on Saturday afternoon and evening. The whole clan had been invited, and a few other friends as well, so there would be seventy or eighty people. We had to provide a feast.

"Do I need to help prepare the food?" I asked Mama in my still-faltering Igbo.

"No," she assured me. Obele had rallied the *ndi ntaru di*, the cohort of women married into the family, to make *jollof* rice, pounded cassava, and okra soup. Ejike had already slaughtered the goat when we arrived. I caught the pungent smell from the next compound, where the animal was suspended over a fire to burn off its hair before it was cut up and added to the rice and soup.

Before we went to bed, I went over to thank the seven women who were stirring the contents of huge iron pots set on tripods over open fires. I took the baby with me.

"*Dalu*. Thank you," I said to one and then another. They were dressed for cooking, in wrappers—six feet of cotton cloth tied at the waist—and blouses that looked well used. One woman had her baby tied on her back with an extra piece of cloth.

"Nno, nwunye Clement. Welcome, Clement's wife," they said. Obele reached out to take the baby, holding him so the others could see. *"O maka.* He's good-looking," a younger woman said, and the others chorused their agreement. I thought their energetic voices would wake him, but he slept on. With their warm greetings and obvious joy at seeing my baby, I felt close to them. I was now part of the extended family, and I belonged here.

A few minutes later, I took Chinaku back to our house. Our bedroom faced the compound where the women were cooking. Well into the night, I could hear them singing and talking. The aroma of the goat meat being cooked was much more pleasant than the burning hair had been.

Benches borrowed from the nearby Anglican church were put in place in front of the house on Saturday morning. I learned later that, taking no chances, the rainmaker, or rain preventer in this case, had been visited and the spirits mollified.

At three in the afternoon, I nursed Chinaku and then dressed in the fanciest item in my wardrobe, a fitted dress of woven Akwete cloth in blue, green, and red. I asked Rosa to dress Chinaku in his blue cotton kimono with embroidered flowers. Clem wore his Igbo wrapper at home but was not yet accustomed to Igbo dress for formal occasions, and he wore his suit trousers with a loose paisley-print shirt that he loved.

Around four o'clock, people started to gather. Clem and I had seats of honor with Clem's parents and uncles in front of the house. Mama wore her best wrapper, a blue print with matching blouse and head tie. Papa was dignified in his long gown of the same fabric. He had added a felt cap of dark blue and a walking stick.

When the space in front of the house was full, Ejike stood up. *"Ndi be anyi, kwenu.* My people, rejoice." The guests shouted, *"Kwenu."* He turned to his left, then his right, with the same greeting. Each time, the response was louder. Chinaku began crying. I rocked him in my arms. "Don't worry. You're safe here."

I knew breaking kola was the first major agenda item of any Igbo event. Ejike reached down and took one of the kola nuts from the plate in front of him. "With this kola, I offer thanks to our ancestors," he said in Igbo as he held up the kola for everyone to see.

"The ancestors have honored us by making our son Clement"—in Igbo, the name Clement was stretched to Cu-le-ment—"a chief engineer. They honored us by giving him a wife from America. Now they have blessed us with a son."

He broke the kola nut he'd been holding into three pieces, took one, and placed the rest on the plate. Then he called several young men to carry the other prepared trays of kola nuts to pass to everyone present, men first, then the women. When everyone had a piece, jugs of palm wine and bottles of Star beer were brought out and served. Most men had their own calabash gourds with them. Some, I suspected, had started their drinking earlier in the day.

Years later, as his son Jonathan ascended the ranks in the Anglican Church in Nigeria, Ejike became a Christian. But now there was no reference to God and no amen. I wondered what Mother would have thought. I guessed she would have been as thrilled as I was to experience this non-Christian way of initiating a baby into the family.

Ejike took the baby from me and held him up before the crowd. "I have given this child the names Chinakueze Iwenofu." He poured a libation of palm wine on the ground as he said, "I consulted the Dibia, who said the ancestors approve."

The wailing baby was handed around to all the senior men. Then the women took turns holding him. He was passed back to me as the women brought out and served the food. After everyone had eaten their fill, a men's dance troupe performed, accompanied by drums, the high-pitched wooden Igbo flute, and Igbo maracas. Then the women, the same group who had cooked and served the food, were joined by more of their colleagues and they began to dance.

"*Bia, gba egwu.* Come dance with us." Obele pulled me up to join her. Rosa took the baby as I rose and joined the circle. I found it easy to follow their steps and, after a minute, lost my embarrassment and enjoyed the music, the movement, and the feeling of belonging. This was, after all, my group—the women married into the Onyemelukwe family. The crowd applauded, Clem most of all, as I sat down, sweating and dusty. The christening we planned to hold later at St. Saviour's Church would seem tame, even boring, after this.

The stub of Chinaku's umbilical cord had fallen off the day before we came to Nanka. Clem had told me to save it and bring it along for the ceremony. Now Papa asked me to bring it to him.

"I bury this cord, which binds Chinakueze to Nanka, to our compound, and to our people forever," he said. "Whenever he returns, he will know that he belongs here. When he is away, he will always know that part of him is here." He placed the cord in the hole that had been dug earlier near the wall between our compound and Ejike's. I felt an incredible surge of emotion for the family that had embraced me so warmly.

I returned to Lagos the next day, leaving a tiny part of my son behind in his father's village. Would he feel this connection? I knew that I did; it was now my village too.

Back in Lagos, I switched from African mode to American and consulted Dr. Spock's *Baby and Child Care*[6] often; it was the bible for American mothers in the 1960s. Dr. Spock said I should trust my instincts, let my child show me his needs, and feed him when he was hungry. This made sense to me, and Chinaku cooperated by doing exactly what he was supposed to. He slept soundly for two or three hours at a time. Rosa and I took turns changing nappies, bathing, and feeding him.

I had another month before I would start at the American School. At night, I took the little yellow carry-cot to our bedroom and placed it by the bed. When he woke up hungry, I nursed him. My breast milk was usually insufficient, so I would go to the kitchen for a bottle or wake Rosa to bring one. Clem could sleep through almost anything, but even he woke up often when the baby cried.

When Chinaku was eight weeks old and I had one more week before school started, I decided to move him into the room with Rosa at night. So after feeding him around 11:00 p.m., I put him to sleep in his crib and came back to bed. As I climbed in, Clem said, "Aren't you going to sleep in the room with Chinaku?"

"What do you mean?" I said, shocked out of my sleepiness.

"You have to wake up to feed him. Why should I have to wake up as well?" At this time, Clem was still working on his first book, and he would sometimes get up in the middle of the night to write. I would usually wake up when he switched on the light. Now he wanted to ostracize me because I would wake him?

I dissolved in tears and anger. He was as surprised at my reaction as I was at his wish for me to move to the other bedroom.

"The mother stays with her baby. That's the custom," he said.

"It's not my custom. I'm not an Igbo woman, and I don't intend to move." I pulled the sheet over my head.

He reminded me of the traditional practice: the man has his own hut. His wife would also have her own, and her children would sleep with her there.

"We're not in the village, and I'm not moving."

He pulled the sheet away from my face and kissed me. "I'm sorry."

Clem didn't apologize easily. I melted as he pulled me close and said, "I didn't mean to hurt you. I'm really sorry."

I relaxed, with the crisis averted. I would stay in our bed and let the baby sleep in the other room. If I didn't hear him when he woke, Rosa would call me.

What other shocks were ahead?

In August, we asked Reverend Payne to baptize Chinaku. The Anglican baptism was similar to the Presbyterian ritual I knew but more formal. It had little emotional resonance for me, though Clem loved it. Compared to the naming ceremony in the village, I found it dry and lackluster. No body parts were left behind at the church.

And then it was time for school to start. The first day at the American International School, AIS, was frightening. Would these children listen to me? The atmosphere was so different from the more rigid and strict Nigerian teaching I was used to. Children were encouraged to speak up, to be curious, and to ask questions. Yet, within the first week, I was completely comfortable with the children, and I found the teaching style much more natural for me. I quickly became friends with other teachers. I more than made up for my inexperience in American teaching with my enthusiasm and dedication.

I was so excited at the new job that for the first couple of days I hardly thought about my baby at home. By the third day, I began to miss him. On the way home, I would picture myself holding him. But I wasn't worried. I knew that Chinaku was in Rosa's capable hands.

I became familiar with Woodward's Gripe Water, a standard treatment for upset babies that had come to Nigeria with the British. I think it must have contained a sleeping potion, and it did seem to help when Chinaku was occasionally fretful.

I learned more Igbo. Still, there was sometimes confusion between Rosa and me. Occasionally, Clem had to help us out, though he didn't know many of the Igbo words having to do with babies. There was no Igbo word for nappies, and the word we used, *akwa*, means cloth. But if pronounced with the wrong tones, it means egg. Formula, baby bottle and nipple, sterilize, diaper pins—these were all foreign concepts and there were no Igbo words for them.

And if having a new baby and a new job were not enough, I invited my sister to visit. Beth had asked to visit me earlier, when I was still a Peace Corps volunteer, and she had just graduated from high school. I suspected she really wanted to get out from under Mother's supervision. Given the stories my mother related about her escapades, I didn't think it was a good idea.

But now she had completed a year of college, I had a house, a husband, and a child, and I was eager to have her. I invited her to come in November. That way, we'd have her November 21 birthday, when she'd turn twenty, my December 13 birthday, when I'd be twenty-five, then Christmas and New Year's together.

She nearly collapsed in my arms in the airport arrivals hall. "Oh my God! That was the worst experience of my life," she said, wiping the sweat from her face with her sleeve.

"What happened?"

"I was waiting to board when all the lights went out. People started screaming. It was chaos," she said. "Half an hour later, there was an announcement about a power outage. I didn't know what they were talking about." I knew the flight had been delayed by many hours, but I hadn't learned the reason. She continued her saga as we collected her suitcase and walked to the car. "They took us to some crummy hotel. I had to hold a candle to walk up the stairs. The elevator wasn't working."

The flight had departed the next day and, because of the blackout, had insufficient food. So she was hungry in addition to being exhausted and fed up.

"Clem, we're here," I said, calling up the stairs. He came down in his wrapper, his usual dress after work. I thought she might comment, but she was still too wrapped up in her story.

"How was your trip?" he said innocently, reaching out to embrace her.

"You can't even imagine," she said. While I went upstairs to check on my son, she told Clem about the power outage, forgetting she was talking to an electrical engineer. He was full of questions about what happened, but she had no answers.

I brought a sleeping Chinaku, her very first nephew, for her to admire, then sent him back to bed with Rosa while I led Beth to the table.

I had asked Gabriel to prepare egusi soup and pounded yam, but she wouldn't try it. Despite her hunger, or maybe because of it, she wasn't ready for experimenting. I told the cook to prepare sandwiches for her as she finished telling Clem about the terrible trip.

The next morning, I left her at home with Rosa and the baby and headed off to school. Other teachers were talking about the Northeast blackout. The power outage had affected an area from Canada to New Jersey and lasted for many hours.[7] This was the largest electricity failure in US history.

"You were part of a historic event," I said as I put down my books from school and took Chinaku from Rosa in the afternoon.

"Whoop-de-do," she said. "It was still awful. I never want to have that experience again."

How would she feel when the power went off in Ikoyi, as it surely would while she was here? I imagined that she would ridicule Clem, who after all was chief electrical engineer of the electricity corporation. Or how would she fare in the village that had no power ever?

When I came home from school on Friday, she met me at the door. "I thought you were crazy to leave Chinaku with a twelve-year-old girl. But she really knows what she's doing."

"What happened?" I said, glancing past her to see if Rosa might be holding an injured, crying Chinaku. "I picked him up from his nap this morning, and I even changed his diaper. But he wouldn't stop crying. She took him, and in two seconds he was cooing."

I was relieved that she and Rosa seemed to manage together, despite the language barrier. In fact, she was helping Rosa learn English, since I tried to speak Igbo whenever possible to help my skill at the language.

On Saturday, Clem came home from his half day at work. Gabriel served our regular Saturday beans and yam, and Beth agreed to try it. With plenty of catsup added, she found the dish of cooked red beans, with palm oil, crayfish, and yam, acceptable.

"Hurray—something else you like." She also liked plantain, which she'd had with rice on a couple of evenings, and that night she was willing to try egusi soup, made with ground egusi, or melon, seeds. She wasn't up to eating the pounded yam and soup with her hand, as I did, but she did find it unobjectionable, even tasty.

"I have a question," she said, turning to Clem as we got up from the table. "Why don't you wear regular clothes? All I ever see you wear is a suit, when you go to work, or that." She gestured to his wrapper just like those women wore, a six-foot-long piece of brightly printed cotton fabric that he wore bunched over at the waist to hold it in place.

"My wrapper is the proper Igbo dress for men," he said, sounding somewhat offended. "And it's comfortable."

"Why don't you wear it to work then?" There was no answer.

With her questions, she helped me see how different my life had become. "Why can't you go to the kitchen yourself if you want a drink of water?" she said one evening when I'd called Gabriel to bring water upstairs for me. Another day, she said, "Why does Rosa have to eat in the kitchen?"

Clem and I agreed that we would visit Nanka for Christmas. I wanted to show Beth more of the country, and I also wanted to show her off to Clem's family. They had only met my parents during the wedding a year earlier. It was time people in the village knew a little more of my family.

Three days before we were due to leave, Beth came down with malaria. She had been careful with her mosquito net but careless with taking her Paludrine, the malaria prophylaxis. "I'm going to die," she said as she shivered under the blankets I piled on top of her.

"No, you're not," I said as I handed her the chloroquine tablets and a glass of water. "I know you feel awful, but I promise you'll be better in a couple of days."

"How do you know?" she said.

"Because I had malaria my first Christmas here. Remember when I called you all on Christmas Day that year? I said I was fine. Actually, I was just as sick as you are now."

By our departure day, she felt well enough to travel. As Clem drove, I explained the family. "You'll meet Clem's parents. You can call them Mama and Papa like everyone else does. And Papa's three brothers will be there. Ejike lives right next door with his wife, Obele. She'll come to greet us when we arrive. Obi is the youngest uncle and lives very near. We'll see him and his wife, Mercy, right away. The other brother Ebueme lives a couple of miles away. He has two wives, but you probably won't meet them until they are passing on their way to the market."

"How can he have two wives?"

"Traditionally, most Igbo men had more than one wife. But now many Igbos are Christian, and they usually marry just one. But Ebueme is not Christian."

"That's weird," she said. I realized again how different we were—I found the differences fascinating and loved learning. For her, something different was just weird.

"Did you tell her about the masquerades?" Clem said.

"No. You should." I wanted to hear how he would describe them.

"They are spirits that live underground. They come out for a few hours on special days, like now for Christmas and New Year's and for the new yam festival. They speak in spirit voices," he said. "They are called *mmo* in Igbo." He sounded like he really believed in these spirits. Why didn't he say they were men in costumes?

"What do you mean, they're spirits? Are they people or animals?" she asked.

"They're spirits. And you can't look too closely. In fact, women shouldn't look at them at all, or they may beat you."

"How do they become *mmos*?" I said to encourage him to reveal more of what he knew.

— 71 —

"They have to be initiated. I wasn't in the village when I was a young man, so I don't really know the process," he said. I was relieved that he was admitting their humanity.

"It sounds like a secret society," I said. He nodded in confirmation.

As we drove, Beth pointed out a woman who had a load of firewood on her head and a baby tied on her back. This was no longer strange to me, but to Beth it was amazing. Likewise, a man riding a motorbike with a woman and two children as passengers struck her as not only odd but also dangerous.

I loved her unguarded comments. On my first trip to the East, three and a half years earlier, I was a new Peace Corps volunteer, traveling with other volunteers. Although we had noted the strangeness, we were determined to be uncritical. She had no such reservations.

It had been only a few months since I'd seen Clem's parents for the naming ceremony. My Igbo had improved with Rosa's help, and I was eager to demonstrate. So I introduced my sister to them in Igbo. They were gracious and welcomed her in their limited English. I greeted other relatives who came to welcome us, repeating my Igbo phrases proudly.

Clem and I dug into the pounded yam and egusi soup Mama had prepared and Beth was able to eat enough to be satisfied.

Though I had a few moments of nostalgic yearning, especially with my sister nearby, I didn't actually miss having a Christmas tree. Giving presents wasn't a tradition for Clem, so I ignored that too, and I certainly didn't miss snow for the holidays.

The village provided enough excitement. The Christmas Eve service at the Anglican church, walking distance from our compound, was packed with people in their fanciest clothes, embroidered cotton and sateen in bright colors, with the women in head ties of red, green, and gold, the men with felt caps. The congregation sang the carols, some familiar and some not, in Igbo.

We walked home under the tropical night sky, with children surrounding us, saying *"Onye ocha.* White person." Even adults we didn't know greeted us this way.

Of course, we looked completely out of place in the sea of dark skin. Beth, blond, blue-eyed, and tall, and me, close to her height with brown hair and hazel eyes, were both dressed in flat shoes and no hats. We didn't have gaudy jewelry. To the people in the village, not only our skin color but our whole manner seemed very plain.

We were objects of curiosity for adults and children alike. I didn't mind the stares. Those who knew me called me not by my own name but by the name of my son, "Mama Chinaku."

The next day, after lunch of rice, chicken stew, and plantain, the air throbbed with anticipation and apprehension as everyone awaited the masquerades. Children were dashing into the road, pushing each other and scampering back into the compound as they watched and listened for the first signs. Suddenly, I heard a sharp, rapid rattle and saw the children looking for places to hide. "I don't want to admit it, but they still frighten me," Clem said, gripping my hand. His mother, standing near us, was trembling.

"Don't look," she called softly in English.

But how could I not look? The first masquerade strode into the compound. He wore dirty tan leggings and boots, blue cloth tied around his knees, a thick raffia skirt, and a blue knitted shirt that hid his neck. Long sleeves hung over his hands. He had a wooden mask over his face, surrounded by more of the same blue fabric. Around his waist, he wore a woven raffia belt with smooth, shiny palm seed husks, so closely placed that they struck each other when he ran.[8] His two followers carried long, thin whips that they used to strike the legs of anyone who came too close.

He stalked around the compound while women cowered and children pretended boldness. A few of the older boys ventured forward, but the *mmo*'s assistants chased them back. After a minute of impressive fast starts and stops with rattles shaking, he began speaking in an eerie, unnatural voice, high-pitched and unclear. I understood "Mama Chinaku" but nothing else.

"What's he saying?" I asked Rosa, who was holding Chinaku closely and peeking out from a corner of the veranda. Clem seemed too frightened to answer.

"He wants you to give him something."

I reached into my pocket, pulled out a shilling, and handed it to his assistant. I saw other women looking at me with admiration for my willingness to come so near. "Don't they see that these are just guys dressed up?" Beth said. "Why are they so frightened?"

"They use the *mmos* like some people use the bogeyman—to scare children. If you've been told since you were little that the *mmo* will get you if you aren't careful, you might be scared too."

New Year's Eve brought another service at the church. On the way home, we heard the small fireworks called knockouts that boys were setting off along the road. More masquerades appeared on New Year's Day. This time they knew Beth's name, too, and called out to her.

She was ready to leave when we returned to Lagos, with plenty of stories of her flight coming, the village with the masquerades, and the uncle with two wives. She had enhanced my experience with her questions and reactions. I missed her when she left in the second week of January. For years, her malaria returned periodically, giving her a regular reminder of her visit.

With the house quieter, I was feeling very settled. I thrived in the atmosphere of the American School. I loved watching Chinaku begin to crawl and explore. Clem's book was progressing well. I helped with editing, often spending an hour or more at night going over his manuscript and correcting his long, run-on sentences.

But within days of Beth's departure, Nigeria delivered a major shock.

7

A Year of Coups

"Aren't you finished yet?" Clem asked on Saturday evening. I was working on the last chapter of his manuscript. "I need to get this to the typist so I can give it to Julian next week." Julian was the Nigerian representative for Longman's, the British company publishing Clem's book.

"I'll finish tomorrow. Beth's just been gone a few days, and I've had to catch up on lesson planning." I didn't like to be pressured to finish what I was undertaking voluntarily. Didn't he understand that this was just one of my tasks?

I was seated on the bed, with Clem beside me. Chinaku, now nearly seven months old, was sleeping in the next room with Rosa. The upright, dark wood radiogram, a relic of Clem's days in England, was on. I wasn't paying any attention as the male BBC announcer droned on with his rising and falling cadence: "Manchester United, two (voice up), Manchester City, zero (voice down); Newcastle, three, Leeds United, two." I'd been puzzled by this weekly recitation of scores until I'd learned that many Nigerians bet on the British football results through betting pools, a holdover from colonial days.

I jerked my head up to stare at the radio when a Nigerian voice interrupted the broadcast. "In the early hours of this morning, 15 January 1966, a dissident section of the Nigerian Army kidnapped the prime minister and the minister of finance and took them to an unknown destination. The general officer commanding the Nigerian Army and the vast majority of the Nigerian Army remain completely loyal to the federal government and are already taking all appropriate measures to bring the situation under control."

"Did you hear that?" I couldn't believe my ears. "What about the president?" I knew he was out of the country.

"Wait. There's more," Clem said.

The announcer continued, "The federal government is satisfied that the situation will soon return to normal and that the ill-advised mutiny will be brought to an end. All public buildings and establishments in the federal territory are being guarded by loyal troops."[9]

"You know the telephone and power were off this morning when we got up. Do you think that's related?" I said. "And did you hear the sirens today? What does it all mean? When is President Azikiwe coming back?"

"I don't know. Mutiny certainly sounds like trouble. Maybe there was a coup that didn't succeed," Clem said.

I remembered not just the disruption of services and sirens but also the report from the market brought by our cook in the afternoon.

"Madam, I no find chicken for tomorrow lunch. Too many army tank."

"Tanks in the market?"

"No in market. At Dodan Barracks. Army people all time going in and out, make plenty noise with siren." If the announcement was meant to restore confidence after an unsettling day, it certainly didn't work for me.

Rumors of unrest had been circulating for months. Dissatisfaction with the government was rife. The 1964 federal elections had been hotly contested, and there were stories about rivalry between tribal factions within the military.

Clem's friends Johnson and Ben were pessimistic about the country's future. They both feared for Nigeria, and specifically for the East—the region that was home to the Igbos—if trouble were to come.

"I can't believe it. What do you think has happened to the prime minister?" I said as I went to the window. Did I think I would see him outside? Nothing had changed. The streetlights along Alexander Avenue were on. I saw no cars on the road now, normal for a Saturday evening in our end of Ikoyi.

The same radio broadcast was repeated an hour later following an interlude of martial music with its drums and brass. "Let's turn the radio low and leave it on," I said as we got into bed. I went to sleep uncertain of what the next day would bring.

Sunday morning was quiet. I made pancakes, by now a Sunday morning custom. Gabriel prepared and served our lunch, using meat he'd bought the day before when he couldn't find our usual Sunday chicken. While Rosa sat nearby reading, I fed Chinaku and put him on a blanket on the floor near me in the upstairs sitting room. He'd started making babbling sounds, and I often held "conversations" with him in English and Igbo and encouraged Rosa to do the same. Clem headed for the bedroom for his Sunday afternoon nap. Not even a mutiny could interrupt that!

We went to the evening service at St. Saviour's. The streets, normally busy at the end of the weekend with people going home from visiting friends or family, were eerily quiet. I moved into the pew next to Henry Omoh. "What did you think of the announcement?" I said, speaking softly as I glanced around.

"It didn't provide much information," Henry said. He leaned past me to engage Clem in the muffled conversation. "Do you have any idea what happened?"

"No, I don't," Clem said. "Do you?"

They were both perplexed. So was I. I couldn't get out of my mind the image of tanks near the market.

The first hymn was one I knew well. I wondered if Reverend Payne had chosen it especially for this service when there was such uncertainty in the air.

> Abide with me: fast falls the eventide;
> The darkness deepens; Lord, with me abide:
> When other helpers fail and comforts flee,
> Help of the helpless, O abide with me.[10]

I poured my soul into singing all three verses of the hymn. I paid more attention than usual to the prayers for the country and its leaders. And I thought, as I did every week, how strange that I had to pray for the queen too.

After the service, we exchanged polite greetings with other churchgoers, mostly British, and returned home. The steward was off on Sunday evenings, so I prepared our supper of baked beans on toast with tea. Afterward, we put the TV on for the Nigerian evening news. To our surprise, there was no news. Instead, we were treated to repeats of the popular comedy *Village Headmaster.*

At 10:00 p.m., we moved to the bedroom and turned on the radio. All we heard was more military music, just like the night before.

But we left the radio on again. Clem demonstrated his amazing ability to fall asleep in less than a minute. I couldn't go to sleep. My mind raced with thoughts of what might happen in my adopted country. Would there be another mutiny, or a full-blown coup? Finally, just before midnight, I heard a deep male voice. "Clem, wake up." I nudged him until he opened his eyes. "Listen."

The speaker, the acting president, spoke as if he had a gun to his head. "I have tonight been advised by the council of ministers that they have come to the unanimous decision voluntarily to hand over administration of the country to the armed forces of the republic with immediate effect. I will now call upon the general officer commanding the Nigerian Army, Major General Aguiyi-Ironsi, to make a statement to the nation."[11]

"A military government? I don't like the sound of this at all," I said.

"Wait and hear what the GOC says."

"You've certainly become familiar with military titles quickly. When will you start saluting?" I said. Neither of us knew that this would lead, eighteen months later, to the Biafran War. Clem wouldn't salute then, but he would serve that government in critical positions.

Before Clem could respond, Ironsi began his speech. "The government of the Federation of Nigeria having ceased to function, the Nigerian armed forces have been invited to form an interim military government for the purpose of maintaining law and order and essential services. This invitation has been accepted, and I, General JTU Aguiyi-Ironsi, the general officer commanding the Nigerian Army, have been formally vested with authority as head of the federal military government of Nigeria and supreme commander of the Nigerian armed forces."[12]

"Invited? He said he was invited to form a government? Do you believe that?"

"Shh," Clem said.

Ironsi continued. "The constitution has been suspended," he said. He added that the judiciary, civil service, diplomatic relations, and treaty obligations would continue. Military governors would be appointed for the regions with their civilian counterparts as advisors. He closed by asking "all citizens of the Federation to extend their full cooperation to the government in the urgent task of restoring law and order in the present crisis and to continue in their normal occupations."[13]

We still had not learned the fate of the prime minister or the minister of finance.

I was apprehensive as I drove to school Monday morning. But I encountered no problems even when I passed near the residences of the two missing leaders. There were soldiers around but no roadblocks. The school was less than a mile farther.

Fellow teachers at the American School approached me. "Are you all right? Was your husband involved in the coup?"

"No," I assured them all. "He's chief engineer at the Electricity Corporation. He isn't in the military or the government."

On Tuesday, I learned from the *West African Pilot*, a popular Igbo-run newspaper, that there had been a coup attempt by several army majors, mostly Igbo, to remove the civilian leaders whom they believed held office unfairly. Wednesday's paper brought the news that the premier of the North and Governor Akintola of the West had been killed by coup leaders. Ironsi had not been part of the coup and had remained loyal to the elected government. He was credited with preventing the coup plotters from taking over. So the remaining ministers had turned to him as the top military official.

"Maybe this will be good for the country after all," I said to Clem on Thursday as I showed him the statement from Alhaji Hashim Adaji of the Northern People's Congress (NPC) in the other most popular paper, the *Daily Times*: "The party gives its unqualified support to the military regime and to the major general in particular." The NTV evening news reported similar statements from the leaders of other political parties.

"I think we are fortunate to be rid of that corrupt regime," Clem said. "The soldiers are more disciplined. They will be different from the politicians. This is what our people need."

On Friday, the new military government announced that the prime minister's body had been found along the road not far from Lagos, and on Saturday, we learned that the minister of finance's body had been found alongside. Both had been shot to death. It was ordered that flags were to be flown at half-mast for three days.

After a week filled with drama, I hoped Clem was right and the country could move forward with the military government. Most of all, I wanted a peaceful country for my son and myself.

With each day's news, I had thought of Dick Sklar, our political science instructor in Peace Corps training. He had talked extensively about the tribal animosities and religious differences that made Nigeria an unlikely success as a single country. Now I was seeing these in action. Had I become part of a country doomed to fail? What would that mean?

The Hausa people of the North, the country's largest tribe, were Muslim, as were the Fulani, traditionally nomads but now mostly city dwellers, who had become the northern traditional rulers. They had a single central religious and political leader, the sultan of Sokoto, whom I'd actually visited in his palace on my trip with Dave.

The Yoruba of the southwest were the second largest group, mostly Christian but with a Muslim minority like the chief and others in Ojo. Traditionally, they'd had a single ruler, the Oni of Ife, but he was not as powerful a central figure as the sultan in the North. The Igbos, Clem's tribe and the third largest, were Christian or pagan. They had never had a central ruler.

In 1912, the British had united the disparate tribes and regions into a single unit under their provincial administration. In 1929, the first serious anticolonial action occurred with an uprising by Igbo market women in Aba, eastern Nigeria. Over the next several decades, the newly minted Nigerians began to express an ever-greater desire for self-government. Political parties formed—largely based on tribal affiliation—and the push for an end to colonial status intensified.

At independence in 1960, the northern party won the federal election and formed a coalition government with the National Council of Nigeria and the Cameroons (NCNC), based in the East and primarily Igbo. Each of the three regions had its own government, with the NCNC winning in the East, the Action Party in the West, and the NPC in the North. After independence, a new region, the Midwest, was created and had its own government.

Over the next month, I learned more about the coup. Thirty people, mostly government officials, had died. President Azikiwe, an Igbo, returned to the country but with no government role. Northerners began to comment that only one Igbo had died, and their resentment of Ironsi, an Igbo, as head of the military government became clear.

There had been mild bitterness at Igbo success in commerce for a long time. Now it grew and began to seem ugly. Many Igbo families had lived in the North for generations, and they began reporting harassment. At the same time, Ironsi seemed to struggle with the responsibilities of governing, antagonizing the military governors he had appointed. Almost oblivious to the turmoil in the country, the American School carried on. I finished the school year, my first as a fourth-grade teacher. The principal asked me to return for the next year, and I happily signed the contract, looking forward to another year at the American School.

That summer, 1966, I took Chinaku to meet my parents. I had sent pictures, and my sister had reported on him, but they wanted to meet their first grandchild, and I was eager to take him. I was also relieved to get away from the rumors and mistrust circulating in Nigeria.

"How am I supposed to manage for four weeks?" Clem said from the driver's seat on the way to the airport.

"How did you manage before we were together?" I was touched by his dependence and knew he meant that he would miss me.

If he didn't say it, I would. "I'll miss you. But the time will fly past. You'll see."

This departure was so different from my last flight to the United States two years earlier. Although Peace Corps had officially sent me home at the conclusion of my two years of service, Clem had driven me to the airport. I was full of excitement at sharing the joy of my engagement and wedding plans with my parents and friends.

Now I was a mother, loaded down with diaper bag, bottles, and baby clothes, as well as two suitcases. I was going to introduce my own son to my parents and siblings. Would they find him as enchanting as Clem and I did?

I was apprehensive about the flight too. The stewardesses were helpful as I boarded and found my seat. But they couldn't help as Chinaku had a crying fit soon after departure. I don't know who was more relieved, the other passengers or I, when he fell asleep.

He woke an hour later, eager to explore. I already missed Rosa, and I'm sure he did too. There were still many hours before we reached the United States. He had just learned to walk and didn't like being confined to my lap. How was I going to manage for the rest of the flight, not to mention four more weeks, without a helper?

But we survived and were soon in New York. Ann met us at the airport and took us to her Manhattan apartment for the night. Her pleasure at meeting my son made me feel confident and ready. She sent us off to Cincinnati the next day, where my parents were waiting at the airport. I hadn't seen them since they left Nigeria a few days after our wedding a year and a half earlier.

"Meet your grandson," I said, as I hugged my mother and held Chinaku for her to see. Tears came to my eyes as she reached out eagerly for him. But he didn't want to leave my arms, so she stroked his curly hair.

"He's so handsome," she said. "He looks like Clement, doesn't he?"

"He does," I said. "He's shy around new people, but he'll be fine in a few hours." I hoped that was true. My father, never one to show emotion, actually looked pleased as he let me kiss him. I held Chinaku in the backseat as Father drove us home. I described the long and tedious journey from Nigeria and relayed Ann's greetings.

"Peter and Beth will be home later," Mother said. "They're off with friends."

I was engrossed with my baby and getting him acquainted with my parents, so I didn't mind. But the contrast between Nigerian family closeness and the distance between me and my siblings was striking. After all, my brother had never seen my baby, his first niece, and my sister had left Nigeria seven months earlier. Surely they could have been home to greet us. I had even thought they might come to the airport for our arrival. The car would have been crowded on the way home, but I wouldn't have minded.

My mother reached out again for Chinaku when we pulled into the driveway, and he went to her, so I grabbed baby belongings and one suitcase while Father carried the other. I felt like I was going backward through a time warp as I walked into the living room. I had been there just two years earlier, but with the changes in my life, my perceptions had changed.

There was the dark maroon Chippendale sofa by the near wall and the high-back chair where Father sat after dinner. The same small TV I remembered was against the opposite wall, next to the glass doors leading into the music room. Mother handed Chinaku to me. "I borrowed a high chair but not a crib. Do you think he'll be all right on Beth's bed?"

"I'm sure he will," I said. "I'll just push the beds together so he can't fall."

While Father went to work every morning, Mother and I looked after Chinaku. We took him grocery shopping at the A&P in Fort Thomas and on other errands. There were occasional black women caretakers with white children on the street and in the shops. But a mixed-race child with white women was unfamiliar. There were quite a few stares followed by averted glances.

Mrs. Weber, the elderly lady next door, brought out a blue wading pool for Chinaku and sat outside with us a couple of times as Chinaku splashed happily. I called on the Murphys, who lived on the other side. They were polite but not very friendly. I got the feeling that they had no wish to have me and my black child in their house for long.

From the time I was first a Peace Corps volunteer and Mother had taken the course on Nigeria at the University of Cincinnati, she had followed Nigerian politics. She asked about the people involved in the coup. I filled her and Father in on what I knew. I wasn't yet really worried about Nigeria's future, and I didn't want to alarm them, so I played down the tribal animosity that had become more obvious in recent months.

The time together felt similar to our life years earlier. There were no intimate conversations and, although we admired Chinaku together, little deep emotional interaction. But we were easy and comfortable together. We even had a bridge game when Peter was home one evening. It was such a contrast to the vibrancy of life in Nigeria, where people interacted constantly, often speaking in loud voices and using gestures.

In the village, people spent much of their time outdoors, not enclosed in four walls. Children played while adults mingled all the time, going to market, preparing food, and working the land. Even in Lagos, people visited each other spontaneously in their homes and stopped for real conversation when they met by chance.

No Fort Thomas high school friends were in town that summer, but I had one college friend who lived close enough to see. Susie and I had met in

Cincinnati at the summer event for new students held by the Mount Holyoke Alumnae Club. And she reminded me that we had also met a year earlier when we both played in a piano recital at the Cincinnati Conservatory of Music.

We had rooms across the hall from each other during freshman and senior years in North Mandelle, our Mount Holyoke dorm, and had become close friends. We had been part of a round robin letter exchange for the first eighteen months after college. She had married and had one son as well. We agreed that I would drive to her home for a visit. She called the day before.

"Cathy, I have to ask you not to come tomorrow."

"OK. What day shall I come? I still have a few days here."

"No, it's just not a good idea for you to come. John wants me to focus on my own child."

"What's wrong?" I said, curious to understand. It struck me suddenly that she was embarrassed to tell me that her husband did not approve of my interracial marriage and mixed-race child.

I was surprised and hurt that Susie wouldn't see me. I had so looked forward to discussing married life and child rearing with her. Weren't our bonds of friendship stronger than racism? Then I was angry, and it occurred to me that maybe Susie herself was not comfortable with my choice.

What was wrong with people? In Nigeria, I was sometimes stared at, but that didn't feel like racism, just curiosity. Of course, as I knew from the politics, Nigeria was not exempt from animosity similar to racism.

The very next day, I had new evidence. *NBC Evening News* reported that there had been another coup. Major-General Ironsi had been killed by junior army officers, and a new military head of state had been installed. The next morning, I searched the *Cincinnati Enquirer* until I found a tiny article. The new head of the military government was Yakubu Gowon, a northerner but a Christian.

I called Clem. "I heard about the coup," I said. "Now what will happen? Will northerners want to punish the southerners for the earlier assassinations?"

"I don't know. We'll have to wait and see." My husband is a patient man, and "wait and see" is often his answer. In this case, he was clearly right. There was nothing he or I could do except hope for the best. And a few days later, I was on my way back and would see for myself.

This flight was easier. I knew what to expect, and Chinaku slept more. I was eager to see Clem—this was our longest separation since getting acquainted. I would appreciate having Rosa around again.

Clem was beside himself with joy when he saw me emerge from the plane holding his son. But he was also a little shy, not behaving with his usual bravado. Over the years, I have come to expect this reaction to meeting after a long separation, no matter which of us has been away. The first time, it surprised me. But within five minutes, we were chattering away normally, passing Chinaku back and forth while waiting for luggage.

"What's happened with the military government?" I said to Clem as we got into bed that night. He reported that he had seen little change in the country since the latest military action. The counter-coup leaders didn't seem much different from the earlier military men whom they'd replaced. They had not uprooted all corruption as they boasted they would. In fact, he thought it was worse than before. And he felt that anti-Igbo sentiment was growing, an unpleasant sentiment that was borne out in the next months.

I was happy to be back with Clem. I found our lovemaking more pleasurable. Our separation and the sense of threat in the country seemed to draw us closer though I was still reserved.

In September, I started my second year at the American School. Again, the children in my fourth-grade class were a mix of nationalities, with Americans whose parents worked at Mobil, Shell, and oil service companies in the majority.

Then the country was rocked anew. There was a massacre of at least five thousand Igbos living in the North. People fled from villages, towns, and the larger cities back to the East. The evening news said little, but the *West African Pilot* carried pictures of injured Igbos arriving aboard crammed trains and people carrying bodies to the East for burial. The military governor of the Eastern Region, Lieutenant-Colonel Odumegwu Ojukwu, called on Gowon to end the killing.

"He's an amazing speaker, isn't he?" I said to Clem as we watched him on national TV.

"He is impressive," Clem said. "He does love to show off his Oxford education."

Ojukwu made clear that if the federal government and the governor of the North could not stop attacks on innocent Igbos, then the Igbos would have to take their safety into their own hands. He used the words "pogrom" and "genocide" to describe what had happened and again encouraged Igbos to return to the East, where they would be protected.

"Do you think we will have to leave?" I said. I was settled in my job and my house. I did not want any disruption.

"No, I'm sure they will work things out," Clem said.

Mother wrote with concern about the news she was hearing from Nigeria. I wrote back that we were fine, and we were not in the area where the massacres had taken place. But the bad news continued, and I did begin to fear for our comfortable life.

In early November, I learned that I was pregnant again. Our second child would be born just two years after the first.

"I really hope the country settles down by next June," I said to Clem when I told him the news. "I would hate to have a baby in the middle of this unrest." I didn't suspect that there was greater conflict coming and my child would be born in the newly independent country of Biafra at the start of a bloody three-year war.

With the horrifying atrocities and the massive flight of Igbos to the East, we did not even consider going to the village for Christmas 1966. I was relieved. I didn't want to be confronted by the injured and maimed people who'd fled from the North. I was unsettled enough by reading about the carnage and seeing the TV images. Clem's parents assured us they were safe in Onitsha and would not go to the village that Christmas either.

I did what I could to have a joyful Christmas celebration at home despite the turbulence in the country. I put up a few decorations. Christmas fell on a Sunday that year. We opened our gifts early in the morning after our Sunday breakfast of pancakes and bacon. I had wrapped a set of wooden alphabet blocks in Christmas paper for Chinaku, and I gave Clem a pale green, tie-dyed, embroidered shirt. For Rosa, I bought a sky blue, short-sleeved cotton blouse with a matching tailored skirt. She looked very smart when she put her new outfit on.

I suggested we take Rosa and Chinaku with us to St. Saviour's Christmas service. Although several British families had gone to the UK for the holidays, there were still more white than black faces. We sang the familiar hymns I knew growing up. "Come All Ye Faithful" and "We Three Kings" were among my favorites. I had learned new carols too, and "Once in Royal David's City," which I'd never heard before coming to St. Saviour's with Clem three years earlier, helped my Christmas mood.

After the service, as I looked around, I wondered whether the Igbo friends we didn't see in church had gone to the East for the holidays or had left permanently.

As soon as we got home, I called my parents. I had already written them about the pregnancy. "Are you safe?" Mother asked, having continued to keep up on Nigerian news.

"Yes, we're safe. We just came from church. Reverend Payne sends his greetings."

"Peter and Beth are here," Mother said. "We've just finished our Christmas dinner. We miss you." She put my father on the phone. "You seem to have a little excitement there," he said with his usual understatement and slight sarcasm.

How to answer? "Indeed we do," I said. His flippancy didn't invite sharing my fears with them, especially since I barely acknowledged them to myself. Besides, they had their own news. My father had just retired. His whole career—thirty-five years—since coming to the United States from Germany had been with AT&T.

Mother had mentioned their plans for a round-the-world trip. "We leave in just one month," she said. "We fly to Los Angeles to see the California relatives and then on to Hawaii." She promised to write, and I assured her I would keep them updated on the situation in Nigeria. She had sent me their itinerary, and I could always reach them through American Express offices.

The next evening, Clem and I went back to Bristol Hotel for our Boxing Day anniversary dinner. "Remember when we came here three years ago?" I said. "You thought I forced you to say you wanted to marry me. That evening was almost the end of our relationship."

"I'm glad it wasn't. I was lucky to find you. I am very fortunate," he said. I felt fortunate too as I grasped his hand across the table. My family in the United States seemed very distant, not just in miles but also in emotional warmth.

"I wonder if I would feel closer to my parents if I saw them more often," I said to Clem on the way home that evening. "Now that they're both retired, maybe they can come see us again after they finish their trip."

"They should come," Clem said, "as long as the country is still safe."

But by the time my parents had finished their globe-circling, Nigeria was in pieces. Rather than their coming to see us for a few weeks, I would spend many months living with them.

8

NIGERIA BREAKS APART, BIAFRA IS BORN

CHINAKU, AT A year and a half, now said words I could understand. Every day, he added to his vocabulary, sometimes with English words and sometimes Igbo. Rosa and I laughed as we tried to decipher his meaning and encouraged him when he got frustrated at our inability to understand.

I wanted Clem to be more involved with his children than my father, who had kept us at a distance with his sarcastic tongue and aloof manner. "You have a talkative son," I said to Clem one Sunday afternoon at the beginning of 1967. We sat on the low cement wall that surrounded a six-foot-square outdoor area just off the living room that I'd filled with water. The sun was hidden by the Harmattan haze. Chinaku splashed his hands in the water, sending spray over us.

"*Gini k'o nekwu?* What is he saying?" Clem asked, wanting his son to hear him speaking Igbo.

"*Amam?* Do I know?" I answered. "Maybe he's saying I look funny with water all over me. Or he's saying 'I'm not sure I want a baby brother or sister.'"

Clem patted my tummy, still almost flat. "Are you sure there's a baby in there?"

"Quite sure," I said. We'd celebrated our second wedding anniversary a couple of weeks before. The two years had sped by with our first child, teaching at the American School, my sister's visit, and the publication of Clem's first book.

But the country was heading toward disaster. Igbos felt more unsafe than ever, and Ojukwu talked of secession. On the evening newscast, he declared, "I must warn all easterners once again to remain vigilant. It is not our intention to play the aggressor. Nonetheless, it is not our intention to be slaughtered in our beds. We are ready to defend our homeland." He concluded in his deep Oxford-accented English, "God grant peace in our time."[14]

As January progressed, I felt more and more uncertain about my future and that of the Igbos in a unified Nigeria. And while Ojukwu intensified his calls for Igbos to return to the East, members of smaller tribes in the East were unsettled. They didn't know how they would fare if the East were to leave the federation. Would their rights be protected?

Further complicating the tense situation were discoveries of additional huge oil reserves in and around Port Harcourt, part of the Eastern Region but not primarily Igbo. The federal government was excited about the prospect of serious oil revenue. But with the conflict between the federal and regional governments over control of resources, it was unclear who would benefit.

In February, Clem's mother called. "*O di mpka ka unu ga nata.* It's important that you come home."

I gave the phone to Clem. He spoke in a mixture of Igbo and English. I heard him say we were safe but watchful. "If Lagos becomes too dangerous, we will come," he concluded.

To hear Clem admit we had to be watchful was frightening. What would we do if someone turned on us? Could we protect our son, ourselves, Rosa, and the cook, Gabriel? How long would this go on?

In late February, Clem began coming home with stories of Igbo colleagues at ECN who had left for the East and others who stayed with friends, a different house every night, so no one would know where to find them. I read about Igbos, both military and civilian, apparently killed by army men. For most, there was a reason they were targeted—one had been involved in the coup a year before, another was a civil servant who had refused to promote a Northerner. But some seemed random. Would Clem be a target?

One Saturday evening in late March, we visited Jean and Johnson. "Are you getting ready to move?" Johnson said after Jean served us drinks and the fruitcake she still had on hand from the Christmas holidays.

"No, they can't push me out," Clem said. He loved his title and his management responsibility; he had no wish to give it up.

"I'm thinking about going," Johnson said. "Jean doesn't want to leave, but we will if the situation gets much worse." Hearing Johnson say these words shook me.

We drove home in silence. Back home, I sat on the floor in our sitting room with Chinaku and his blocks. "Square, triangle, and circle," I said, handing him each shape as I named it. I looked up and said to Clem, "Do you think we should go?"

"Do you want to?" he asked.

"No, not at all." I couldn't imagine abandoning my class at the American School and disrupting our settled lives. I didn't want to move when I was six months pregnant.

Mama called again in April. On May 5, Gowon announced the division of the four Nigerian regions into twelve states. Most of the oil-producing sectors were taken from the Igbos and made parts of other, non-Igbo states. Ojukwu railed against this decision, calling it a deliberate provocation. That evening, I read the news account of a lorry load of Igbos killed on their way from Lagos to the East.

My fear grew. Mama called again within minutes after the newscast. She didn't have a TV, but she had heard. "You have to come," she said. "You will be killed just like the people in the lorry."

The next day, I stopped at the flat of my best friend, Carol, an American like me married to an Igbo, and also pregnant. As Chinaku played with her three little daughters, she said, "I'm leaving for Ghana tomorrow. I'm taking the girls," she said. "Walter is going to the East."

"Just like that? You're leaving?"

"I've been thinking about it for a few weeks. I just heard from St. Mary's School in Accra that they have a place for me. I'll have the baby there."

Was I being foolish to think I would not have to leave Lagos? If Carol, who had been in the country and married years longer than I, thought she had to go, what was I doing endangering my husband and son by resisting?

I walked in the door and straight to the bedroom where Clem went after work to change into his wrapper.

"It's time to reconsider," I said before I realized he was on the phone.

He hung up and turned to me. "That was Pius Okigbo's office. He wants me to come to the East to head the fuel commission."

"Wow. That's incredible timing," I said. I told him about Carol's decision.

"Why isn't she going to the East with Walter?"

"My guess is that Walter doesn't have a house in the East. I think she realized she could take better care of herself and her children in Ghana. But tell me about the position," I said.

"He says I would lead the Fuel and Energy Commission to oversee the power and fuel sectors in the East."

"Where would we live? Where would I have the baby?"

"The position comes with a house. And I'm sure there's a good hospital in Enugu. But I don't know if it's the right thing to do."

"Call back and say yes. You can't refuse. This is a sign."

"I need time to think," he said. "We'll see."

I didn't need any more time. When Mama called later, I told her we were coming. "If Clem won't leave, I'm coming on my own."

Then I told Clem. "You have the weekend," I said. "It's just not safe here anymore."

I was ready to face the hurdles, and they were many. I was now eight months pregnant. I had never lived in the East. There would be few expatriate women around, and I knew no one. I would walk out on the teaching position I loved. I would abandon the life I'd worked so hard to build for us in Lagos.

Clem finally saw that I was serious. He had a different problem to overcome. He'd grown up in the East and knew the region and the people. But he harbored the dream of becoming ECN's general manager when the Taiwanese agreement was up in three more years. Leaving would mean the end to that hope.

"You do realize," I said on Sunday, "that an Igbo would never become ECN's general manager in the polarized atmosphere of Nigeria today."

"You're right," he finally admitted. "I could even be fired or arrested as a potential traitor if I stay."

"You could also be accused of treason for abandoning your post at ECN. But that's not so likely. More probable is that people will be relieved if you're gone. Then no one will have to look for an excuse to fire you if they really want the Igbos out."

We would go on the coming Saturday, May 13. We would tell no one about our decision and coming departure unless absolutely necessary. We hadn't heard of Igbos being prevented from leaving, but Clem had a major position in the electricity corporation. Could he really be regarded as a traitor when he took his skills to the East?

With equal amounts of relief and apprehension, I began frantic planning, sorting, and packing.

On Monday, I made sure Clem called to say he accepted the offer and would arrive on Saturday. "Your house won't be ready, but we'll have a flat for temporary accommodation," he was told.

I visited my doctor and asked for a referral to an obstetrician in Enugu. "I still hope to have the baby here," I said, feeling foolish in my lie but realizing that caution was wise. "I'm only asking in case I have to leave before the baby comes."

I dragged out all the suitcases Clem and I owned. I told Gabriel to pack our kitchen equipment, dishes, and canned and dry food. "You are not to talk to anyone about packing," I said. "We are leaving for the East, and you can come with us if you want."

"Yes, Madam, I go come wid you. Tank you. I already send my wife and pikin to the East," he said.

On Thursday, I told the principal, and on Friday, I told my class.

I raced around the house on Friday evening. "Rosa, where are the nappies and Chinaku's clothes for tomorrow and the next day?" I said. She showed me where she had everything laid out for the drive and the day after. "Have you packed your own things?" She had. I sent her to bed soon after Chinaku went to sleep.

I turned next to the kitchen and the cook. The kitchen shelves were bare. Only the kettle and mug for my morning Nescafé and bowls and spoons for cereal were out. He'd washed the evening's dishes and packed them away.

I couldn't rest until after midnight. I checked closets, moved clothes to the "immediate use" suitcases and then back again as I ran out of space. I checked that my wedding dress was in the trunk Peace Corps had used to ship my books and household goods when I first arrived in Nigeria. I put the square, fur-covered jewelry box that my grandmother had given me in the trunk.

I finally lay down, exhausted, my mind still churning, while Clem slept peacefully beside me. Would we be safe on the road? No one knew we were leaving, but what if just being Igbo on the drive to the East was a cause for random killing? What life would I find in the East? Where would I have my baby? Had I given up any chance of a future teaching career in the American School? Would Clem be happy in his new job?

Too soon, it was six on Saturday morning. I sent Gabriel to hire a lorry. By the time he returned, Rosa and Clem, with what little help I could provide in my pregnant state, had moved most of the boxes and suitcases to the downstairs hallway ready to load. The lorry driver and his assistant packed the major items with Clem's supervision. His beloved radiogram, the piano, and my grandmother's painting of Venice that hung on our living room wall went in.

While Rosa carried belongings from the house to the lorry, I left Chinaku on the floor at the foot of the stairs, next to the mortar and pestle and a few pots. I waddled upstairs to use the bathroom one last time. When I came down a minute later, he had found a box of matches and was trying to strike one. I grabbed them so roughly he began crying. What if I hadn't come down that second? I was almost sick with fright and relief.

Clem chose this moment to say for the second or third time, "Can you hurry? What else is there to pack?"

"Don't stand there telling me to hurry! Why don't you get in here and watch Chinaku?" I almost threw one of the boxes at him. I recovered as he helped get the last belongings loaded. By half-past eight, we were in the car. The cook was in the lorry.

I cast one look back as we drove away from Eight Alexander, the site of our wedding and our home. I didn't want to cry, but I felt overwhelmed with sadness at all I was leaving.

Clem was driving the Ford Consul that he loved, and he seemed less sad at leaving. He was, after all, going to what should be an exciting new position.

Soon we were out of Lagos and headed toward the East. "What's going to happen to this country? When do you think we'll come back?" I said. I couldn't hold back my tears any longer. This was the city I loved, where I'd become a teacher, met and married Clem, and had my first child. I was due to deliver in a few weeks.

"We'll be fine. You're just tired from all the packing. Relax."

Suddenly I thought of my parents. In the rush to leave, I had not written them. "My parents have no idea that we're leaving or where I am going. How will they let me know if something happens?"

"You can write them from Enugu. There are post offices there."

I was determined to feel sorry for myself. "And I'm about to have a baby."

"Do you need to go to the hospital right away?" Clem was suddenly frightened.

Now it was my turn to tell him to relax. I recovered my equilibrium and most of my good spirits as I laughed at his misunderstanding. "No, I'm not actually having the baby at this moment."

We saw Nigerian soldiers in Benin and kept driving. We crossed the newly completed Niger Bridge to Onitsha and continued. In Enugu, we found the flat where we were to stay temporarily. The lorry driver and his assistant helped Rosa and Gabriel bring everything inside. There was barely space to move between all our belongings. I fed Chinaku a little of the jollof rice we'd brought, ate some myself, and collapsed on an unmade bed.

We were in the cramped apartment for two weeks before moving into our house on Coal Avenue. It was a charming two-story British colonial with a red tile roof, whitewashed walls, and hardwood floors. Instead of facing Coal Avenue, the house had its back to the road and a circular driveway that led around to the "front" door. Across the drive from the main door was a sloping field of corn of at least an acre. I wondered who the farmer was. Were we to have the harvest?

Two days after we moved in, I was still deciding where our possessions belonged. Clem came home to say, "There's a major announcement coming tonight." We turned on the radio just in time.

"Now, therefore, I, Lieutenant-Colonel Chukwuemeka Odumegwu Ojukwu, military governor of Eastern Nigeria, do hereby solemnly proclaim that the territory and region known as and called eastern Nigeria together with her continental shelf and territorial waters shall henceforth be an independent sovereign state of the name and title of 'The Republic of Biafra.'"[15]

"Oh my God," I said. "He's really done it. Why the name Biafra? What will Nigeria do now?"

"I thought this was coming," Clem said. "Just wait—you'll see what we can do as an independent country."

"But what will happen?" I said. My worry, which had almost vanished in the days I'd spent absorbing the mood of the East, returned. I couldn't think of anything but the United States' civil war and the eventual defeat of the secessionist South.

"I expect that Nigeria will fight," he said. "They surely won't accept this without doing something. But they'll never defeat us." I was amazed at his sureness. I knew others would feel the same. Were they right? Could Biafra succeed?

"You should be happy," he said. "Did you ever think you would have the chance to be part of a new country?" His joy was transparent—clearly, he wasn't worried about the future. After a few more minutes of listening to Ojukwu, I also became unexpectedly jubilant.

"What should we do to celebrate?" I said to Clem. "We have to mark this occasion. I wish we had champagne. But let's at least open a bottle of wine. That is, if we can find one." I dug in the cartons until I came across a bottle of red wine. I found the opener in another carton. He poured, and we toasted the new country.

"We need to get the TV working," I said. "We have to watch tomorrow night's news."

The next day, everyone I saw at the market, at the grocery store, and at the doctor's office, was excited and defiant. Igbos had their own nation. Like Clem, everyone else was completely confident of the new country's ability to reach heights Nigeria had only dreamed of. The air was filled with anticipation and joy.

I swung back and forth. I tried to think of secession movements that were ultimately successful, but I failed. At least I found the answer to the source of the name when I located my atlas—the Bight of Biafra is just south of eastern Nigeria.

A coal corporation housing manager came that day and hooked up the appliances, including the TV. He was delighted to tell me that that his surname was also Onyemelukwe. I was surprised; I had thought we were unique. He explained that his family was from another town, and we weren't related.

At nine that evening, Clem and I sat in front of the TV with Rosa while Ojukwu announced the new national anthem, "Land of the Rising Sun," set to the music of "Finlandia." A military band played as he unveiled the flag with its rising sun centered on a black horizontal stripe between red and green borders. I found the music and the speech incredibly moving.

I was ready for whatever would come. My new baby would be a Biafran!

9

NEW BABY AND NEW HOME

"IT'S TIME," I said. "The baby's on the way."

Clem felt no sense of urgency. unlike the moment I'd frightened him in the car on the way to the East. He struggled to wake up. "Hmm? What? What time is it?"

When I finally made him understand that it was five-thirty and time to go to the hospital, he still hoped for more sleep. "Let's wait and see," he said.

I was already dressing. "We're not waiting unless you want to deliver the baby yourself!"

That got his attention. As he pulled on his trousers and shirt, I woke Rosa to tell her we were leaving for the hospital. Clem raced downstairs, out the door, and into the car, barely waiting for me. He sped out of our driveway as I closed the car door.

"Don't worry. We'll be there in plenty of time." But he was now in a state of panic. At this hour on a Sunday morning, there were no other cars, so his frenzied driving was not a threat. We reached St. Thomas Hospital in half the time it had taken me for my two appointments. He pulled up in front of the three-story cement-block building and ran inside, leaving me to get out of the car and grab my bag. "Don't worry," I said to his back. "I'm coming."

Everything about this birth was completely unlike my experience with Chinaku's. My husband was in the country. He brought me to the hospital. I was given a bed right away in a large, airy room. I shared the room with one other patient. The nursing sisters were very attentive.

Within an hour of arriving, the labor pains grew more frequent. "Let's go to the delivery room," the nursing sister in charge said, as she led me down a short hall. The delivery, assisted by a midwife, was fast.

"You have a lovely girl." She held up the squirming, crying infant—my daughter. In a few minutes, I was holding her, filled with relief that this birth had been so easy and overjoyed that I could show her to Clem right away. I cradled her, felt her curly dark hair, and sketched her bow mouth with my index finger. She stopped crying. Half an hour later, I walked back to my bed while the nursing sister carried our baby. Clem helped me get into bed before he realized we had a new baby. "What happened? Are you all right?"

Then he saw the baby in the nursing sister's arms. "I can't believe it. Is the baby all right? Wasn't this too fast?" In his shock, he forgot to ask the baby's gender.

"I've had practice. Just look at her. Isn't she lovely?"

Tears came to his eyes as he looked at his daughter for the first time. Then he couldn't take his eyes away.

"You can touch her," I said, giving him an encouraging smile. Slowly he reached out and stroked the baby's hand where it poked through the swaddling blanket. Then he held her hand while he gave me a long, gentle kiss.

That afternoon, Clem brought Chinaku and Rosa to see the new addition to our family. We didn't have a phone in our new house, but he went to the telephone exchange that evening to call his parents and ask his father for the baby's Igbo name. He sent a cable to my parents at the American Express location where we thought they would be on their round-the-world trip.

I was home for Chinaku's second birthday on June 29. That day, Clem's father sent a cable with the name *Ijeoma*, go safely, because of our safe return to the East. I loved that name, but I wanted to call her Elizabeth, or Beth, after my sister and aunt. Rosa knew my sister and was easily persuaded. With the situation in our new country so uncertain, there was no talk of a naming ceremony as we had done for Chinaku.

On July 6, Nigerian troops began their assault. Radio Biafra reported Nigerian troops approaching Nsukka, the university town forty miles away. Ojukwu spoke almost nightly to his "fellow Biafrans" to assure us that our brave troops were standing up to the invading army.

But on July 14, the news changed. I had Beth on my lap, and I'd just finished nursing her when the television news anchor reported that Nsukka had fallen into enemy hands.[16]

The rest of July and into August, we heard regular reports of battles around Nsukka. It did indeed seem that the Biafrans were holding their ground. Ojukwu was full of praise for the soldiers and encouragement for all loyal Biafrans. His frequent speeches were confident and enthusiastic, and I began to believe him.

In early August, I received a note from the American consulate in Enugu to say that, in the next couple of weeks, they would be evacuating Americans to the embassy in Lagos. They would take any Americans in the breakaway Biafra who wanted to go to Lagos, and they would arrange transport to the United States for those who wanted to return home. All Peace Corps volunteers in Biafra were being evacuated. Did I want to leave with them?

I thought of my two children. They would be safer out of Biafra. But we were a family now. Even if the consulate agreed to take my spouse, and I didn't think they would, Clem wouldn't leave. He was committed to the Biafran cause. I was torn.

"What do you think?" I asked Clem. "I don't want to leave. I certainly wouldn't go to Lagos without you. I don't really have a home in the United States now that my parents are traveling. Maybe my sister would take me in, but with two kids, it's difficult."

"I hope you won't go anywhere. I need you with me." That's what I wanted to hear. I would stay.

I did go to the consulate to register our daughter's birth so she would have her US citizenship and a passport. I tried to convince the American vice consul that her birth country should be listed as Biafra on both documents.

"I understand what you're asking. But the United States has not recognized Biafra, so the documents would not be legal," he said. "I have to record her birthplace as Nigeria." His insistence probably saved me from difficulties later in the war when I needed her American passport.

On August 9, I was in the supermarket when I heard people exclaiming over that morning's news, which I had missed. Biafran troops, led by a Yoruba brigadier, had entered the Midwest and taken over the region. I was as excited about the Yoruba leader as I was about the victory. I believed that if a Yoruba military leader was supporting Biafran independence, led by Igbos, maybe the country could come to its senses and agree on peaceful secession.

This military success led to boasting by Ojukwu as well as most other Igbo men, including Clem. "You are fortunate to be Igbo," Clem told his two-year-old son. "You will see. When you grow up, you'll be a proud Biafran."

I kept to myself my concern about the possibility of succeeding without foreign help. Surely the massacre of so many Igbos in the past year, in what many called a pogrom, merited world attention. If other countries would come to our aid, we would have a chance. But despite messages condemning the killing, neither the United Nations nor any countries stepped in.

Then the air raids started. At first, I laughed at these. Radio Biafra assured me that the Nigerians did not have many experienced pilots. I had heard the rumor, later confirmed, that two Nigerian air force planes had been commandeered by Biafrans when they returned to the East. No bombs hit targets in Enugu. I felt almost as if this were a pretend war. And it was the rainy season, though we were in August break, so flying was not always possible.

But around noon one day in late August, I was nursing Beth while Chinaku ate his lunch of fried plantain. I heard a loud rumble that seemed to rock the area where we lived. My first thought was that an overloaded truck was passing on the busy road that ran by the house. A couple of minutes later, there was another reverberation. I realized this was no truck. "Did you hear that?" I said to Rosa.

"Airplane," Chinaku said as he began waving his arms back and forth like a plane's wings. "Big bang." I caught the sound Chinaku heard. It was a plane, and it was dropping bombs. It wasn't close, but it was certainly within the city.

I wasn't sure what to do. "Rosa, take Chinaku. Come on, we're going to the bedroom." Rosa sensed my panic. She grabbed Chinaku's hand. She barely gave him time to get his footing as she pulled him after her. I carried Beth as we ran to the guest bedroom on the main floor. "Get under the bed," I directed Rosa and Chinaku, who was crying by now. I held Beth and scrambled under the other bed.

"Don't worry. You're safe," I said from under the bed, as much to reassure myself as to reassure Rosa and Chinaku. Any sense of a pretend war vanished. Ten minutes later, just as I was wondering if we were out of harm's way, the cook came to the bedroom door.

"The plane be gone now," he said.

How did he know? I couldn't be sure. But I wasn't prepared to spend the rest of the day under the bed. So I crawled out, still holding Beth. Rosa emerged from under the other bed, clearly shaken. I embraced her and then reached under to grab Chinaku, but he didn't want to come out. "Come on. Let's go finish your plantain," I urged him.

I turned to Gabriel. "Do you want to go to your family?" I asked him. I had forgotten all about him in my fright.

"No, madam. I done see them already. They fine."

I handed the baby to Rosa and reached under the bed for Chinaku. "Hold on. I'm going to pull you out," I said as I took hold of his leg and tugged gently. "Do you want me to pull you all the way to the dining room?" He giggled at my suggestion, and I was relieved that he seemed to be over his fright. I wasn't over mine. But he and Rosa didn't need to know that.

When Clem came home at the end of the day, Chinaku ran to him. "I heard a plane," he said, "and Mommy made me get under the bed." I filled in the details. Clem told me where a building had been hit and suggested we drive over to look. I saw the rubble of a multistory, concrete-block structure that had been under construction. It wasn't yet occupied, and fortunately the builders were not there that day. But what if people had been in the building? It was too horrible to contemplate.

The next day was quiet. But a day later, we again heard explosions, and I again dove for cover with the children and Rosa. That night's news carried the report of a bombing death. Had I made a mistake to stay with Clem when I'd had a chance to leave? I began to see people driving out of Enugu with their cars loaded to the hilt, clearly abandoning the city. I was on autopilot, caring for my children during the day and worrying about our safety and the country's future in the night.

"Did you hear the broadcast today?" I asked Clem when he came home on the last day of August. "Ojukwu said we should build air raid shelters. So he expects the air raids to continue."

"We have plenty of space. Call the gardener and tell him what you want," Clem said.

"What I want is to be safe. Can you imagine a bomb falling on us?" I said, with tears near.

"Don't worry," Clem said. "Ojukwu knows what he is doing."

"I want you to find a helper and dig a tunnel, long enough for three or four adults and the children to fit inside," I said to the gardener the next morning, leading him to the top of the hill at the edge of the corn field. He seemed mystified, so I asked Clem to help with the explanation in Igbo.

"Yes, sir. I go do um now," he said. Soon after Clem left for work, the gardener and his helper went to work. By the end of the day, we had our air raid shelter. I placed bottles of water inside. We used it twice in the next two weeks. I began to wonder if we should leave Enugu and take refuge in Clem's village of Nanka. Was I putting our two little children at risk just to stay in a city?

One day in mid-September, the planes sounded especially close to our part of town. Clem was at work. By then, the cook had sent his family to his village. I called him and Rosa, and we all headed into the shelter. I held Beth while Rosa pulled Chinaku along. After huddling uncomfortably for half an hour, I heard no more planes, and we emerged. Beth had dirt all over her. Chinaku was calm now but had been crying with fright when we'd rushed in. This was crazy.

As soon as Clem came home, I told him about the afternoon experience. "I've had enough. We should go to Nanka as long as Enugu is a target." I didn't have to work hard to convince him this time.

So we packed up after just three months in Enugu. I hated moving again. What kind of life was this?

I should have known we wouldn't be back, but somehow I still believed Ojukwu's assertions that Enugu would soon be safe again. So I had the cook pack our gas tabletop stove, a few plates, the mortar and pestle, and a few other kitchen items, leaving the nonessentials like good china. I packed our wedding certificate, Chinaku's and Beth's birth certificates, our passports, our wedding album, and the scrapbook filled with telegrams we received after our wedding. I grabbed my little jewelry box and my wedding dress. I took Dr. Spock's *Baby and Child Care*, the book that had guided me through Chinaku's infancy and into his toddler years and that now was my guide for Beth's early days.

After he helped us pack, I let the cook go. He had to look after his own family, and I didn't want the responsibility of another person to care for. I would have Rosa to help me in the village. I felt only a little sad leaving Enugu behind, but I was very nervous about what lay ahead. The last time I'd been to the village was nearly two years ago for the Christmas holidays at the end of 1965. At that time, when we'd spent two weeks over the Christmas holiday in Nanka while my sister was visiting, Clem's parents had been there with us, and I had depended on them entirely for our care.

This was a very different situation. Although his parents went to Nanka frequently and kept the house in good condition, they were in Onitsha now. I would be in charge of the house, and I had no idea how long we'd be there.

All the way from Enugu to the village, I imagined what the days would be like—no department store, no water, no electricity, and no hospital nearby.

I knew there was a big market in Nanka every fourth day, and I'd gone with Mama and my sister a couple of times. But how much was available there now? When was the next market day? When Mama was there, she used the outside kitchen, where she cooked over an open fire on an iron tripod. Where would I cook?

Clem tried to be reassuring. "I lived in the village with my parents for many years. We never starved," he said. "I was hungry when I lived with the catechist, but that wasn't for lack of food—only because the catechist's wife was stingy." His consoling words were no help.

We drove into the compound in midafternoon. The relatives greeted us so warmly that I momentarily forgot my concerns. Chinaku ran off with other children. I set up my indoor kitchen with Rosa's help while Clem's cousin Georgina held Beth. I saw that Mama had left water in a large earthen jug on the floor from her most recent visit.

I had brought food and drinking water for the evening meal and food we could cook for the next two days. I found the matches and put a kettle of water from the jug on to boil. I'd have to boil and filter all drinking water. This wasn't new; we'd been doing that in Lagos and Enugu already. But where would we get water? It was time to start learning. I asked Georgina.

"From Odudunka," she said. "Rosa can come with me tomorrow morning."

"How far is it? Can she go several times?"

"It's not far. I will go with her twice for you," Georgina said.

Georgina and Rosa went twice each—I did the math. A pot or plastic jug held three or four gallons; that would be twelve to sixteen gallons for the whole day. Would that be enough? I'd never measured our water use, but I would be careful now.

I thought of my high school camping trips. I'd driven hundreds of miles with friends, first with Sue, Gail, and Karen to the Smoky Mountains and then with Sue, Karen, and Carolyn to Florida. We'd carried tents, sleeping bags, and cooking utensils and cooked over the campfire or on the smelly kerosene camp stove. We'd lugged water from the stream and from the campsite's central faucet. That was entertainment! I wished my friends were here now.

I was in a village in rural Africa, miles from a city, a telephone, plumbing, or electricity. This was anything but entertainment. I had two small children. Each camping trip had been just a week. I had no idea how long this would be. I had no friends around to share the experiences.

I had just fed Beth when Chinaku came into the compound surrounded by five or six older children. They ran off as Chinaku came inside. "Mommy, I'm hungry," he said. I was getting hungry too, and the light was fading.

I realized I'd better find the kerosene lanterns. I remembered how awkward they were to light from our last visit. Then I had an even more important thought: I wanted to use the outhouse before it was completely dark. I dreaded the thought. At least I could make my first trip while we had some daylight.

I found the lanterns, asked Rosa to give Chinaku his supper, and made my visit to the outhouse. I came out knowing I could face it for as long as I had to. What choice was there, after all? The odor was unpleasant but not overpowering, reminding me again of our camping trips. But no way was Chinaku going to be toilet trained to use this. The wooden seat was high, over a deep hole. I didn't even want him to know where it was. I had brought his potty, and he could use that as long as we were in the village.

I really wanted a warm bath, but that entailed heating water on the gas stove, carrying it to the outside enclosure near the latrine, and bringing the soap and towels from upstairs, where I'd hurriedly unpacked. Tomorrow would be soon enough for that.

Where was Clement? Although we usually ate dinner together, we often were doing separate things before and after. And since getting to Enugu, he had been late several times with his new responsibilities. But didn't he know I would need him on my first night in the village?

Still, I put that thought away while I took Chinaku upstairs to bed. Rosa already had taken Beth up to her yellow cot. She'd set up Chinaku's blue fabric crib beside her bed. After his afternoon of running around the village, he had no problem falling asleep. I went down again just as Clem came in.

"Where have you been? I needed you," I said, as I resisted crying.

"I was with Ejike and Obi. They wanted to tell me what is happening in the village and hear about the fighting in Enugu," he said. "I knew you'd be all right."

"All right is an overstatement," I said. "This is pretty overwhelming."

"I'm sorry. I forget that it's all strange for you. What do you want?" He put his arms around me.

His clear concern broke through my resolve to be brave, and I let the tears fall as he held me. "I want you to make this war disappear! But if you can't do that, eat your dinner and stay with me."

Our first day in the village drew to a close as we got into bed around nine. I felt safer than I had during the last few days in Enugu. The quiet enveloped me. The only sounds were muffled bleats from the goat shed next door and Clem's gentle snores.

The roosters crowing woke me the next morning. Then I heard Rosa get up to fetch water just as the sun was rising. When she returned forty-five minutes later, I was downstairs with the children.

Georgina and another girl had earthen pots balanced on their heads. Atop Rosa's head was the plastic jug we'd brought from Enugu. "Good morning, Ma," the girls chorused as they approached. Rosa was barefoot like the others and had her wrapper tucked tightly across her chest. Her arm muscles were visibly less developed than those of the others, for whom this was a daily task. Georgina lifted her own container to the ground and then helped Rosa remove hers. One girl after another poured the water into our storage pot and headed out again.

When they returned from their second trip around nine, sweat was pouring off their faces and bodies. I redoubled my resolve to be very frugal with water use as I thanked them. Still, I had to bathe the children.

Rosa pulled a metal tub from the outdoor kitchen and partially filled it with water from her plastic container. She added water from the kettle I'd been heating to make the bath body temperature. While I held Beth in the tub and Chinaku splashed the water around the veranda, she ran upstairs to get soap and towels. Then I was ready for my own bath.

I felt slightly guilty asking Rosa to heat another kettle of water for me as I brought my soap, shampoo, and towel. Think like a colonial, I said to myself. The situation is not of your making. But I couldn't help myself. I took the skimpy half bucket to the shed by the kitchen and washed and rinsed carefully.

It was time to find out when the next market was. I knew the names of the market days now—Afo, Oye, Eke, Nkwo. The town of Nanka had its market on Afo, the first day of the Igbo week, when all the sellers would be in their stalls or at their tables. I would be able to buy meat—on the hoof or already butchered—fish, vegetables, prepared foods, and household goods. Firewood, hardware items, and fabrics were available. On the other days of the market week, a few sellers would be in the market, but I wouldn't find the same variety. Ekwulobia, about five miles away, had its market on Eke, and it was even larger than Nanka's, with sellers and buyers coming farther. The nearest Oye and Nkwo markets were small.

The visit to the market two years earlier had been a tourist trip. Now this was where I would buy what I needed to provide for my family. "Obele or Georgina's mother can tell you all you need to know," Clem had said the night before. "They go to the market regularly, and you can go with one of them."

I went through the doorway in the dividing wall. "Damn!" I said as I bumped my head on the low beam. There was Ejike seated outside his obi, his square hut, watching as I came through rubbing my head. "*Kedu?* How are you?" I said.

"*O di mma.* All is well."

"*A putago?* Are you up and about?" I was still learning the intricacies of the extended greetings.

"*Eh.* Yes."

I continued the litany of greetings required of a polite first meeting of the day, even with a close relative. I felt like I was on stage, performing for an unseen audience. Would this feel normal one day?

I walked on to Obele's hut, a few feet further. After exchanging greetings, I asked her when our town's market day was. "*Echi bu Afo.* Tomorrow is Afo," she said, "and I'm going."

I would make a list today and go to market tomorrow. I headed back to our compound, bumping my head again. Rosa and Georgina were in the kitchen taking turns cleaning up and holding Beth. The stew we'd brought from Enugu was still in the pot where Rosa had heated it for us the night before. "You should throw this away," I said, picking up the pot and handing it to Rosa. With no refrigeration, I couldn't keep leftovers.

"If you heat it well, it will last for tonight," Georgina said as she struck a match and lit one of the burners. I wasn't sure I believed her, but I had no alternative—why not try? With Rosa's help, I put together a list for market the next day.

Clem was downstairs by this time. "Please don't disappear like you did yesterday," I said. "I need to get ready for your days away."

I think he remembered my tears of the night before and quickly agreed to my request to accompany me to Georgina's home. He had his bath, demonstrating none of the restraint that I had felt. He ate his usual cornflakes, using the last of the powdered milk I had mixed. Together we went through the gate past Ejike's obi. This time I ducked my head. Clem went through the same greetings with Ejike as I had before we headed out through the gate. I recalled coming through this gate when I was a Peace Corps volunteer in 1963. What amazing changes had happened in my life in the few years since then!

Now we followed the path to Georgina's parents' home. They didn't have a gate, but they had a mound to step over to show the separation. Their house stood thirty feet back from the entrance. It was a traditional village house—a single story, with a passageway from the front through to the back, and two rooms on either side. It had mud walls and a smooth mud floor, but with the modern touch of a tin roof. "*Pom, pom,*" Clem said, using the common substitute for a doorbell.

Obi came around the side of the house. "*Nno*. Welcome," he said. "Missus! *Bia, kene ndi biara*. Come, welcome our guests." Mercy appeared, holding a large wooden stick used for stirring pounded cassava.

As we took seats on the wooden benches along the hallway, I looked at Georgina's mother more closely. She was dark and slender. She had narrow lips and a straight nose, different from the round-faced Onyemelukwes. She had a distinctive accent, and she spoke fast. She usually had an opinion and had no fear of speaking her mind. Georgina looked like her but didn't speak like her.

After the usual greetings, I thanked them for letting Georgina help us out. I wasn't sure if she had come on her own or been sent, but I wanted them to know I needed and appreciated her. Their three sons followed us back to our compound. Goddy, the youngest, was a smiling toddler, near Chinaku's age. As soon as Chinaku saw him and his brothers, he disappeared with them for the next few hours. I nursed Beth and then found a broom, just like the one Mama and Papa had given Clem and me three years earlier to signify their approval of our marriage. I attacked our bedroom first, and then took Beth downstairs while Rosa and Georgina cleaned the other rooms upstairs.

Over the course of the day, Clem's other uncle and more relatives came to see and greet us. I kept up with conversations as best I could. By the end of the day, I thought I must have used every Igbo word I'd learned and added new ones to my vocabulary. I had met more people than I could hope to remember. I nursed Beth three or four times in between visits and cleaning. As the day ended, I gave her a bottle and handed her to Rosa while I sat down with Clem and Chinaku, now dirty and tired, to eat the stew, unspoiled despite its day out of the fridge, just as Georgina had promised.

Ojukwu had assured all Biafrans that our soldiers would hold Enugu, and we could return in a few weeks. Even if his prediction was not fulfilled quickly, I would survive. Other Peace Corps volunteers had lived without electricity or running water for two years, after all. I was just having the experience later.

I was exhausted mentally and physically. But I also had a feeling of accomplishment. I had secured our water supply. I knew when the market was and would go in the morning. I had visited the nearest relatives. I had Georgina as an extra helper. Half the village had welcomed me, or at least it felt that way. Everyone knew who I was and would watch out for my son as he wandered around in the company of other children. I wrote a quick letter to my parents for Clem to mail the next day.

In the complete dark and quiet of a village night, I had no trouble falling asleep.

10

VILLAGE LIFE, THE MARKET, AND THE WAR

THE ROOSTER FROM next door woke me again early the next morning. Then another from farther away joined. Soon it was a chorus. I groped on the floor to find my watch and the flashlight—5:30 a.m. I tried to sleep again, but it was impossible. I lay on the bed feeling refreshed and safe—no more bombs, I hoped. Then I remembered that Clem would be leaving soon, and I would be on my own in the village. I'd need all my skills at adapting to a new environment.

I heard Rosa leave to fetch water. I went downstairs and turned on the battery-operated radio to see if there was any news. I imagined for a moment how I'd feel if the war had ended and we'd be able to go back to Lagos. I'd start teaching again, I'd see my friends, life would return to normal. Then I heard Beth stirring upstairs. I brought her down and sat on the veranda railing to nurse her.

"*Ejekom afia*. I'm on my way to market," Obele said, pausing after coming through the doorway between her compound and ours. She had bent low to allow the tray on her head to get through the doorway without being knocked off. I saw dozens of small packets wrapped in banana leaves stacked on her tray.

"What is that you are carrying?" I asked in Igbo.

"*Utaba*," she said. At my look of puzzlement, she held the fingers of her right hand up to her nose while gripping the tray with her left. She sniffed. I was mystified.

"I'm coming later," I said, as she walked toward the gate. When Clem came down, I said, "What's *utaba*?"

"Snuff," he said, with the gesture I had seen Obele use, and imitated the quick snorting sound men make when inhaling it. "Why are you asking?"

"Obele is taking it to market to sell." Now her earlier gestures made sense. I hadn't seen snuff in use, but I did remember reading about it during Peace Corps training. From deep in my memory came the reference to precolonial times in Igbo-land when the village men shared snuff. My friend Art had asked the instructor whether this was an anachronism—hadn't snuff been brought by the English?

"No, Igbos were already growing and grinding tobacco when the Europeans arrived," the instructor had told us. What else would I recall from training, now that I was living in a village instead of a big city? I wished I had my books with me. But we'd left them in Enugu, along with most of our possessions.

As soon as Clem had departed for Enugu, and Rosa and Georgina had returned from their second trip for water, I asked Georgina to go with me to the market, leaving Beth with Rosa. Chinaku was nowhere in sight, so I reminded Rosa to keep an eye out for him and tell him where I'd gone. Georgina ran home to change while I checked my list with Rosa. What would we need for the next four days until the next Afo? We might be in the village for only another week or so, maybe a month. But at least we needed meat, yams, tinned tomatoes, and fresh vegetables and fruits.

I handed the basket and plastic bags to Georgina as we got into the car. She'd changed into a dark cotton skirt, white pullover blouse, and sandals.

"You look pretty," I said to her in English. Had I dressed well enough for the Nanka market? I was wearing my favorite brown A-line skirt that I'd had since Peace Corps training, with a sleeveless jersey top that sparkled. It would have to do.

We passed dozens of women and a few men walking uphill to market. Quite a few carried large bundles on their heads. From our house, it was about two miles. But others lived another two miles downhill. Many people, like Edwin's family, lived on side roads, a mile, even two, off the major thoroughfare. How did they carry these burdens so far in the heat and humidity?

We were still driving on the left then, so I parked where I saw a couple of other cars, in front of a row of adobe, single-story buildings, all the same reddish-brown color as the soil. A few men sat on wooden chairs outside a café or bar. Across the road on our right were piles of yams and cassava spread on the ground, with their owners standing patiently, chatting and waiting for customers.

We stepped around their mounds and headed into the market. I was overpowered by the rich, fruity smell of palm oil. No wonder. Beyond the yam sellers were three palm oil presses. At each, three men turned a six-foot cylinder to extract the oil from the palm kernels. The matted reddish-brown fiber residue covered the ground. I copied Georgina as she greeted the workers, "*Dalu unu.*" This phrase, I'd learned, means thank you to more than one person. But it's used to greet people at work, to say something like, "More grease to your elbow."

Everyone nearby greeted and welcomed me as we made our way to the stalls of vegetable sellers, where tomatoes and onions were piled neatly. "*Oyibo.* White person," I heard all around me, "*Nno.* Welcome." I was an object of interest and curiosity. "*O bu onye be Onyemelukwe.* She's from the Onyemelukwe family," I overheard a couple of people say.

I nodded and smiled. I hoped I would see Obele. "*Nno,* Mama Chinaku. Welcome." It wasn't Obele but seemed to be someone who knew me as more than the strange white woman. I turned to see a familiar face. "Do you know me?" she said in English.

"Yes, but please remind me who you are."

"I am Irene, Edwin's sister." Now I recalled meeting her at Chinaku's naming ceremony and during our Christmas holidays in the village. She was charming and had a warm smile. She was my height. Her face resembled Edwin's, with even features and a nose that was narrow for an Igbo. I remembered that she was married and lived near the market.

— 113 —

She wore a blue-and-green wrapper with matching blouse and head tie. We exchanged greetings in a mix of Igbo and English. Her tomatoes and onions looked better than the others around. Even if they hadn't, I would have bought what I needed from her.

I asked for directions to the meat sellers. Irene led us, though I could almost have followed my nose. As we approached, I was assaulted by the fleshy scent of newly butchered animals. There were eight or ten butchers, each standing behind a wooden table where his meat was arranged. Behind the butchers were the live cows and goats, ready to be slaughtered if needed. The ground between was covered in blood.

I looked around for the stand with the fewest flies and approached the Hausa butcher who had brought his cattle from the North. I recognized beef fillets, but otherwise the cuts were a mystery. I was pretty sure he would not speak Igbo, so I addressed him in English.

"How much for this?" I said, pointing to a hunk of beef.

"Two pounds."

"*Hubba*," I said, using a wonderful Hausa word that indicates shock or surprise. "I'll give you one pound."

"Pay one pound, ten shilling."

After more back and forth, I told the butcher to wrap the meat and handed over one pound, six shillings of Nigerian currency, still in use in Biafra. Did this Hausa man feel as out of place as I did, surrounded by Igbos, most of whom did not speak my native language?

We wanted chickens, but they were not near the meat sellers. I went back to Irene to ask her where we'd find them. Again she guided us to the main road, where I found raffia cages of five or six chickens. This section of the market also had eggs, margarine, and bread.

By now we had all we could carry. Georgina held the two chickens tied together at the legs and the bags with meat and vegetables. I held the eggs and bread.

We were just turning to head back to the car to store our purchases, buy our yams, and head home when I saw Obele. She was seated on a low wooden stool opposite the church. Like the women in a row with her, she was selling cigarettes and candy. But she seemed to be the only one with the packets of snuff. I greeted her and her colleagues in Igbo, sending the other women into shouts of surprise and gales of laughter.

Shopping in Nanka would never be boring.

The next evening, Clem returned from Enugu, bringing with him the Venice painting from my grandmother's house, our good dishes, and more documents. He had retrieved all the notes and drafts for the beginning of his second book, but he had to leave the piano, the radiogram, and most of my books and papers. My high school and college yearbooks and the Peace Corps "face book" and curriculum from our training were left behind. Would I ever see them? "I won't go back to the house again soon," he said. "It's too near the Nsukka Road. I've been given a room in the Government Rest House."

"That sounds ominous. Are the Nigerian soldiers so near?"

"No, it's just a precaution. And with no cook in the house, I need to eat somewhere." For the next month, Clem would sometimes spend the night in Enugu, returning to Nanka on other nights and every weekend. He brought news of the latest military happenings and the Biafran government's moves.

I was concerned about Clem's being in Enugu in case there were more bombs or the Nigerian Army invaded. But he didn't seem worried. I got used to being on my own a good part of the time and established a routine. I boiled water three times a day, nursed Beth whenever she was hungry, and prepared occasional bottles to supplement. I went to market every four days. Georgina helped Rosa with washing diapers, cleaning, and cooking. With no electricity and no refrigeration, I worried about keeping food from spoiling. I adopted Georgina's method of reheating leftover stew or soup in the morning to pre serve it for lunch or even the next evening. It worked.

"Our brave soldiers are holding the city of Benin. The people of the Midwest are joining the cause of their brothers and sisters in Biafra," Ojukwu said in a radio broadcast on September 19. He announced the creation of the independent Republic of Benin, tearing away another section of Nigeria to join Biafra in its fight for independence. I was amazed and thrilled at this news.

"Isn't it wonderful about taking the midwestern part of Nigeria?" I said after hugging Clem when he returned the next night. "But why isn't there any news about Enugu?"

"There isn't anything to report," he said. But his mouth set in a straight line and his downcast eyes told me more. I didn't press him.

Just three days later, I heard Ojukwu say, "The people of Benin have abandoned us." Apparently the new "republic," which Ojukwu had declared so boldly, had fallen. That night as I was getting ready for bed, I learned from the BBC that Nigerian troops, having retaken Benin, were advancing eastward toward Onitsha. They were treating all Igbos along the way as traitors and carrying out vicious attacks.

If the Nigerian soldiers crossed the Niger Bridge, I thought, they would overrun the city of Onitsha quickly. I wondered what Clem's parents were thinking. I expected them to arrive in the village any day. And if Onitsha fell, how safe would we be in Nanka?

One morning in early October, I was holding Beth on the veranda when Ojukwu's voice came over the radio. "The Niger Bridge has been destroyed. The Nigerian Army will never enter Biafra from the west." I guessed that the Biafrans had blown up the bridge to prevent the Nigerians from crossing. There was no other bridge within one hundred miles and none that led directly into Biafra.

Now the war was even more of a tragedy. I'd crossed the Niger Bridge before it was even completed because of Clem's ECN role. I'd crossed it again coming to the East the month before Beth was born. Now my physical tie to the happier, peaceful life in Nigeria was severed. I could think of little but the futility of war.

And it wouldn't prevent the Nigerian Army for long. There were the ferries we had used before the bridge was built. I was more eager than ever for Clem to return to give me an update.

"They will never make it across the Niger at Onitsha," he said. And over the next three weeks, I listened to the Biafran news reports as they mocked attempts by the Nigerian Army to cross. The Nigerians lost many troops and tanks in the effort, though I was never sure how much was propaganda and how much was truth.

But there was disaster on the other war front. Enugu fell to the Nigerians. Clem announced that the capital was moving to Owerri. "Listen to this," I said to Clem one morning. "BBC says that with the fall of Enugu and the shortage of fuel, there is the possibility of Biafran surrender."

"They don't know what they are talking about," he said. "We may even lose the coal fields in Oji, but we are going to distill petrol. We will have fuel. Just wait." Biafran military and civilian leaders redoubled their efforts. Clem started driving to the new capital, an hour trip, on Mondays, coming home on Wednesday night, and then driving back for two or three more nights, before coming home on Friday night or Saturday.

Finally, in November, Clem said that the Nigerians had abandoned the attempt to take Onitsha by crossing the Niger River. They were instead approaching the city from the north and were getting close. Two nights later, his parents arrived.

"*Kene Chukwu*. Thank God," Mama said, holding up her hands in a gesture of prayer. She continued in Igbo, "I thought we would die." Her face was a picture of terror. "You cannot imagine the confusion in Onitsha. The artillery was so powerful, it was shaking the house." I could understand much of what she described, and Rosa or Clem translated as needed.

"The Nigerian Army was near and getting closer. Papa had to pay double to find transport. The road out of Onitsha was mobbed," she said. I was very happy they were safe. I stretched the meal I'd prepared and brought them food as they sat in the parlor shuddering over what they'd witnessed.

Mama described the day when the Niger Bridge was blown up. "I heard the blasts, the loudest noises I have ever heard. I didn't know what it was. People were running from the market and the lorry park all the way to St. John's Cross."

Papa added, "I thought it was a bomb. I told Missus to stay inside. I thought the market was destroyed."

"But later I went to see," Mama said. "The bridge was gone completely. I think people died on the bridge. The area smelled like burned flesh."

She told us that she'd seen the corpses of Nigerian soldiers who tried to cross the river. "Their bodies were dragged from the water and were lying on the road."

Before they went to bed that night, Papa said we should pray. We sat together in the dark with one lantern between us as he thanked God again for their safe delivery, for having the house Clem had paid for, and for success for Biafra.

What would it be like to live in this house together for two or three months or longer? I had to reorient my thinking. This was Mama's house, after all, even though the money to build it had come from my husband. She surely had a routine that was different from mine.

Within a few days, we had basics worked out. Mama would be up very early, by six or six thirty. Sometimes she swept the compound. More often, she would wait until Rosa or Georgina came back from fetching water and direct one of them to sweep. She would clean up from the prior evening's meal, make a fire, reheat any leftovers, and prepare *garri* by mixing dried ground cassava with boiling water, to go with leftover soup for breakfast.

I would rise around seven, nurse Beth, and get a simple breakfast together for Chinaku and me and Clem when he was home. We had packaged cereal and powdered milk at first. Or I prepared *akamu* and bought or fried *akara* to go with it.

Sometimes I cooked on the gas stove in my indoor kitchen. But mostly I came to depend on Mama for her soups and stews. She was an excellent cook. I believe cooking over a wood fire added to the flavor. And then reheating made the dishes even tastier.

My favorite, and Clem's, was bitterleaf soup, with its labor-intensive preparation. We would buy the bitterleaf, which looked like spinach, in the market or from a neighbor nearby who grew it. Mama or Rosa would wash the leaves several times, using our precious water, to remove the bitterness. Then Mama would heat palm oil until it was golden, add chopped onion, ground crayfish, salt and red pepper, and meat or chicken and stockfish, which she had boiled ahead of time. Finally she'd add the leaves and water. After an hour or so, she would boil cocoyam, pound it to a consistency like mashed potatoes, and add scoops of it to the soup.

When the soup was done, she would make pounded yam or garri to serve with it.

When Mama saw how much I liked the soup as long as it didn't burn my mouth, she moderated her use of pepper. I learned how to make this and other soups, okra, *agbonu*—a seed that made the soup draw like okra—and egusi, or pumpkin seed. Some dishes took even more time to prepare than bitterleaf soup. I found that an Igbo woman could easily fill her whole day with fetching water and firewood, gathering ingredients, and cooking.

Chinaku loved fried plantain. I began to give little bits to Beth, who gobbled it up. Clem had a soft spot for rice, which we had with stew, made with meat or chicken and, rarely, fish. Sometimes we boiled yam to have with stew, or mixed yam with crayfish, oil, and vegetables to make what we called yam pottage.

Mama or I, and sometimes both of us, would go to the market every Afo. With the large number of families that had returned to the village, some from homes in the North and some, like us, from Lagos or Enugu, it was crowded.

We had very different styles of shopping. I expected to bargain, but I would concede on price well before Mama would. I sometimes became impatient with her need to argue for every last penny in savings from the buyers. But I liked to walk around with her as she was greeted by the many women she knew.

I had struggled again with breastfeeding, as I had with Chinaku. I had thought it was important that I try even harder to have sufficient milk for Beth, since with the disruptions I wasn't sure if I could buy the evaporated milk I would use in formula. Beth cried a lot, probably because she was hungry, but I was afraid to supplement her feeding very often. Dr. Spock's *Baby and Child Care* told me that giving her formula was certain to lessen my meager milk supply. But before Christmas, I'd given up.

"We'll have to boil more water and sterilize bottles again," I said to Rosa, who'd become an expert when Chinaku was smaller. I'd already been buying evaporated milk for tea and akamu. I now bought enough for Beth's bottles six a day. I tried to make just enough for each feeding, since we couldn't store it very long.

With December came the Harmattan. The dusty wind blowing south from the Sahara made the temperature and humidity fall but left a sandy grit on surfaces and haze in the air. Soon it was Christmas, which would fall on a Monday. "What will we do to make Christmas feel special?" I said to Clem on the weekend before.

"Of course, we will go to church in the morning," he said. I should have known. We'd attended church in Lagos together with my parents on Christmas Day in 1964, the day before our wedding. We'd gone to church on Christmas in the village in 1965 when my sister was with us. In 1966 in Lagos, we'd attended St. Saviour's again. And we'd been to the nearby church on a few Sundays since arriving in the village. "In the afternoon, you will see the *mmo*."

Wartime, I thought, was no time for presents. Clem had told me that when he was a child the most he ever expected at Christmas was a single article of clothing or a pair of new shoes. I knew he wouldn't miss gifts. The children were too little to notice. With the war and daily village life on my mind, any attempt at a mock Christmas tree or gifts seemed totally irrelevant. But I did look forward to the change of pace promised by the masquerades, or *mmo*,

After church on Christmas Day, Mama killed the two chickens we'd bought for Christmas lunch and cooked the stew and rice while I fried plantain. As we finished eating, the distinctive sound of the masquerades' rapid footsteps brought us to the veranda to watch.

"You really are afraid, aren't you?" I said to Clem, who was half-hidden behind the post on the edge of the veranda as the first masquerade of the day entered.

"Don't look them in the face," was his response. "Hold Chinaku's hand."

This *mmo*, like the ones I'd seen before, was covered head to toe. His body was shrouded in dark blue fabric. He had four tall white feathers on top of his thick blue net face cover. His commanding movements and spooky voice, and the whips of his assistants, made the nearby children quake with fright. Chinaku and Beth were a little scared, but they seemed to pick up my own fascination rather than their father's fear.

During that Christmas period, I could forget we were at war for a few days. Our town of Nanka was not on a major road to anywhere and was not in danger. I'd grown accustomed to the pace of village life. My Igbo improved daily.

There were no other white or foreign women that I knew except Jean and Anne, who were with their husbands twenty miles away in opposite directions. Most of the time, I felt I belonged, despite being so clearly an outsider. I only got annoyed at my lack of anonymity when too many children followed me, calling, "*Onye ocha*," or when I just wanted to shop in the market like everyone else was doing but had an audience.

My coping skills were called into play daily. What was the use of complaining? I'd made the decision to stay when offered the chance to leave. I didn't regret it, though there were moments when I wondered if I had done the right thing to ensure the safety of my children.

I got used to being confronted by people from Clem's extended family or clan who would ask in a rather aggressive manner, *"Imarim?* Do you know me?"

I would usually smile and admit in Igbo, *"Amarom gi.* I don't know you." They would then explain the connection, and I would try to remember the face to go along with the relationship.

The first few times I was called, *"Nwunyem.* My wife," I was taken aback. "What liberties does this entitle someone to?" I asked Clem.

"None." He laughed. "He's just telling you that you belong. You are one of the wives married to our clansmen," he said.

Every once in a while, I would say to myself, how did I get here? How long is this war going to last? Can Biafra really succeed? But most of the time, my days were consumed with caring for the children, shopping, and getting food on the table, the normal tasks of every day.

The greatest stress of living with my parents-in-law came from trying to superimpose my own sense of child rearing, as instructed by Dr. Spock's *Baby and Child Care*, on village life. Beth still slept morning and afternoon, but I insisted Chinaku also take a nap every day. I would call him if he'd gone off again and take him upstairs.

Dr. Spock didn't know that children in an African village are cared for by older children during the day. They sleep when they're tired, on the ground or on a mat, in their own compound or a neighbor's. And they go to sleep in the evening when it's dark, around seven thirty year-round. I was too young and naïve to realize how silly I was being.

By late January 1968, Biafra had created its own currency and outlawed the use of Nigerian notes and coins. This was fine for a couple of months. Then inflation and scarcity hit. Imported goods from Europe or Asia had disappeared early in the war. Now it was even hard to find some of the locally produced products, like the evaporated milk for Beth's formula that had been coming in from Nigeria, now enemy territory.

"I can't keep driving home every two or three days," Clem said on the first Monday in February as he was preparing to leave for work in Owerri. "Petrol is scarce, and we need to reserve as much as possible for the army. I'll be back on Saturday."

That meant one fewer dinner and breakfast to provide in our house, which was good. Although his salary was enough to take care of us, with inflation it was becoming more challenging to provide full meals. I wondered if we had done the right thing when we told our next-door cousin Mbokuocha that she should send her son Okeke, closest in age to Chinaku, over for evening meals.

"I would love to go somewhere other than the market," I said when Clem came home after five nights away.

"We can visit my sister Monica. You can stay for a few days with her."

I packed a few clothes for myself and the children. Clem drove us to her home. Her school, where she was the English teacher, had abandoned classes and sent the students home after the Christmas holidays when it became too difficult to get supplies.

"I was going crazy with just my husband and two children around all the time," she said. "You came just in time to keep me sane."

She had friends in the school compound, but I understood what she meant about feeling isolated. I gave her updates on her parents and other relatives in Nanka, and she told me stories about people in her school. Chinaku was just a few months older than her daughter, Nonso, and Beth was near the same age as her son, Emeka. We watched them play and discussed their development to our hearts' content until the next weekend when Clem came to collect us.

I wrote to my parents regularly, sharing anecdotes about the children or village life. They had settled, at least temporarily, in Germany. They sent their replies to Clem's office in Owerri, and he brought me their letters.

But as February turned to March, six months of village life, with no electricity, no running water, and no social life as I had known, was wearing me down. I had no friends with whom to share confidences. My husband was away most of the time. When would it end?

Then the weather seemed to turn even hotter. The Harmattan was over, and the rainy season hadn't started. I knew the average temperature for Nigeria was over eighty degrees, though I had no way to measure. The days before the rains started were especially trying as the sky grew heavier, but there was no relief from the oppressive heat. On some days, the village seemed like a prison, and I wondered if I would ever get out. It would be another six months.

11

THE MONEY CHANGER, THE SNAKE, AND DEPARTURE

"Our Igbo scientists are very clever," Clem said one evening in March as I spooned rice onto his plate. "It's shameful how we let Great Britain dictate to us. We stopped thinking for ourselves. This war is turning into a great opportunity."

"You already told me about refining petrol. What else?"

"The inventors are working on weapons. We can't be sure we can continue to import arms." He was amazingly confident at age thirty-four as civilian head of Biafra's power and fuel sectors. He reminded me that Igbo people had guns before colonization. "We have all the ingredients for explosives, and we have chemists. We should have something usable soon," he said.

"Biafra is lucky to have you," I said. "I'm not making much of a contribution, am I?" I was tired of being cut off from the outside world and any opportunity to work.

"You are taking care of our children and helping out my parents. Isn't that enough?"

"Do I have a choice? It's like I'm getting my Peace Corps experience now. When other volunteers were in villages, I was in the big city. Except now I have two children and no job, not to mention a war."

"You also now have a husband to look after you," Clem said.

"A husband who is hardly ever here."

"That's not my fault," he said. "I would be here every night if I could." I held my tongue. I didn't want to argue and didn't want to burden him with how alone and on the sidelines I felt. I couldn't take away from his pride and the work he clearly relished.

And I was proud of my ability to speak Igbo and be a part of village life. I could bargain like an Igbo woman, and if I were hidden from view, I could convince someone that I *was* Igbo by my command of the language.

But this was not my tribe. No one shared my background or cultural references. I had no friend like Carol here in the village. Even though my Igbo was good, I didn't share the experiences or context of my fellow *ndi anutara di*, the women married into the family, or other women in the village. I couldn't hold a deep conversation.

Then there was the war. How realistic was Clem to think that Biafra could ultimately be successful in its quest for independence, no matter how brilliant the scientists and engineers? I didn't like to think about how the war would end or how much longer I would remain in the village. So I pushed the thoughts away as I ate.

That night, I tossed and turned as Clem slept soundly. Diplomatic recognition had come only from Tanzania and Zambia. Great Britain was unwilling to give up on its prized colony Nigeria and was clearly supporting efforts to reunite the country. The United States remained distant from the conflict. France had hinted at recognition but did not follow through. The United Nations paid little attention.

A few European mercenaries had joined Biafra's military, and a few weapons came in from Lisbon and other unnamed sources. Portugal allowed access for Biafran flights. But without outside financial and military help, I was afraid the cause was doomed. My sleep, when it came, was fitful. I awoke at the first crow of the roosters to worry again.

Ever since the Nigerians had taken Onitsha in November 1967, they'd tried to advance further to the east to join up with their forces sixty miles away in Enugu, which had fallen in September. If the Nigerians could con-nect these two major cities, they would cut Biafra's territory by a quarter. I was relieved that our town of Nanka was about thirteen miles south of the main road, so I didn't expect fighting to reach us, at least not now. I had no idea what would happen to my children and me if the Nigerians tried to move south.

"Listen," I said to Rosa one morning a week later. "Isn't that like what we heard in Enugu? Not the planes, but the guns."

"It sounds the same. It's the artillery. But there are two different sounds."

The shelling was a distant boom, boom—muffled but distinctly audible. We listened all day. The sound was intermittent, with pauses of an hour or more between a series that lasted four or five minutes. We continued to hear it for the next few days. Clem's cousins, John, Atu, and Georgina, all said there were two different types of armaments in use, and they could tell when it was Biafrans and when Nigerians, but I couldn't distinguish.

Added to the artillery on ensuing days were occasional blasts that remind-ed me of the bombs I'd heard in Enugu. Again, I didn't know which side was active. "Mommy, *bia nene*. Come look," Chinaku said, as I was clearing our dishes from breakfast. "Plane," he said, pointing to an unaccustomed aircraft in the sky.

"*Nke onye?* Whose?" I squinted up, shading my eyes from the tropical sun already far above the horizon. I hoped Atu, who had just come into our com-pound from next door, would have an answer.

"*O nke anyi.* It's one of ours," he said with assurance.

I shouted with joy, "Hurray, Biafra!" Chinaku held my hand. "Do we have to run?" he said, not understanding my excitement.

"No, we don't have to run. We're safe here." I hoped I was telling the truth.

I looked at Beth, completely comfortable and unworried. She was now able to pull herself up to a standing position at the veranda railing, just the right height for her. She would spend hours there with the little girl from across the road and Mbokuocha's daughter Mboku. All three were around nine months old and all the same height. The three of them would line up and move along the railing, watching the activity in the compound and squealing with delight as people passed and called out to them.

When Clem came home a week later, he kissed me and held Beth while Chinaku struggled to get his attention to tell him about the plane.

I usually fed the children in the evening before Clem and I ate, but that Sunday, I held Beth in my lap and Chinaku sat at his low table when Clem came into the dining room. I lit the candle I had placed in the mound of pounded yam.

"What's this?" he said.

"Happy birthday to you," I sang while the children clapped. "Tomorrow is April 1, your birthday. I thought we should celebrate."

"I didn't even remember," Clem said. "I'm amazed that you did. Thank you," he said. I kissed him. Then I served our dinner of yam and okra soup with a little goat meat and the stockfish that Clem loved. And I pretended for a few moments that life was normal.

After the children were asleep, Clem and I sat in the upstairs parlor with a lantern and the radio. "The market is becoming a nightmare," I said. "No one has change. Can you bring home small bills next time?"

"I will try," he said, "but I don't think there is an adequate supply in Owerri either." I knew people hoarded in a time of scarcity, but I was still frustrated.

I was beginning to doze when I heard Ojukwu's voice on the radio. "The brave soldiers of the Biafran Army have ambushed and destroyed ninety-six vehicles of the Nigerian Army," I heard him declare. "We have halted the advance toward Enugu. We will drive the invaders back into the Niger River with our Ogbunigwe."[17]

This was the biggest Biafran victory since the invasion of the eastern part of Nigeria in the fourth month of the war. "This must be a birthday present for you," I said to Clem. "Are these the weapons you were telling me about?"

"Yes. They're still not perfect, but they were effective." I reached over to give him a big hug.

The following week when Clem got home, he took us to see the ambushed vehicles. We parked with other cars along the side of the road and joined people walking on a field. An enterprising man had set up his own little business guiding tourists to see this evidence of the Biafran victory.

We followed his gaze as he pointed to a spot on the ground ten feet in front of where we stood. There it was—a hand sticking out from the earth. "Other soldiers are buried around here too," he said. "The Biafrans killed many Nigerians." I felt my skin crawl at the grisly sight. I regretted letting Clem convince me to bring the children, but they didn't seem upset.

We drove on into town, getting as close as we could to the battle scene. The damaged Nigerian tanks and trucks lined the road for nearly a mile. I was glad that we saw no more evidence of bodies. But there was a pervasive smell of explosives and decay that stayed with me for hours.

The Abagana massacre was a tremendous morale booster for Biafrans. Though I applauded the victory and believed it did help demonstrate the resilience and determination of the Igbo people and the new country of Biafra, I doubted it would change the eventual outcome. Clem still seemed confident of victory. But even with victory, Biafra would have a difficult time making it as an independent country. More years of privation would lie ahead, I thought. And if Biafra lost? I had no idea.

The next time Clem was home, we took the children to visit Clem's friend Ben and Anne, his British wife, in Ben's town, ten miles from us. Anne was clearly fed up. "When is this crazy war going to end?" she said.

"I wish I knew. You must have heard the shelling in Abagana even more than we did," I said.

"Yes, we did. I told Ben I wanted the Nigerians to win and put Biafra out of its misery," she said. Ben cringed at her disloyal words.

"How are you making out? Beth is looking a little thin, isn't she?" Anne said.

"I know. It's hard to find enough milk. And now the scare of contaminated tins has made it worse." Rumors had started two weeks earlier that the Nigerians were poisoning evaporated milk cans.

"You should go to Catholic Relief Services. Their headquarters is right here. I've been to them for milk for Chime." Anne's younger son was just a few months older than Beth. I followed her advice. Although I was embarrassed needing to ask, they were very happy to see me and assured me that I had done the right thing.

"We see so many children who are malnourished. It is a pleasure to see your children who look generally healthy," the head sister said in her Irish accent. "Let's be sure we keep them that way." They gave me powdered milk and sugar and encouraged me to come back. I did, several times, each time feeling less ashamed and more grateful.

Each trip to the market was becoming more of an ordeal. Yam and vegetables, grown locally, were plentiful, but fish, which had come primarily from the Niger River, was no longer available. Beef had always come on the hoof from northern Nigeria, where the climate permitted cattle to thrive. Now few cattle sellers from the North were coming into Biafran territory, so beef, when available, was very expensive. The cost of chickens seemed to go up every week—that is, every market week of four days.

And getting change was nearly impossible. There was a drastic shortage of currency in smaller denominations. The Nigerian currency, though banned, was still used, but people hoarded it for the chance they would be able to buy smuggled Nigerian goods.

The conversation with each vendor was frustrating. *"Achorom tomatoes. One? I want these tomatoes. How much?"* I would say.

"Shilling ino. Four shillings."

When I proffered a one-pound note, the seller would say, "No change."

One day, completely exasperated, I visited Goddy, the chemist, across the road from the church. His was the second in the connected row of five single-story cement-block shops with tin roofs. "Goddy's Chemist Shop" was the unimaginative but brightly colored, hand-painted sign over the entrance. I stepped into the store. Goddy had been in the troupe of dancers that had performed at our wedding. He was short and wiry and friendly. I had seen him several times since returning to the village. His shelves were nearly empty of medicines, but he had a warm smile for me. "I don't know what to do. I can't buy anything because I have no change."

"Wait here," he said as he disappeared into a back room. He returned to count out twenty-five small bills and coins as I handed him a large note.

"*Dalu.* Thank you," I said, with tears in my eyes. He became my savior, and I visited his shop every four days when I came to the market. Occasionally I would buy something; more often I would just get change.

In May 1968, Clem took on a second job as civilian chairman of the National Airports Board, charged with planning, construction, management, and operations of the two airports. One was an airstrip recently carved out of the jungle at Uga, near Johnson's town. Uli was the major airport. Another two airstrips were under construction. He was responsible for thousands of people. Alex Ekwueme, later Nigeria's vice president, was his head of planning.

He loved the responsibility and power, and he poured all his energy into helping Biafra survive. But his efforts didn't help me with the responsibilities I had to protect our children and help them learn about the wider world.

Shortage of kerosene made me reluctant to use the lantern when I went to the outhouse in the early morning. One morning at dawn, I entered the dusky shelter with no light. Suddenly, I noticed an unusual shape on the wooden seat. I moved forward cautiously, wondering who had left an article of clothing. Then I realized it was a snake coiled around the base, looking at me over the hole! I guessed it to be at least eight feet long and nearly a foot around. From deep in my memory came the picture I recalled from Peace Corps training of the signature blotch markings of a python.

I was more frightened than I'd ever been in my life. "Help! Come! Snake!" Mama came running with John and Christian close behind, having heard me all the way from the other compound. They called Atu, who picked up long bamboo poles as he ran across our compound. The three boys pushed and pried the snake away from the wooden seat and guided it out the door of the tiny building. It slithered slowly away.

"Why don't you kill it?" I said, still trembling.

"No. We can't. Tradition does not allow it. The python lives and moves close to the earth," Atu said. Goose bumps rose on my arms as he talked. "We are taught that it is a friend of the earth gods, so we dare not harm it."

So the snake was protected. But I wasn't! This was very unfair. Could it even harm Beth? I knew that in theory pythons stuck to smaller prey, like chickens. But Beth was little, and the snake was so large. I kept an eye on her when she was in front of the house, and I made sure that I used the outhouse in daylight or with the brightest kerosene lantern, the Tilley lamp, at night. I even had someone stationed near the outhouse for the next couple of days when I was inside.

"Do you really think the gods would mind if the snake disappeared?" I said to Christian when we spotted it three days later, coiled up in the stone wall between our compound and Mbokuocha's. Two days after that, it was in the log out front, at the side of the entrance into our compound. Of course, we couldn't be sure it was the same snake, but I had no doubt!

"I am so terrified, I don't know what to do," I said to John and Atu that afternoon as we looked at it resting peacefully. I had never before used my status as a foreign white woman, unaccustomed to African life, to gain an advantage. But this was a desperate situation. I usually honored and respected Igbo traditions. Now I hoped that someone would disobey this custom and put an end to the snake's threat to my peace and security. This was just about as frightening as the war itself! It was certainly more than I had bargained for when I said, "For better or worse."

"*Agwo onwugo*. The snake is dead," Georgina said as she poured the water into our kitchen pot the next morning.

I wasn't positive I'd understood her. "Say it again."

"The snake is dead," she repeated.

"How? What happened?"

"I don't know how it died. But I know it's gone."

The rumors started that morning. No one was admitting anything. But the common knowledge was that several young men had not only killed it, but also cooked and eaten it! Protein was in short supply by this time, so when I heard this, I was glad it hadn't been wasted, though I shuddered at the thought.

The *umunna*, the men of the clan, held a meeting the next day to deliberate on how to address this affront to custom. They decided to send Obi, Clem's youngest uncle, and Nnadi from across the road, to the Dibia, the intermediary between the spiritual and temporal world, to ask for forgiveness.

"Did you know that they had to take a white chicken, two yams, and a jug of palm wine to propitiate the gods?" Atu, one of my saviors, said. We were sitting on the low veranda wall. We hadn't seen the sun in days, but at least there was a break in the rain. I could smell the palm oil for the soup Mama was preparing. I didn't think the price was too high at all.

I retold the whole experience to Clem over dinner when he returned that weekend. He was sympathetic but didn't seem suitably impressed with the depth of my fear or the excitement.

On Saturday afternoon, we sat inside Ejike's dim hut watching the rain through the open door and drinking palm wine. Christian, one of Clem's cousins who'd helped dislodge the snake from the outhouse, was a gifted storyteller. He liked to speak English with Clem and me, but he told the story in Igbo now for the benefit of Clem's uncles, Ejike and Obi.

"It was just getting light. I could hear her shouting, 'Help, save me,'" he said, using his imitation of my voice and American accent. "You should have seen her face when we came." His wide eyes and shocked expression made Ejike bend over with laughter, while Obi slapped his thighs.

"The snake was huge. I'm sure it's the same one that took Obele's chicken last month." He spread his hands. Striding the width of the hut, he said, "It was so long it would not have fit in here."

"Why don't you tell us what happened to it?" I said.

"How would I know?" His look of innocence couldn't convince me. But I wasn't about to challenge him. I didn't want to risk the anger of Clem's uncles or the further wrath of the gods.

For the next couple of weeks, I watched to see if any snakeskin objects appeared. Nothing.

Two weeks later, Clem was home again. He was still upstairs in bed on Saturday morning when Georgina came.

"My mother says you should come for roasted yam," she said in Igbo.

"Are we to come now?"

"Yes, it's ready now."

Clem hated waking early, but it was already eight thirty, and I roused him despite his protest. When he finally understood what treat awaited us, he stopped grumbling, splashed water on his face, brushed his teeth, pulled on trousers, and followed me through Ejike's compound, out the gate, and on to Obi's compound. I carried Beth. Chinaku ran ahead.

Obi had placed one wooden bench and two chairs near the steps outside their house. "*Nno dani*," he said, motioning to the seats as if they were thrones for royalty. "Missus," he called to his wife. She appeared from behind the house to place a tray with two yams on a rickety table between us. Each yam was about ten inches long, its skin nicely charred and scraped. I inhaled the smoky smell of the wood fire that clung to the yams. Georgina followed with a bowl of thick, red palm oil sprinkled with salt. The yams were scored so we could break off a wedge, an easy size and shape to hold and dip in the oil.

"I haven't eaten this since I left for UK," Clem said as he took a large piece and dipped it in the palm oil before chewing it with gusto. I too found this a pleasure, a way to break the boredom of boiled or pounded yam.

"Why haven't you had it in the years you've been back?"

"I don't know. I usually visited my parents in Onitsha. I think of this as food for the village. I never thought to ask."

When Obi and Mercy saw how much we enjoyed the feast, more roasted yam breakfasts followed. I persuaded them to prepare it later, so Clem could enjoy his sleep for another hour.

In June, Clem's mother decided to go behind enemy lines to buy fish. I tried to dissuade her, while she told me how much I would enjoy the change in our diet. We had two nervous days before she returned with two huge baskets of dried, smoked fish, neatly coiled on skewers, and stories of her exploits. I could see where Clem got his resolve.

She was right about how much I would enjoy it. She used some in our soup for the next few days. She took the remainder to the market and made a tidy profit. After this success, she repeated her trip and purchases a month later without mishap.

I thought I should follow her example of contributing financially with buying something relatively scarce in Nanka. So the next time I was in Ekwulobia, with its bigger market, I bought a large stalk of bananas with many bunches of five or six each. I thought I could sell by the bunch to people who would take them to the Nanka market. But each day, as more of the bananas ripened, we ate them, until the stalk was empty.

Around the same time, refugees from other towns started arriving in Nanka. They had to leave their own towns and villages when the Nigerian Army came in. The school halfway between our house and the market became refugee housing. There were probably two or three hundred people in all.

Their presence was welcomed at first. This was wartime, and Igbos needed to support each other. But after a month, women in Nanka began to resent the refugee women who were invading their market territory and undercutting them. The village elders had to mediate and set rules. The "foreign" women could sell but only along the road and not in the main market.

Occasionally, I would see a mother and her children begging. "How are they living?" I said to Clem.

"The Biafra Refugee Commission is bringing in some relief supplies. But they can't keep up with the demand. There are settlements like this all over." The refugees' presence made the inflation and currency shortage worse, as more people were struggling to buy the diminished amount of goods. I wondered how long Clem's salary would be sufficient for us.

"Make sure there is no light showing tonight. Go to bed early," Mama said one night as we stood outside. The clouds had parted long enough to see a few stars, but there was no moon. "The night masquerades are coming tonight."

"Are they like the masquerades we saw at Christmas?"

"No, these are even more frightening," she said. "You can't see them, but you will hear them."

Around nine, I put out the lantern and fell asleep. Much later, I was awakened by the eerie music of the Igbo flute and the shaking of the dried shells the masquerades wore around their waists or ankles. As I leaned toward the window to peer out, I heard a high-pitched nasal voice calling out from the darkness, "Mama Chinaku." The sound sent chills up my spine, and I decided I didn't want to see the masquerades, even if I could. I pulled the sheet over my head until the masquerades had passed our compound, moved on to Obi's, and gone further until I could no longer detect their presence.

I was relieved that they were gone and very glad I had nothing to feel guilty about. Then I wondered if they knew that I'd wished the snake dead, even encouraging the young men to kill it. Maybe they were reminding me that I'd offended the spirits after all.

During the height of the rainy season in June, when I thought I could bear no more of the isolation of village life and the constant rain, Clem suggested we visit Port Harcourt. He had someone to see related to his airport work. We stayed in the one operating hotel in the city.

On our third day, Chinaku got sick. He had no appetite and wanted to do nothing but sleep. I could tell he had a fever. We found a doctor who looked him over, took his temperature, and said our son needed antibiotics. He wrote a prescription and handed it to me, saying, "I don't think you will actually be able to find these. No one has antibiotics anymore." He wished us luck and assured us that Chinaku would recover even without drugs. Still, I had to try. I used precious petrol and two hours going from one pharmacy to another unsuccessfully.

"Let's go back to Nanka. Goddy, the chemist, will help us," I said. We arrived back home in the evening. Early the next morning, when I was dressing to drive to Goddy's, Chinaku came into our room, completely recovered.

"He was sick because he was not in his home," Mama said. I couldn't argue!

Beth turned one on June 25, and Chinaku turned three on June 29. As for Clem's birthday in April, I stuck candles in our pounded yam, and we sang. In between, Biafra celebrated a year of independence, though the new country was already shrinking as Nigeria's army achieved victory after victory. And the rain was constant. I would wake up to rain, go to sleep to rain, even go to market in the rain.

The veranda was slick with water. Chinaku found that he could slide on his tummy from one end to the other. He introduced the new entertainment to the other children. For hours, they would take turns, slithering along, shouting with glee. Mama would caution them, *"Nwayo, ne anya.* Slowly, be careful." I, on the other hand, saw no harm and encouraged them.

I thought about my family on July 4. My sister probably watched fireworks somewhere, maybe at Coney Island. Peter was in Indiana, or perhaps he had gone to Cincinnati for the summer. I didn't even know then that he was actually in Vietnam. I wondered whether my parents were still in Germany, where they had ended their world tour.

Though I wasn't aware of it at the time, *Life* magazine's July 12 issue in 1968 came out with a cover photo of starving Biafran children, most notable for their large, mournful eyes and diseased hair. The word "kwashiorkor" was introduced to Americans and the world. The image of children afflicted by this disease of protein deficiency, with distended bellies, ribs showing, and hair turning yellow, became a powerful call for action, though the calls did not succeed.

At the same time, Clem and I finally reached the painful decision that it was time for me to take the children out of Biafra. I'd received a letter from my parents, who were in the United States, so I knew where to write. I would ask if they could pay for a flight with the Biafran government to get me to Lisbon and then on to meet them. Apprehensive about their reaction, I sent the letter off with Clem. Would they be overly worried? Did I really want to leave? And what was best for the children?

In late August, I received Mother's letter. She had paid for the flight from Biafra to Portugal. I should go to the American Express office in Lisbon, where I would find instructions and money. Clem told me I would be notified a day ahead. I was still uncertain. I had no idea how much longer the war would last, and the scarcity would become worse. Biafra continued to lose territory. But leaving Clem would be difficult. I wavered day by day.

The harvest season came in late August. I was approaching the beginning of a second year in the village, and I could hardly wait for the new corn, which could provide some variety in our boring diet. Maybe I could wait out the end of the war.

Then two more intruders and food poisoning helped me decide. One morning, I went to the outside kitchen to get boiling water from the pot for tea. I nearly stepped on a millipede. It was slimy and disgusting, about eight inches long. I didn't know if it was poisonous, but it repelled me even more than the cockroaches that were often around in the night. I grabbed a piece of kindling from the stack near the fire. At my touch, it coiled into a tight knot. I picked it up, ran out of the kitchen, and threw it over the back wall.

After supper two days later, I was coming down the stairs from taking Beth to bed. I had turned onto the second half of the staircase when I saw a snake draped over the rafters above my head. Had it been there when I walked up the stairs a few minutes earlier? I was focused on Beth in my arms then and not paying attention to my surroundings. It was only a couple of feet, nothing compared to the snake that had met its death a couple of months earlier, but I was almost as scared.

How could I leave Beth alone upstairs? How could I walk under the snake to go back to her? Neither alternative seemed possible. I screamed. Papa heard my shouts and came quickly.

"Where did it come from? What's it doing in our house?" I cried.

"Don't worry. I'll be right back." He returned in a minute, with Atu following. They dislodged the snake and carried it off. I hardly slept that night as I heard, or imagined, rustlings in the ceiling over my head.

In the middle of the night a few days later, I was wakened by sever e stomach cramps. I didn't have time to get to the outhouse to vomit. Luckily, Clem was home, so I woke him with difficulty and told him to grab a bucket. The pain increased with more vomiting and diarrhea until I thought I would die. Clem sent someone to call the nurse Osisioma, who came quickly and confirmed food poisoning. He was able to give me something to calm my stomach, but I was shaken.

I'd had enough. So when Clem came home on the first Friday night in September with the news that I could leave the next day, I was ready. I told Mama and Papa that night. Mama cried, with a mix of sadness at our departure and relief that her grandchildren and I would be safe. Papa called us to a meeting and had us pray for safe travel, the end of the war, and the protection of the Biafran soldiers and civilians.

By noon the next day, word had spread, and relatives and friends from other parts of the village came to say good-bye. I didn't have much to take, just a few worn-out clothes for me and the children and a few diapers that easily fit in one suitcase, so packing took just a few minutes.

We gathered in front of the house. "Don't forget us. We will pray for you," Mama said. "And greet your parents for us. We think about them often." She gave me a fervent hug and turned to Chinaku. "Remember, this is your home," she said as she embraced him. She held Beth and then placed her in my arms as we got into the car. My cheeks were wet with tears as I waved to Clem's family, not knowing when, or even if, I would see them again.

We drove out of the village in midafternoon. The August break was over, and clouds covered the sky as rain started falling. Chinaku was excited at going on a plane but a little worried too. "Is the plane going to drop a bomb?"

"No, no bombs ever again," I said.

"You're doing the right thing to take the children away," Clem said as he drove. I could see that he was trying hard not to lose his composure. I kept my hand on his arm.

I sat on one of the few wooden benches at the airport as we waited for darkness. Clem led us to the plane, carrying a shielded flashlight to show the way. He gave each child a hug and a kiss, and then held me so tight I wasn't sure I could break loose to follow the children up the ladder. He let go, I climbed in, and I watched through the window as men removed the raffia and palm branches that hid the plane. The landing strip's few lights were switched on just long enough for the plane to take off.

The ascent was rapid, and the plane was dark. I understood that the pilot feared an attack by the Nigerian planes. But after twenty-five minutes, everyone seemed to relax a little, and a few minutes later, minimal lights were turned on. I looked around at the other passengers. In the four rows of seats, there was one other woman I recognized, with her two children, and two others I didn't know. I saw two Roman Catholic sisters and a priest.

Then I looked behind and saw at least twenty men sitting, some on the floor and others on crates. Several had guns across their laps. Most were Biafran, but there were a couple of white men as well, perhaps some of the mercenaries.

I was flooded with relief that the children and I were among the people getting out, mixed with sadness at leaving Clem behind and worry about him and his family. Would I ever see him again? Would the attrition of territory continue slowly with no definite end for months? I hated to admit it but hoped that the end would come quickly. What would happen when the Nigerians defeated the Biafrans, as seemed most likely? And how was I going to take care of Chinaku and Beth until we were together again as a family?

12

MADEIRA, AN INTERLUDE
IN PARADISE

"It's been so long since I've had bread like this. It smells wonderful," said a woman across the table from me in the hotel dining room in Lisbon.

"This is real butter," I said. "Can you believe it?" I heard similar comments from tables near me. The linen napkins, ice water, and china dishes seemed like items from heaven. We were all foreign wives who had been with our husbands in Biafra for over a year. No matter how much I liked yam and plantain, I savored this food.

The next morning, I awakened from a solid night's sleep with no roosters crowing at dawn. I relished the running water as I showered and bathed the children.

At the American Express office, my mother's letter was waiting. She said to call their good friends Ernest and Hildegarde, who were spending September in Lisbon. She had enclosed an American Express traveler's check, which I cashed on the spot. Back at the hotel, I phoned the number for the friends. They asked me to come right over and bring my things.

In their apartment, the children were very quiet. The whole setting—a well-furnished apartment in a major city, with no one they knew in sight—was strange to them, and after so long in the village, it felt strange to me too.

"Have you talked to your parents yet?" Ernest asked. He picked up the phone. In excellent Portuguese, he asked for my parents' number in the United States. A minute later, I was speaking to my mother for the first time in nearly two years. Tears of relief and comfort welled up in my eyes as she told me there was an apartment waiting for us in Funchal. I assured her that we were all right and would be fine until they arrived.

Hildegarde brought out cakes and tea, while Ernest picked up the phone again, speaking rapidly in Portuguese.

"You have flights to Funchal day after tomorrow, if that's all right with you," he said when he hung up ten minutes later. I'd finished my tea, Chinaku had gotten crumbs on the carpet, and Beth had finished the bottle I'd given her.

"I don't even know where that is," I said. He explained that Funchal was the capital of Madeira, a semitropical island that was part of Portugal and an hour away by air. "Your parents rented the apartment hoping that you would come."

The Deliglises were happy to have us for two nights but were equally happy to see us go, I suspected. "I've called Johnny, your parents' landlord. He'll meet you at the airport in Funchal," Ernest said as he walked with us toward our departure gate, holding Beth's hand. I let Chinaku carry the new, small suitcase Hildegarde had bought me. We waved as we boarded, and Ernest called out, "See you in Madeira."

Johnny had no problem spotting us as we stepped off the plane. "Welcome to Madeira," he said as he kissed me on both cheeks, hugged Chinaku, and swept Beth into his arms. His warmth made me comfortable immediately. He exchanged greetings with other passengers and staff as we waited for our luggage.

"You like plane landing?" he asked in his limited English.

"It was very exciting. I've never seen a landing like that."

"Only best pilots fly in Madeira, never new pilot."

I could see why. Planes arriving in Madeira then had to come in over the sea, negotiate a narrow passage between rocky hills, hit the short runway, and apply their brakes immediately. At the end of the runway was a drop of three hundred feet into the ocean. Two emergency boats always waited in the water below.

The town of Funchal, with its red tile roofs, white adobe houses, and palm trees spread out on the hills, looked magical.

"Is beautiful, no?"

"Yes, it's beautiful."

Soon the hills were above and around us, and we were passing the harbor in downtown Funchal. The sidewalk was busy with shoppers, women with baskets over their arms, a few in bright dresses and head scarves and several in black, and men in work clothes. He drove on and headed up a hill on the opposite side of town.

There were grape arbors on my left, and one- and two-story, white stucco homes on my right. I caught the scent of the flowers I saw outside every house we passed—red and pink bougainvillea, jasmine, and others I couldn't name. Everything looked pristine and charming. He turned into a driveway near the top of the hill.

"*Venha aqui.* Come here," he called up the steps. A stout, brown-haired woman in her thirties or forties appeared and came down to greet us.

"Here is Therese. She will take care for you," Johnny said. She cared for us well, even though we couldn't converse. I was very grateful for her presence. She served delightful meals, washed and ironed our clothes, and did the necessary shopping.

I was fortunate that my parents weren't there when we arrived, so I had a few days to get used to living in a European environment again. It felt odd being surrounded by people with whom I had no connection, after the year in the village where everyone knew who I was and where I fit. When I gave Johnny a letter to Clem to mail for me, I felt like I was communicating to a different universe. I wondered how long it would be before I heard back.

And in a week, just as I was feeling a desperate need for adult company, my parents arrived. Johnny met them at the airport. I was waiting on the patio in the warm noon sun when they drove up.

They looked little different from two years earlier. Father's balding head, high forehead, large nose, and slightly sardonic smile were completely familiar. As usual, he wore a long-sleeve white shirt and tie with his suit. Our greetings were restrained as ever.

"You're a big boy now, aren't you?" Father said as he bent down to put an arm stiffly around Chinaku. Mother leaned over to give him a hug and kiss on the cheek.

I held Beth out. "She's lovely," Mother said, "and she looks like you." We followed Therese, who'd come down to take their bags into the apartment.

"Where is Rosa?" Chinaku said, looking a little disappointed. "*O ga bia ebaa?* Is she coming?"

"She's in Nigeria. We left her with Daddy and your friends in Nanka." I hoped my parents wouldn't feel it was a bad sign for Chinaku to be asking for someone else when they'd just arrived.

"Who's Rosa?" Mother said, clearly not disturbed, motioning to Chinaku to sit beside her on the sofa.

"She's Clem's cousin, and she's been our nanny from the time Chinaku was born. Her mother took care of Clem when he was a baby."

"Has Therese taken care of you? Have you had enough to eat?" Father said, pointing to the kitchen, where Therese had gone to prepare lunch. "You don't look too much the worse for wear."

"She's been wonderful," I said. "I looked a lot worse when I arrived in Lisbon. Life in the village was stressful, though the actual fighting didn't reach there."

I couldn't help comparing the warmth Johnny and Therese, strangers to us, showed when they'd first greeted us to my parents' European reserve. And these were my parents' own grandchildren. The contrast was even greater when I thought of the Nigerian enthusiasm and expressiveness that I'd become accustomed to.

My parents asked about the war and my year in the village over the next couple of days, but I held back. Did they want to hear about the danger Clem and his family faced remaining there? I sensed that Father's way of reacting to any stories of difficulty would be sarcasm. I didn't want that. And I didn't want to destroy their happy memories of our wedding and meeting Clem's family.

My mother had already been working on her Portuguese on their earlier visit. With her musical background and knowledge of Italian, she was soon able to speak well enough to be understood. I followed her example and was able to pick up a few words quickly. My accent was as good as, and sometimes better than hers, though her vocabulary was greater. She read what she could from the daily paper, *Diario de Noticias,* and gave us a synopsis of the day's news.

I wanted Chinaku to communicate with my parents quickly so I stopped speaking to him and Beth in Igbo. Soon he was at home speaking in English and could communicate with Therese in Portuguese.

The apartment was cramped with two active children, and we moved to a bungalow on the other side of town. I checked the mail every day. I had written to Clem several times again. But I didn't get a response for weeks. Had my letters reached him? Was he even still alive?

At last, his reply came. My first letter had taken four weeks to reach him. His reply took two. I kept writing every week, filling him in on our lives and how we all missed him. He wrote with news of family members and the war. "Port Harcourt has fallen, and we can't get petrol," he wrote in late December. "We are totally dependent on the gasoline we can distill from the oil smuggled from Cameroon." I understood that the noose was tightening around Biafra.

Madeira was famous for its New Year's Eve fireworks. Several cruise ships would be on hand at year's end for this display. I didn't want to see fireworks right then; it was too close to hearing the artillery and bombs. But I thought Chinaku was over his fear and would enjoy watching.

Father took him up the hill to an overlook where they had an excellent view of the harbor. They returned with Chinaku in tears and Father angry.

"Your son is not very brave," he said as he pushed Chinaku toward me with a look of annoyance. "I told him he wouldn't get hurt. But he just wanted to hide in the backseat."

"I'm sorry. Were you very scared?" I held Chinaku and dried his tears as I spoke to my father. "I was wrong to think he would have forgotten the bomb blasts."

But Father showed no consideration. How could he not understand what it's like for a child to be afraid? I tried to remember a time I'd felt sympathy or received consolation from him. My memory bank was empty. It took me a few days to get over being angry.

We went regularly to the English church. I'd come to know the *Book of Common Prayer* well in Nigeria. The priest was British, and the congregation was a mix of Anglicans and other expatriates who wanted a church service in English.

"Why don't we ask the priest to baptize Beth?" I said to Mother, as we stood outside the church after the service one Sunday in early February. "Do you think he would?"

"Let's find out," she said. I admired my mother's manner, straightforward, practical, and direct.

"I would be delighted," he said when we put the question to him. "We have a lot of funerals here, but there hasn't been a baptism for a very long time."

We set the tentative date for one month hence. On the morning of the baptism, I dressed Beth in a white, gauzy, long dress, with lace decorating the front and the sleeves that I'd found in the department store. I wore the tangerine-colored suit with paisley lining that I'd ordered from Mother's seamstress. With my knee-length skirt and tan heels, I felt very elegant—until I saw our neighbor Vida. She was beautifully coiffed, with her hair in a glamorous bun topped by a graceful blue hat, a royal-blue silk dress, and blue high heels.

"Dearly beloved," the priest began. I listened to the familiar litany, watching him in his white robe and maroon stole and glancing now and then at Beth in Vida's arms and Chinaku standing next to another neighbor, Helder. The priest took Beth in his arms, dipped his hand in the font, and placed it on her forehead while he said the baptismal words over her. "Clem would love this," I said softly to Mother as we watched.

"You were baptized just like this," I whispered to Chinaku. "But Daddy was there. I wish he were here now."

Other than Clem's letters, I had little news about the war. With no idea how much longer it would be before I could return to my husband, I began to think about working. I could teach English, and Mother and I talked about offering English language classes together. After all, she had been a teacher for longer than I had.

But then I had a letter from my close college friend Joan, with her wedding invitation. My parents offered to send me to the United States with the children to attend her wedding in Boston and then to visit my sister in Fort Thomas. I planned to return in three or four weeks, so I left without really saying good-bye. But I wouldn't return to Madeira for three years.

13

THE UNITED STATES, THE MOON, AND THE WAR'S END

I'D LAST SEEN my sister Beth three and a half years earlier. She'd returned to the United States from Nigeria with the malaria to remind her occasionally of her visit. She'd married a year later.

I held her in a long hug. "So this is my namesake," she said, picking up my daughter. "She's so cute. Can she give me some of those curls?"

"How was the Boston wedding?" she said. "Very snooty?"

I was surprised how much like Father she sounded, mocking people she didn't know. "Not at all," I said. "I did get curious looks as people saw the children. I thought it was just that I had brought children to a wedding reception, but later I realized it was because they are biracial."

"Did you get the same looks in Madeira?" she asked as she drove to our old house, where she now lived with her husband, Tommy.

"No, the Portuguese assumed the children were from there. And the English in Madeira are so proper they would never be seen staring."

She pulled into the familiar steep, narrow driveway where I'd learned to reverse between the cement walls. "I have to warn you," she said. "Tommy has dogs." Two huge Great Danes rose from the carpet in the living room and approached as we entered. They were bigger than Chinaku and twice the size of Beth, and they made the living room look cramped. The children hid behind me. With my heart pounding, I tried to move away, but the dogs kept coming. Tommy finally called them off.

It was not an auspicious beginning. I had little sympathy for pets now. Why should someone spend money and time on owning dogs when children were starving in Biafra and there was a war in Vietnam? I couldn't recall the feelings I'd had before about our own dogs; the whole idea seemed alien to me.

Apart from the dogs, my sister and I had a good time together. I had expected to be ready to fly back to Madeira after a few days in the United States. But I didn't want to.

What I really wanted was for the war to be over so I could take my children back to Nigeria and resume a normal family life. But lacking that possibility, I decided I should make the best of what opportunities I could find, earn a living, advance in my teaching career, and give my children a sense of us as a family.

I knew my sister and her husband couldn't support us. I read that the new federal preschool program for low-income children, Head Start, was hiring teachers. I applied and got hired, not to teach—no teaching certificate—but for administrative work. There was day care in the same building. I made friends with other staff members.

The home front, however, was uncomfortable. After four weeks with Beth and Tommy, the relationship was strained. Tommy did not like having my biracial children in the house. "I'm sorry. I don't want you to go," Beth said, "but Tommy thinks it's better for us and the dogs."

I began looking for another place to live. I knew there was a row of single-story wooden houses near the Presbyterian church, right on Fort Thomas Avenue. The next Sunday morning, I noticed a sign outside that said an apartment was available. That afternoon, I took Beth's car, spoke to the landlady, and agreed to come back with my children to look at the apartment.

I returned later that day. "I was here earlier about the apartment," I said. "I'd like to take my kids in to have a look."

"Oh, I'm so sorry. I already rented it," she said. I was stunned. How could she do that?

"I told you I'd be back this afternoon," I said, my anger coming through in my voice.

"I'm sorry. It's gone," she said. I was naïve and didn't fully connect her rejection to race, though it was at the edge of my consciousness, along with Tommy's wish to have us move out. I saw no choice but to look elsewhere.

I began looking at notices in the *Cincinnati Enquirer* for rental apartments and made a couple of phone calls. And I asked the director of Head Start about jobs for the fall. He sent me to a Catholic school in Covington, Kentucky, that didn't require a teaching certification.

When I spoke with the head nun, I described my teaching experience, the Biafran War, and why I was separated from my husband. By then, everyone in the United States and a good part of the world had seen pictures of the starving Biafran babies. I told her that the Nigerians were blocking access by aid organizations and drawing an ever-tighter net around the remaining Biafran territory.

She hired me to teach fourth grade and told me there was an apartment for rent next door. It was on the ground floor, dingy, with two small bedrooms, a kitchen, and a bathroom. It came with basic furniture, slightly tattered floral curtains in the living room, and pulldown shades in the bedrooms. I took it to move in a week later.

The next day, I bought a well-used, light-green VW bug with the money I'd saved working and the refund on the ticket back to Madeira and drove it to my sister's.

And a few days after that, I bid farewell to her, her husband, and his hateful dogs, and we moved out. I had another month of work at Head Start, a job awaiting me after Labor Day in September, a place to live, and my own transportation.

And I was excited about the moon landing coming up. A colleague at Head Start invited me to bring the children and watch with her.

"It's unbelievable!" I said, my eyes glued to the twelve-inch black-and-white TV screen in her living room. It was nearly 11:00 p.m. "It's like something out of a fairy tale."

Neil Armstrong had just taken his first steps on the moon. It was July 20, 1969. I had been back in the United States for two months. I looked at my sleeping children. Chinaku had turned four on June 29. His head of tight black curls was on an embroidered floral pillow at one end of the sofa. Beth, now two, with hair similar but a little softer, slept at the other end, her head resting on a folded blanket. Her feet just touched his.

"That's one small step for man, one giant leap for mankind," Armstrong said as he stepped off the ladder from the Apollo Lunar Module lander and stood on the moon's surface.

"This is so exciting. I have to write to my husband with the details," I said to my hostess, who was seated in an armchair beside the couch.

"Won't he see this? I thought people are watching all over the world," she said.

"All over, yes, but that's very different from everywhere in the world. Even without a war, there's no TV in his village in Nigeria. In fact, there's not even electricity." I was reminded again of how little Americans knew about countries in Africa.

After watching Armstrong and Aldrin plant an American flag on the moon's surface, it was time to leave. I carried Beth and pulled Chinaku, barely awake, into the car for our drive back to our tiny apartment in Covington, Kentucky.

I was fed up with this peripatetic existence and life without my husband. The few news reports from Biafra grew more frightening every week, with more photos of starving children in major media. Then I heard about Senator Ted Kennedy's efforts to get the United States to pressure Nigeria to end its blockade of humanitarian relief. It was time for me to at least make some effort. So I wrote a letter to Congress. After a couple of weeks, I heard back that my letter had been entered in the Congressional Record, though no action had been taken.

My life was split. Most of the time, I was focused on caring for, educating, and entertaining my children and preparing for the teaching job to start in September. Then I would remember the war, and I would shudder to think what was happening to my husband, his family, and the country. When would it all end?

On the first day of school, I spelled out my name on the blackboard. Then I wrote it again, broken into syllables, and said it for the students. After a few tries, they were all able to say it. Within a week, I knew every child's name and reading level.

I visited some of the children at home to help me understand their backgrounds and the environment of this Catholic neighborhood. I used the visits to explain a little about the Biafran War and why I was in the United States without my husband, a question clearly on the parents' minds. Then I would learn a little about the family, how many siblings there were, and what the father did. Usually I took my children with me. "Your children are so...cute," I heard. I understood the slight hesitation. Mixed-race children were almost unknown in northern Kentucky then.

Beth and Chinaku were not challenged at their day-care center. But I didn't see an alternative. I read to them every evening and encouraged them to draw and count. I taught Chinaku the alphabet and a few words.

In early October, the leaves began to change colors. I had forgotten how beautiful the fall was, and how chilly the air, as I hurried the children into the car. Soon I would have to buy winter clothes and coats. I wasn't looking forward to that extra expense. I knew my parents were willing to help, but I didn't like to ask. At least I was settled for the moment.

One night in October, I was sitting at the wooden desk in the apartment preparing lesson plans for the next day. I heard a scratching sound. Was one of the children awake? Out of the corner of my eye, I saw a movement on the floor near the couch. It was definitely larger than a cockroach, which I'd seen now and then and sprayed so heavily with Raid that I was afraid I'd make the children sick. This was gray and furry, with little pink ears.

I stifled a scream. It wouldn't help to wake the children. A few days later, just when I'd deceived myself into thinking the intruders were gone, I heard the scrambling again and spotted another rodent.

That was it. On the advice of my friend Kathy from Head Start, I found and rented a two-floor, two-bedroom apartment in subsidized housing across the river in Cincinnati. It was light, spacious, and clean. The children could play outside in the small front yard. Unlike in Covington, where the neighborhood was entirely white, there was a mix of white and black families around us.

I found a day-care provider, Jenny, who lived nearby. The children and I liked her right away. She would provide more educational experiences than they were getting, and it was convenient.

In November, the first snowstorm of the winter hit. I hadn't driven in snow since leaving for Nigeria in 1962, six years earlier. "Like a Bridge over

Troubled Water" had played on the radio as I drove home, slipping and slid-ing, down the steep curving hill in Northern Kentucky where I was taking evening classes, and then up Cincinnati's snow-covered hills. "I wasn't sure I could make it," I said to Jenny when she met me at her door. I'd arrived later than usual and was still shaking.

"You'll get used to it," she said with a smile of encouragement. "The chil-dren loved it. They didn't seem bothered by the cold." She helped them into their coats, still a little damp from the time outside. At least the children would enjoy the winter. I doubted if I would.

My parents came from Portugal for the Christmas holidays. They stayed with my sister, her husband, and the Great Danes. I drove over on their first evening. I hadn't realized I'd missed them so much until Mother was holding me and then my children in her arms. The children were shy for a couple of minutes but quickly remembered their grandparents and loved the extra atten-tion. "What do you hear from Clement?" Mother asked.

"Not very much," I said. "His last letter was two weeks ago. I'm sure he's having a hard time. He sounds pretty discouraged. But he says he and his fam-ily are still safe in the village."

A couple of days before heading back to Madeira, Mother and Father came over with a TV for me. I began watching evening newscasts. And right after New Year's, I fell in love. Johnny Carson, host of his own late-night TV show, entered my life and became a fixture every evening when I finished lesson plans for my students and my own homework.

For the first two weeks of 1970, there was no news from anywhere in Africa. Then on January 15, 1970, I was stunned to hear the newscaster an-nounce Biafra's surrender. I watched with deep sadness as several leaders of the Biafran government filed into a room at Dodan Barracks, where Major General Yakubu Gowon, Nigeria's head of state, greeted them with a warm smile and handshake. How could he? He had defeated them.

Major General Philip Effiong read a declaration on behalf of the Biafrans, ending with, "The Republic of Biafra has ceased to exist." What would happen to the military and civilian leaders who'd been at the forefront of Biafra's efforts to gain independence, including my husband? Was he in the village; was he alive? I had no idea and no way to communicate. I hadn't even sent him my phone number, knowing he wouldn't be able to use it with Biafra so cut off. Now what?

"What's wrong, Mommy?" Chinaku said as he looked at me and back at the television screen, which showed a map of Africa with Nigeria highlighted. "Is Daddy there?"

"I don't know where Daddy is right now," I said. "We have to wait to hear from him. But maybe we can go home soon."

"You mean to Grandmommy's?"

"No, I mean to Nigeria." I turned from the TV to pull the children closer to me. "Do you remember Daddy?"

"I know Daddy," he said with his hands moving like the windshield wipers on the car we'd used to get to Uli Airstrip. "He drove us to the airport."

As the news sunk in over the next couple of days, I wasn't sure what to think. Suddenly I could anticipate returning to Nigeria, which I had made my home. Yet I didn't feel jubilant or excited, and I didn't rush into planning. Instead, I felt uneasy and ambivalent. "I need to finish the school year," I said, dismissing the questions from my colleagues and my parents in their next letter. And, "I haven't heard from my husband yet. We don't have a place to live in Lagos," were other ready excuses.

It's true that I wanted to finish the 1969–70 school year at St. Aloysius. But I was also a little afraid of how I would feel back in Nigeria. When I had departed in September 1968, Biafra had still had the hope of surviving as a viable country. I had shared that hope, though with diminishing confidence. Even though I had spent my last year in Africa in a village with no electricity or running water, struggling to buy basics, where I was the only foreigner for miles around, it had become familiar.

So many questions raced through my mind. What would Lagos be like now? How would we interact with Yoruba and Hausa friends from before the war who had been the enemy during it? Would we feel like, or be treated like, defeated rebels? On the more practical side were more questions. Would I be able to get my job back? Where would we live?

And even deeper questions hovered at the back of my mind. Did I still love my husband, whom I felt I barely knew now? Would I feel about him as I had when we fell in love? Would he still love me after this long separation and the hardships he'd endured? How would the children adapt to another change in their environment and, more importantly, to a father they didn't remember?

While I waited to hear from Clem, I let the questions simmer. When his first letter after the surrender finally came, I discovered that he was not yet settled and wouldn't want us back yet. He had gone to Lagos and was at ECN but uncertain about his position. He was staying at the ECN Rest House and didn't have a place to live.

In the end, my decision to return to Nigeria and my husband came naturally. Clem wrote in late April to say that the Electricity Corporation had made him head of reconstruction of the former Biafra. He expected to have housing by early June. Could we come then? My answer was clear as I read his letter. Yes, I wanted to return. I loved this man, and I loved his country. I wanted to continue to build our family together.

In May, I began focusing on the return to Nigeria. I wrote to Ann. "Why don't you and the kids stay with me for a night before you fly out?" she replied. Her invitation was most welcome. I'd made arrangements to send the car to Nigeria with a shipping company in New York. I wouldn't have to pay until it arrived in Lagos. I would arrive at Ann's in the evening and deliver the car to the company's office on the docks the next morning. She would take us to the airport for our flight late in the day.

Kathy helped me pack and load the VW, which Chinaku had christened Sunny Jim. Very soon, it was clear that I couldn't fit all our stuff inside and still have space to sit. I bought a luggage rack, which Kathy helped me fasten onto the car. I said good-byes.

I hadn't been away since arriving a year earlier. It was exhilarating to be on the road, even though so much was unknown. I wondered how the children would react to being back with their dad. I had been their only parent for the past twenty-one months. Chinaku was just three years and three months when we left Biafra, and now he was almost five. Beth, two years younger, couldn't possibly have any memory of her father. I didn't have photos with me.

And we'd been mostly in a white society. Would it seem strange for them to be surrounded by black people?

Early in the afternoon, I pulled into a roadside stop in western Pennsylvania. After a quick restroom visit, we got back in the car. I turned the key. Nothing happened. I tried again. Nothing. The battery appeared to be dead. I went up a couple who were approaching their car. "Would you be able to help me out with a push? My car won't start."

They turned away without even answering. I guessed the mixed-race children were the reason they wouldn't assist. I gathered my courage and approached another couple. "Of course," they said as they got behind the car. With my faith in humanity partially restored and the engine kicking in, we were back on the road. I didn't stop until I pulled into a motel for the night. I parked on a slope so I could coast out if necessary. Sunny Jim behaved in the morning. At each stop during the day, I left the engine running while I dashed inside with the children.

Ann lived just over the George Washington Bridge in upper Manhattan. When I pulled up in front of her building, I was afraid to turn off the car. I double-parked and said to the children, "Stay right here, and don't move. Don't let anybody get in the car."

I ran into her building with my heart racing, explained in a few seconds what the problem was, and raced back down, Ann following as she explained where I could park overnight. The children and car were still there.

When the children were asleep and we sat with our second glasses of wine, Ann said, "What will it be like to get back to Nigeria?"

"I have no idea," I said, at a loss for how to describe my fears. Ann was perceptive and understood what I was unwilling or unable to acknowledge. "You're returning to your husband. Isn't that what you want? Don't the children want that?"

"I hope so. I feel like I'm walking into an arranged marriage to someone I don't really know. He's been through some terrible experiences. And he has no idea what my life's been like for the last two years. Do I still belong in Nigeria?"

"Cathy, you went off to Nigeria in the first place without having any idea how you would manage. You're very brave, or very crazy, but I think it's the former." I loved Ann's approach to life. "You'll be fine. Besides, I want to visit Nigeria one day, so I need you there."

The children were squirming with excitement at the airport the next afternoon. When Pan Am announced the flight to Rabat, Lagos, and Johannesburg, Chinaku jumped up, pulling Beth after him. Ann grabbed them for a hug, and then turned to me. "Let me know that you arrived safely." We embraced, I thanked her, and I let her go, not sure when I'd see her again or when I'd come back to the United States.

As I fastened my seat belt and put the children's belts around them, I though how different each flight from the United States to Nigeria had been. For my first, I was with dozens of other Peace Corps volunteers, filled with hope and excitement. The second time, I was traveling with my family to meet Clem in Germany before returning with him to Lagos. The third, I was eagerly returning to my husband with Chinaku from visiting my parents in the summer of 1966. Now I had been away from Clem for nearly two years, and I had two children who didn't remember him.

"You're going to see your daddy when we get to Lagos," I said to Chinaku and Beth, as I had many times already. "He'll be so happy to see you." Was I trying to reassure them or myself? The children slept, and I nodded off, woke and worried, and nodded off again. After ten hours, we landed in Morocco. I took a snapshot of the children on the tarmac to record their first steps back in Africa. We were back on the plane in an hour and in Lagos six hours later.

"Look, Daddy's here," I said as I saw Clem at the bottom of the plane steps.

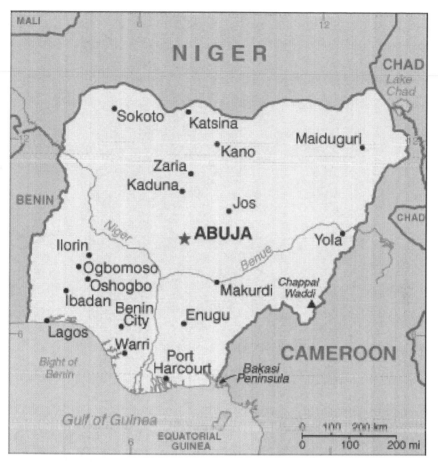

Nigeria's major cities and rivers (with new capital Abuja)

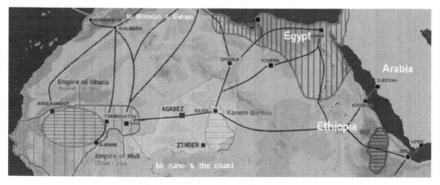

Early empires and trade routes

Kano Central Mosque in January 1963 when I traveled with John Harris and his friends

Fulani cattle as I met them on the road to Ojo in 1962-63, but there were no electric lines then

On the camel in Niger, with the camel herder in control, during the trip
with Roger and John in 1963

Centuries-old 50-foot mosque called Gobarau, a tourist attraction in Katsina,
said to be the first multi-story building in West Africa

My second year class at Awori-Ajeromi Secondary Grammar School in 1964

Our wedding photo as it appeared in Life Magazine, January 8, 1965

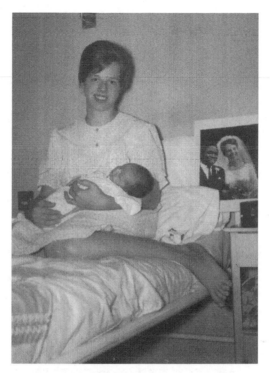

7 Holding our first child at Island Maternity Hospital in June 1965; I brought our wedding photo to display since Clem was away in Taiwan

8 With my family at the Cincinnati airport as I was departing after three weeks in Fort Thomas, Peter holding Chinaku, summer 1966

Chinaku, Beth and me with my parents on the balcony at Bairro das Virtudes, Funchal, where we stayed during the Biafran War, October 1968; Chinaku in his new car

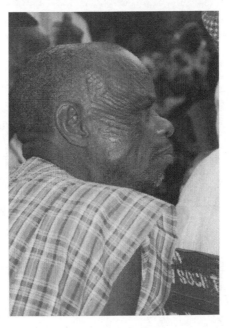

One of our relatives with typical Igbo facial markings seen on older men

Weaver birds occupying a tree along the road to Benin

Beth and her friend Gwen prepared for the 1976 bi-centennial parade in Sacramento

Our three children, Sam wearing the new shirt I brought back
from my 25th Mount Holyoke reunion in 1977

At family reunion my mother organized in Sleepy Hollow, Michigan in summer of 1978

Sam and Beth with Clem 1979

A masquerade holding his whip, the crowd watching for his next move

Sam and I on stage at the American Womens Club Fashion Show in Lagos, 1981

Girl at the market selling bananas and groundnuts (peanuts) 1984

Funchal, Madeira at the hotel pool where we swam before going
to my parents for the evening, 1983

We had this formal family photograph taken in London in 1985,
the year before I returned to the U.S.Nig

14

RETURN TO NIGERIA

"I DON'T WANT A black daddy!" Beth said.

Clem laughed at her words. "You don't mean that," he said. But I could see that he was hurt. We'd just stepped off the plane after our flight from New York and were standing on the tarmac at Lagos International Airport. It was late afternoon in June 1970.

I was embarrassed. "She's just surprised," was inadequate, but it was all I could think of. I had clearly fallen short in preparing the children for this reunion. I'd been away from Nigeria and my husband for nearly two years, kept apart by the Biafran War.

I thought about the past two years. The children had been with white people since leaving the day-care center in Newport, Kentucky, in late fall 1969. I had just assumed they knew their daddy was black and that it didn't matter.

He embraced me clumsily, and I returned his grip, neither of us remembering how to hold the other. He was overcome with emotion as he let me go and knelt to hug Chinaku.

"You're really here," he said. "Finally."

I felt numb. It had been so long that I didn't know what to say. His round face and shy smile were completely familiar, but I had forgotten how he sounded.

Beth would have none of him. She hid her face in my neck. I realized my own hesitation had to disappear right away if I wanted the children to feel at home with this apparent stranger. I dropped my bag and carry-on, put Beth down, and gave Clem another hug and kiss. Then I told him to take my things and hold Chinaku's hand as I picked Beth up again, and we walked together into the airport.

"How did you get to come right to the plane?"

"How was the flight?" he said in the same instant.

"It was long, but…"

"I told the airline people that…" I was eager to find the words that would overcome our awkwardness but uncertain how. Clem seemed to have the same problem.

In the baggage hall, I stood next to Clem while Beth and Chinaku circled my legs. As we waited for our luggage and I heard the Nigerian languages and Pidgin English spoken around me, my uncertainty diminished. Yes, I belonged here again. The children would soon be comfortable with Clem and Nigeria, I knew.

"The last days of the war were terrible," Clem said, turning to me as he drove along Ikorodu Road, into Lagos, and on to Ikoyi and our new home. "I was prepared to go into the bush near the village when Biafra surrendered. I figured out what I would take with me to survive," he said.

"It must have been horrible. Were you frightened? What did Mama and Papa do?"

The tall buildings and crowded streets of Lagos were so different from the huts and small houses in Clem's hometown. The city was vibrant and buzzing, completely different from the slower pace of village life. Other sights were the same—women with bundles on their heads and babies on their backs, and people speaking in loud voices as if in argument. I had missed it all deeply.

"I was so unhappy at the surrender," he said. "While I was debating what to do, Gowon declared amnesty. Then I heard that men had gone to Lagos and returned safely."

"How were you getting news?" I said.

"Radio Biafra's final broadcast was to tell us Ojukwu was gone, and the war was over. Radio Nigeria took over within a couple of days. That's where I heard the Nigerian government ask us to report to Enugu for direction. They said that anyone in Biafra who had worked for the federal government or the parastatal organizations like ECN should come. So I decided I should go."

The children were listening, though I was sure they didn't understand the conversation. I wondered if they even understood his Igbo-accented English.

"In Enugu, we were directed to go to Lagos. They said we should report to Electricity Corporation headquarters for reinstatement. We were given a petrol allocation."

"So 'No victor, no vanquished,' was really true?"

"Yes, that's what Gowon said, and we had to believe him. When I got to Enugu, Onyeaso was there. You remember him?"

"Of course. He was at our wedding and came to the hospital when Chinaku was born." I was drawn back into our familiar life before all the craziness had started.

"We decided to go to Lagos together. Neither of us knew what would happen."

As he described his return to Lagos, I felt tremendous sympathy for him. He'd been so proud of the resilience, creativity, and drive of the Biafrans. He'd played a critical role in the war effort, though always on the civilian side. He'd returned to Lagos as a crushed rebel. His injured pride was still evident six months after the war had ended.

He continued his story. "We got to Lagos in the evening. We didn't know where to go. We considered sleeping in the car in the parking lot of Ikoyi Hotel."

"So what happened?"

"Onyeaso suggested we call on his former boss, a Hausa man. To my surprise, he welcomed us, gave us a meal, and arranged for us to stay in the ECN Rest House."

Within a few days, they were told their new assignments. Clem's new position was a big step down from being chief electrical engineer. "But I was in no position to complain," he said.

Like all Biafrans, they were given twenty pounds of Nigerian currency to last until they received their first pay. And as soon as he had housing, Clem had written to tell me to return.

He drove into the parking lot of a block of six flats at Thirty-Three Lugard Avenue, less than a mile from the house we'd lived in before the war. The children had fallen asleep in the backseat but woke up as he turned off the engine.

The building reminded me of my first home in Ikoyi eight years earlier. By the time I lived there in 1962, all the other apartments were occupied by Nigerians, teachers like me or midlevel civil servants. This building looked more modern but more stark. It was larger, with a flat roof and big steel-framed windows. The yellow paint looked fairly fresh.

Clem led us up the wide central staircase to the second floor and our new home. The smell of palm oil greeted us as we walked into the spacious sitting room. "It's not like Alexander Avenue," he said apologetically, as he set down my carry-on luggage. "But we have a place to live."

It certainly wasn't like the spacious house at Eight Alexander with its lawn large enough to hold five hundred guests for our wedding reception. But it looked comfortable.

"We'll be fine now that we're together again," I said. "How long have you been here?"

Before he could answer, Chinaku returned from his quick exploring. He stopped short at the sight of a man wearing an apron who appeared from the kitchen. He was dark and slender, about the same height as Clem, with close-cropped hair. He looked about thirty. He came forward and said with a slight bow, "Good evening, Madam."

"Who's he, Mommy?" Chinaku said. "Does he live here, too?"

"This is Felix. I hired him a week ago when I moved in," Clem said.

"Good evening, Felix." I turned to Chinaku. "No, he doesn't live with us." I had not even remembered that we would have a cook. Clem sent him to bring our luggage up from the car. "You can change him if you want," Clem said as soon as Felix left the room.

"You did the right thing to hire someone." I took a look into the kitchen, which appeared well-tended. "I'll see what I think after a few days."

Back in the living room, I knelt down to the children. "Felix is going to help me with cooking and cleaning. You can ask Daddy where he lives." I was shocked by how little I'd told the children about Nigeria. Why hadn't I prepared them? I was sure the cook was living in what we'd always called "boys' quarters." I couldn't utter those words now. "Boys' quarters" sounded too colonial, like a reference to slave housing.

"He lives in the boys' quarters behind the building." Clem had no hesitation about the phrase.

Beth was still very quiet, watching Clem with caution, while Chinaku headed to the hallway and into a bedroom. "Come on, Mommy, I'll show you my bedroom," he said, taking my hand.

Beth took my other hand, and we followed him to a room with twin beds already made up. "I guess it's for you too," he said to her.

Felix came back into the apartment with our suitcases. "Will you please bring the luggage here?" I called to him. Turning to the children, I said, "Felix needs to know your names. Can you tell him?"

"I'm Chinaku." Beth didn't answer, so he added, "She's Beth." Felix repeated the names. Chinaku was easy for him, but Beth came out as "Bette" as it had in the village two years earlier. "She no have Igbo name?" he said.

"Yes, she's Ijeoma, but we call her Beth." I gave the name "Beth" careful pronunciation, hoping he could get it right but was not surprised when he didn't.

"Can you show him your suitcases?"

Beth touched the suitcase that held her clothes and toys. Felix placed it on the floor near one of the beds.

"Which one be yours?" he said to Chinaku, who pointed out his own. Felix put it near the other bed and carried the others to the master bedroom.

"Let's get your pajamas out and your toothbrushes and toothpaste," I said. "We'll need to get water from the kitchen to use. You can't drink the water unless it's been boiled." Longer explanations about bacteria and sanitation could wait for another day.

Felix came back. "Food is ready," he said. A meal of pounded yam and egusi soup was waiting on the dining table.

"What can Beth sit on?" I said to Clem. He placed a couple of books from the coffee table on one of the chairs and reached out to lift her up.

"No." She pulled away. "Mommy, you lift me."

"Guess what?" I said when we sat down. "You get to wash your hands right here. Then you get to eat with them." Felix put a saucer with a bar of soap on the table. He held a bowl of water for Clem, me, and then the children.

"Mommy, is this water safe?" Chinaku said.

"Not to drink, but it's safe to wash your hands in, as long as you dry them."

I cut into the mound of pounded yam and placed a wedge on each of our plates, starting with Clem's. This was followed by a couple of spoons of the soup, reddish with palm oil but with the white bits of egusi and the dark green of the vegetable on top.

"Look. You take a bit of the yam in your hand. Then use it to scoop up the soup." I demonstrated. "Watch how Daddy does it."

Clem slowed his movements so they could see.

"I've missed this food. But I didn't miss the pepper," I said with a quick intake of breath as my eyes filled with tears. "Can you eat it?" I looked at Beth and Chinaku, who were taking tentative bites. I wondered if their earlier introduction to the pepper in Nanka was still in their unconscious memory.

"It's burning," Beth said, spitting out a mouthful.

"You're a sissy," Chinaku said as he swallowed. I could see he had to hold back tears, but he was determined.

"His cooking seems all right," Clem said. "At least his soup is better than what I was getting at the Rest House."

Felix brought fruit salad to the table for our dessert. Holding a piece of reddish-orange fruit on my fork, I showed it to the kids. "Do you know what this is?"

"It's watermelon," Chinaku said without hesitation.

"Peach," Beth said.

"Good guesses, but it's neither. It's pawpaw."

"It grows on a tall tree," Clem said, raising his arms as high as he could. I smiled as I saw them watch him. I relaxed and felt my knee touch his under the table.

"Have you been to church?" I said.

"I have. Reverend Payne asked about you. We'll go on Sunday," he said and pressed his knee firmly against mine.

Having a planned event, even something so simple, felt good. "And now it's time for bed," I said to the children as their eyelids drooped. "Say goodnight to Daddy."

Chinaku walked around to Clem's chair and gave him a quick kiss on the cheek. I lifted Beth down from her elevated seat as Clem stood up from the table. Beth reached out as if to touch him. Then she stopped herself, pulled back, and grabbed my hand instead.

"Tomorrow she'll be fine with you; you'll see," I said hopefully.

I left Clem in the sitting room while I got them into their pajamas. I'd forgotten the boiled water and called to Clem to bring me a bottle and a glass.

"Am I your steward?" he said, handing them to me.

"You're their daddy. They need to get used to you." I wanted him to realize that he had to work as hard as I did to recreate a real relationship. "It's just an excuse to get you to come see them."

He said good-night again. Once they were in their beds, I sang them the lullaby from Hansel and Gretel, as I had often done in the States.

Clem had the day's paper open in the sitting room. "You seem settled. I'm going to unpack," I said, giving him a kiss before turning back to the bedroom. Half an hour later, I had most of my clothes in the closet or in the drawers, and I was exhausted. "I'm done and going to bed," I said, poking my head into the sitting room again. I was in my nightgown with the sheet and light blanket over me in the double bed ten minutes later.

Clem changed into his wrapper, turned out the light, and got into bed so our heads were just inches apart on our pillows.

"I missed you so much. When you left, I didn't know if I'd ever see you again," Clem said, putting his arm over me and pulling me closer.

"I know. I felt the same. But here I am."

He leaned closer to kiss me. I responded to his kiss, but when he started to touch my breasts, I pushed his hand away and said, "I'm too tired. Give me a few days." He didn't object, and in a minute his quick, gentle breathing told me he was asleep. I thought nothing could keep me awake, but it was at least half an hour of wondering how we would recreate our relationship before I fell asleep.

"Mommy, get up." Beth was at my bedside. It was barely light.

"What time is it?" I couldn't see my watch. "Come on, sweetie," I said and pulled her into the bed beside me. Clem reached over me to stroke her face.

"Say, 'Good morning,'" he instructed her in a gentle tone.

"Good morning," she responded in a tiny voice.

"How about 'Good morning, Daddy,'" I whispered in her ear.

"Good morning, Daddy," she said so softly I wasn't sure he heard. It was a start.

Clem's turquoise-blue tin cylinder of Paludrine, his malaria tablets, was on the table at breakfast. "I had forgotten all about malaria," I said while putting Beth into her chair on top of the books, "but when I went to the doctor to get shots before coming, he prescribed malaria prophylaxis for me and the children."

"I had malaria during the war, and I'm never forgetting again," he said. "So you still say prophy...whatever. Do you really know what it means?"

I laughed. He had always made fun of "malaria prophylaxis," the words I'd learned in Peace Corps training, for the medicine to prevent malaria. I had taken it weekly and given it to the children as soon as they were old enough. I had brought a supply back with me. Clem took a daily medication he could buy in Lagos.

For the next few days, I concentrated on making the children comfortable in their new life. Clem left for work at eight with a kiss and hug from me and Chinaku and, by the third day, from Beth as well. When he returned, I hugged him, usually pulling the children into the embrace. I told Chinaku to carry his daddy's briefcase into the bedroom while Clem changed into his wrapper, so that became a habit. While we waited for dinner, I made sure the children were with us. I asked the children to tell Clem what they had done during the day. Bit by bit, I reestablished our sense of family.

Most days it rained. I'd forgotten the intensity of the thunder, lightning, and downpours in June, the height of the rainy season. It scared me the first time, and I held the children close as I reassured them and myself that we were safe.

By the end of the week, Beth was not only kissing Clem good-bye in the morning but was also waiting for him when he returned in the evening. As soon as he'd changed into his wrapper and sat down in the living room, she climbed into his lap and didn't move until dinner. At bedtime, she hugged him and pulled him along to the bedroom to tuck her in.

Chinaku, too, was easy with him, sharing his handiwork for approval. "Look, Daddy, see what I made." He held out a paper with his drawing one evening.

"That's a big lorry," Clem said.

"It's not a lorry. It's a truck."

"It's both," I said. "Here in Nigeria, it's a lorry. In America, it's a truck. They're both right."

That night, I was ready to resume our lovemaking. My jetlag was gone, the children were safely asleep in the next room, and I was over the first few days of strangeness at bedtime. I was happy to be home and growing together again as companions, partners, and lovers.

Felix turned out to be an acceptable cook and steward. I couldn't convince him that his soups and stews could still be tasty with no pepper. He would use just a little, and I would say it was too much. By the end of the second week, we'd reached a rapprochement, so I no longer had tears running down my face at dinner.

We celebrated Beth's birthday on Thursday, June 25. Felix made rice, fried plantain, which was already a favorite of the children's, and chicken stew. As he cleared the table, I went to the kitchen for the cake I'd made, lit the three candles plus one to grow on, and signaled Clem to turn out the light. I brought in the cake and led off our singing, which brought a huge smile to Beth's face and tears to my eyes. We repeated it for Chinaku when he turned five, four days later.

Presents were minimal. At Kingsway, I had found a picture book, *About My Body*, for Beth, which she studied carefully. For Chinaku, I'd found Matchbox cars, realistic miniatures of every type of vehicle. He loved the three I bought for him—a Mercedes sedan, a jeep, and a Jaguar.

The birthdays had reminded us that we needed to think about school for the children, especially for Chinaku. "You remember that we said we'd send them to the Lagos public schools?" I said as I cleared the remains of the cake from the table and gave a piece to Felix.

"Whoever said that?" Clem said.

"We both did. But that was theoretical, before we actually had children. I don't think so anymore, do you?"

"I think we should talk to Mrs. Payne on Sunday," Clem said. "You know she's headmistress at St. Saviour's."

"You don't think that's too British?" I knew the neat, one-story, red-tile buildings, half a mile along Alexander Avenue from our first house.

"We'll see," he said. "I think there are Nigerians at church whose children are there."

A week later, we were in Mrs. Payne's modest office at the school. Her first question surprised me. "Don't you want to send your children in the American School?" she said.

"No, I don't. I like the British system, and it's what Clem grew up with."
We paid our deposit and registered Chinaku to start Class One in August
with other four- and five-year-olds. When we inquired about Beth, now
three, Mrs. Payne referred us to Mrs. Vernon's nursery school.

Mrs. Vernon was German. "Yes, I can take your daughter," she told us
in her carefully articulated British English. "We follow the same calendar as
St. Saviour's." I was thrilled—I knew Chinaku would receive solid teaching
at St. Saviour's. And Beth could follow in a year or two.

With the children's school plans settled, I was ready to settle my own. I
drove Clem to work one damp day in July so I could have the car. The rain let
up as I drove along Marina and straight across the bridge to Victoria Island.
The American School was still there. I had so many memories, not just from
teaching before the war but also even earlier. This site had been a trade fair,
which I'd visited when I arrived in Nigeria in 1962. It became the American
School two years later. Now it was surrounded by military barracks, and the
parking lot was smaller. Still, I was in completely familiar territory as I entered.

"I'd like to speak to the principal about teaching," I said to the recep-
tionist, who had risen from a desk to come to the counter. She was a tall
Nigerian woman I hadn't seen before. "I taught for two years before the war.
Is Mr. Anderson still the principal here?"

"No, the principal is Mr. Mondau. I'll see if he can talk to you now." He
rose from his chair and gestured me in even before she came back.

"You said you taught here before?" he said, sitting again behind his clut-
tered desk.

"Yes, I taught fourth grade for two years, though I had to leave at the
start of the Biafran War," I said. "My husband is Igbo." I wasn't sure if that
was sufficient explanation for an American, especially if he was new. "I was in
the United States for the last year, teaching fourth grade. I also took education
courses," I said, offering my transcripts from the three classes.

I filled him in on my background. "I taught at two different schools as a
Peace Corps volunteer, and then at one of those schools for my third year. In
1965, I came here to AIS."

"We do have an opening for a fourth-grade teacher," he said, pulling a
contract from under a stack of papers. "I'll ask Regina to type in your details.
If you agree, you can sign it and bring it back tomorrow."

"I've got a job." Clem was as happy at my news as I was when I told him that evening. "I'll need to get a nanny. Let's go see your parents and see if Rosa will come back to Lagos."

In late July, we drove to the East, no longer the independent Biafra I'd left two years earlier, but now part of Nigeria again. Chinaku entertained himself with imitating the windshield wipers on our Ford Consul and then on every other vehicle we passed. Beth was happy with her picture books, crayons, and drawing paper. I turned around frequently to point out sights.

"Look at those palm trees with the birds' nests." I pointed to several tall trees on the right. "See those nests? Those are for the weaver birds. And guess who makes the nests?"

"The mommy birds," Beth said.

"Nope. Only the daddies," I said, laughing. "And they have to build a very good nest before a mommy will marry them." This bit of information had delighted all the female Peace Corps volunteers during our training. Now it tickled my children.

"Did I tell you about Mama's mother?" Clem said when we got through the crazy traffic of Benin and headed for the Niger River and Onitsha on the other side. "You remember she stayed with us in Nanka?"

"Yes, of course I remember. What happened to her?" I asked.

"She got home safely from Nanka. But near the end of the war, people were fleeing from Agulu. She couldn't keep up, and the others had to leave her behind. Patrick, her grandson, came to tell us after the war was over."

I shivered at the image of her dying alone at the side of the road. I knew we'd visit Agulu in the next couple of days. I was sad that the children wouldn't get to meet their great-grandmother. I knew Clem missed her, and I would too.

Soon we were at the base of the Niger Bridge. I remembered when it had been blown up in the war. I was surprised to see that we were going over it.

"It's a pontoon bridge that the Nigerians put up. It's what I used to come to Lagos a few months ago," Clem said. The structure creaked as we drove slowly across the corrugated surface in the single line for traffic. I was relieved when we were on solid ground again. Twenty minutes later, we were at the house in St. John's Cross. It was late afternoon, and the rain was light.

Mama cried as she embraced us. "*Nno unu.* Welcome." She didn't want to release the children. "Chinaku, Ijeoma, *nwam, unu natara.* My children, you've come back," she said over and over, holding them. Papa, too, looked very pleased.

"Why did she call Beth by another name?" Chinaku said. "Doesn't she know her real name?"

"Ijeoma is Beth's real name too," Clem said. "That's her Igbo name."

"Did she think we wouldn't come back?" I said to Clem.

"Let's just say we were all a little worried. She hasn't forgotten those stories of English women taking their children away and never returning."

We spent the night in Onitsha with them. Their house had not been damaged. The death of Clem's grandmother was the closest personal loss. The other family death was Clem's cousin Pius, who had been friendly with my sister when she was in the village with me in 1965. He had died serving in the Biafran Army.

The next afternoon, we drove to Nanka. The road was in terrible shape. "You can see no repairs have been carried out on the infrastructure yet," Clem said while he negotiated around the cracks and holes in the pavement.

"Is this punishment for the rebellion?"

"They say the whole country's roads need work. I'm sure the roads here are not a priority."

I filled Chinaku and Beth in quickly on a few key people. "You know Papa, Daddy's father. We just saw him in Onitsha. His oldest brother is Ejike. His youngest brother is Obi. You'll see them as soon as we arrive. Their wives too."

Even before we reached our compound in Nanka, word that we were on the way had reached our relatives. Our car was surrounded in seconds after we drove under the gatehouse. Ejike and his wife, Obele, were prominent. Obi was there with his wife, Mercy. Several children, a range of ages, milled around.

Ejike didn't hug or kiss. That wasn't part of Igbo male behavior. He shook hands with Clem and demonstrated his welcome with a hand on my arm and with his words. "*Mama Chinaku, nno.*" His wife, Obele, was not so reserved, and we hugged enthusiastically. Obi repeated Ejike's words of welcome, while Mercy and I embraced. The children looked a little puzzled at this multitude of people and the voices all mingled in greetings.

"*Chinaku, bia.*" Isaac and Goddy, Obi's sons, grabbed Chinaku and pulled him away with them. Georgina, their sister who'd been such a help to me during the war, took Beth's hand. I was delighted with the welcome and knew the children were completely safe. There was no doubt that Clem's family felt I belonged here, no matter how much I looked like an outsider.

The older boys, John, Atu, and Christian, carried our suitcases into the house. Felix took his cooking gear to the kitchen. As always, we'd bought bananas in Onitsha. Clem liked to store them in our bedroom, so we sent those upstairs, too. Just as I turned to go into the house, Mbokuocha came into the compound with her booming, "Mama Chinaku." While most people's garments were well-worn, they were clean and neat. But the hint of unwashed clothes followed her. Still, we hugged and exchanged greetings. The image of her daughter lined up with Beth and the other neighbor girl along the railing during our months in the village sprang to my mind immediately.

The next day, we went to Agulu. "It's too strange, knowing that your grandmother won't be here ever again," I said to Clem as we rounded the long bend in Agulu center before turning down the road by the market. I turned to the children to remind them once again that we were going to Mama's brother Okeke.

We parked in front of a large, two-story house that faced the rutted dirt road leading from the market and entered the wide wooden door. "Eh, see who is here. *Ndi Nanka biana. Nno.* The Nanka relatives have come," many voices shouted as we were recognized and welcomed. I loved this outpouring of excitement, just as in Nanka. "*Wete oche.* Bring chairs," one of Okeke's two wives ordered. As children scrambled to bring chairs out from several of the rooms, we followed Patrick, Okeke's eldest son, to see Clem's uncle. I caught the slight odor of an old man spending too much time in his hut. Added to that was the scent of spilled palm wine. It was all familiar and, in this setting, not offensive.

"*Dalu nna. Kedu?* Greetings, Father, how are you?"

"Why do you call him *nna*?" Chinaku whispered at my side. "You said that means 'father,' and he's my great uncle."

I leaned down and spoke softly. "I say 'father' because we're greeting an older relative. I would use it as a sign of respect for any man his age."

Okeke was seated comfortably on a low stool in the dark obi, the central house of the compound. "*Nno unu, oche di.*" Okeke gestured to the bench along the wall, which I could barely see in the dim light. *"Nwunyem, wete kola.* My wife, bring kola nut," Okeke called.

My eyes adjusted. He looked less healthy than the last time I'd seen him. He couldn't move easily. His hair was completely white, and his moustache was flecked with gray. But his round face and smile were just like Mama's.

His older wife brought two kola nuts on a plate with two garden eggs, or *afufa,* and *ose oji,* the peppery, peanut butter-like dip. Afufa had always seemed like a poor excuse for a fruit. The size of a small tomato but green, it has the bitter taste of a cucumber that didn't get ripe. The only use I could see for it was to modify the heat of the pepper if I inadvertently took too much. But many people like to eat it with kola.

"When the kola nut reaches home, it will tell where it came from," Okeke said in Igbo. He passed the plate to Clem, who took one of the nuts as custom dictated.

He added, "With this kola, we honor our ancestors, who brought Mama Chinaku, Chinaku, and Ijeoma back to us." Then he broke the nut into several pieces and gave the plate to Chinaku to pass around.

I could see one of the wives begin cooking. As we emerged from Okeke's hut, I said to the nearest child, "Please tell your mama that we don't want to eat."

We were going on to Nne Julie's, Mama's sister, who was an excellent cook. We accepted the warm soft drinks, quickly bought from a nearby stand, and soon said good-bye and drove back out to the main road and on to our next destination.

To my surprise, Nne Julie was expecting us. I had forgotten how fast news traveled on the "jungle telegraph." The road we took by car was in poor condition, and we bumped along the four miles. The footpaths were probably less than a mile, and someone had clearly run to tell her.

"She looks like Mama," Chinaku said when she released him from her arms and pulled Beth to her.

She'd already started cooking. She fed us pounded yam with bitterleaf soup. After we'd had our fill, we drove on to Rosa's home where she'd stayed with her mother after I'd left for Portugal, another four-mile drive and less than a mile by foot.

"Rosa took care of you both when you were babies, right up to the time we went to Portugal," I said. "I hope she'll come back with us now. She taught me to speak Igbo too."

Rosa hugged the children with enthusiasm. She didn't hesitate. I think she'd had enough of village life. She packed her belongings and jumped in the car. They were quiet in the backseat together as we returned to Nanka. She began helping Felix with the cooking that evening, and by the time we headed back to Lagos three days later, she was bathing the children and giving them their meals. The children were completely comfortable with her, as she was with them.

In August, my shipment arrived. The VW, Sunny Jim, seemed to like Lagos and behaved well most of the time. It was wonderful to have a car! And I was relieved to have my cooking equipment, books and linens, and the children's books and toys that we hadn't brought on the plane.

I drove both children to their first day of school in late August. I held Beth's hand as we walked Chinaku into the school compound at St. Saviour's with his snack and drink. The one-story classrooms and office formed two sides of a U, with a large assembly hall at the bottom of the U. The children seemed to be a healthy mix of foreign and Nigerian, boys and girls.

Chinaku seemed confident and easy with other children. I wasn't worried when Beth and I left him, but I was struck by sudden sadness at my first child's starting school. How quickly he was growing up.

I took Beth to Mrs. Vernon's and led her up to the veranda. Mrs. Vernon met us and introduced Beth to the other children. Then she took us into the cloakroom, where twelve pegs were placed on the wall at just the right height for the two- to four-year-olds to hang their snack bags and belongings. She'd already placed Beth's name over one. She took Beth back into the room, where the other children sat with the aide, and suggested I leave quietly.

I assured myself that Beth was all right, then turned and walked out to my car, feeling again the momentary pang of sadness as my second child entered the wider world. But at the same time, I was thrilled that we'd found places for both children where I was sure they'd thrive. And I had a job starting the next week.

Nine years later, I came to know the house well when I was part of the amateur drama group Festival Players. We met often for planning meetings at that house, then occupied by an Englishman. The pegs were still there in the hallway.

15

ANOTHER BABY AND ANOTHER MOVE

I DROPPED BOTH CHILDREN at their schools for their first few days. But when my own school started a week later, Clem took over. Each morning when he pulled up at St. Saviour's, Chinaku jumped out of the car with barely a good-bye and ran into the school compound, eager to join his friends and his teacher.

Beth, on the other hand, who'd shocked us by saying she didn't want a black daddy two months earlier, now couldn't bear to be parted from him. When he took her hand to lead her into Mrs. Vernon's, she clung to him and cried miserably until he picked her up. Then he had to forcibly detach her from his arms and hand her over.

"What am I supposed to do?" he said after the third day. "I feel so wicked when I leave her."

"You're not wicked. She's suffering from separation anxiety," I told him. "Dr. Spock said it's fairly common with children Beth's age."

Mrs. Vernon also tried to reassure him, saying, "Beth stops crying when you drive away. She doesn't speak, but she seems content."

After two weeks, Clem walked in the door from work beaming. "I dropped Beth off this morning, and she didn't cry." I hadn't realized how bothered he was by his daily ordeal.

Another three weeks went by, and he came home with more news. "Mrs. Vernon said Beth can read. All these weeks when she wasn't speaking, she was picking up words." Clem was ecstatic as he told me how clever she was. "She read all the words in a whole book to the other children." I was relieved that we'd survived the weeks of his pain and now could celebrate her achievement.

We'd started going to St. Saviour's Church again for the regular Sunday evening service. We often saw our friends Jan and Geoff, whose son, James, was also in Mrs. Vernon's school. Geoff served on the church vestry, which Clem had just joined. At his first meeting, Clem had recounted his difficulty dropping Beth off in the morning.

"How is Beth doing?" Jan said one evening in October. The rains had nearly ended, and we could stand outside the church chatting after the services.

"She's happy now, and she's even reading," I said.

"You see," Geoff said, turning to Clem, "I told you it would be all right."

"I can tell you I didn't think I would survive," Clem said. "But I made it. She's taking after me with her intelligence."

As the children settled into their schools, I was getting acquainted with my class at the American School. Of my twenty-four nine- and ten-year-olds, three were Nigerian. There was an Israeli, a Scandinavian, two other Europeans, and many Americans. Suzy, a pert, blond American, came to school every day smelling like suntan oil. A group of four exceptionally bright and talented boys quickly became close friends and class leaders. Three of these were American, with fathers in the oil industry, and the fourth was the son of a British mother and Iranian diplomat father.

As if new schools for the children and my new job weren't enough excitement, I suspected I was pregnant. "Did Dozie come back after the war?" I said to Clem as we were dressing for church the first Sunday in October.

"No," Clem said, "he decided to stay in the East. He set up his obstetrics practice in his home. I think he's building a hospital there."

Then it hit him. "Why? Are you pregnant?" he said, pausing with his tie half-knotted.

"I think so." I patted my tummy. "Not a surprise, after the last few weeks." Our sex life had resumed fully. I was more comfortable with it than I'd been before. I hadn't attended any feminist sessions while I was in the United States, but I'd heard about them and read a little. I learned that I was normal even if sex wasn't always exciting for me. I only learned to enjoy it fully a few years later, and it wasn't from Clem.

Clem grabbed me around the waist and danced me around the room. Then he stopped short. "Maybe you shouldn't move so fast."

"It's fine. I'm not sick, just pregnant." I felt fine, and I loved how excited he was.

At church half an hour later, he held my hand and whispered, "Let's ask Henry Omoh about a doctor."

"There's a new private hospital, St. Nicholas," Henry's wife told us. "That's where I had my last baby. You should go there."

It was within half a mile of the church and Clem's office and not far from Island Maternity Hospital, where Chinaku had been born. After school on Monday, I drove to the three-story building occupying half a city block and went up the wide cement steps through the glass doors. There were lots of windows—it would be light and airy. I was able to see a doctor within half an hour. My pregnancy was confirmed with a due date in March. It seemed very far away.

With the time I had, I decided to prepare better for this birth. I had heard about natural childbirth during my year in the States. I found that St. Nicholas was holding classes in the Lamaze method, where the woman is taught how to breathe for maximum relaxation. I enrolled for the six Saturday morning classes.

"Skip work, and come with me," I said to Clem as I dressed for the first class. "I've heard that some husbands help their wives with breathing right and then actually stay with their wives during the delivery." He was just getting out of bed and would leave for the office soon.

"Me? Never. That's not for African men to do," he said, screwing up his face. Then he laughed. "You know, you should have the baby in the goat shed, like a proper Nanka woman."

I could play at his game. "But we don't have a goat shed."

"I could get one built in plenty of time," he said, heading for the bath.

"That's OK. No goat shed. I think I'll just go to the class." I gave him a kiss and put on my sandals.

I wasn't surprised. I knew there were African customs that Clem would never give up and foreign customs he would never adopt. He stayed out of the kitchen and was not involved in household management. He regarded himself as the head of the house. At that time, in 1970, I barely chafed at this.

I wrote to my parents with news about my teaching, my pregnancy, and my Lamaze classes. I sent the children's drawings and writing. Mother wrote back about their friends, their bridge tournaments, and the English Church. She said my sister was also pregnant, and her baby was due a couple of months before mine. My brother Peter was still living with Beth and Tommy in Fort Thomas. I hoped he was feeling more welcome than I had been. But, of course, he didn't have mixed-race children that offended Tommy's sense of propriety.

I'd never before been bothered by the heat, but the last few weeks of that pregnancy were pure misery. January through March, before the rainy season starts, is the hottest time of the year. The school didn't have air conditioning, but when I was busy with the class, I didn't notice. When I got home, I retreated to our bedroom, getting as close to the air conditioner as I could. I was desperate to be cool and even remembered fondly the cold weather of the winter the year before in the United States.

Apart from the heat, the pregnancy was easy. I hoped the delivery would be equally easy. I stopped teaching on the Friday before my due date. "I'll be back before the end of the school year," I promised, as I handed over my class to the substitute.

Monday passed slowly. I'd already packed my suitcase for the hospital, and I was ready. But the baby wasn't. At last, after a restless night, I felt the first contractions. Clem was dressing for work Tuesday morning. "I think it may be today," I said as he ate his oatmeal.

"Let's go," he said, dropping his spoon and jumping up.

"No, not yet. Go to the office. I'll let you know."

By eleven thirty, I was sure. We didn't have a phone, so I sent Rosa to Mrs. Vernon's to call Clem, who raced home. "Take the elevator to the second floor," the receptionist at St. Nicholas told us. "Someone will meet you there." Clem was so flustered I had to guide him to the elevator and push the button.

The nursing sister took us into an admitting room, where she instructed me to lie on a gurney. "I will get the midwife," she said, hurrying out.

My contractions were now fast and regular, and I felt a strong urge to push. "This baby is coming," I said to Clem through clenched teeth. Maybe he would be with me, whether he wanted to or not. But instead, he ran away in total panic, leaving me completely alone. I wondered for the next minutes what would happen if no one came. Would the baby fall on the floor, dangling from the umbilical cord?

Two minutes later, the midwife came. With her steady encouragement, after half an hour of pain and pushing, my baby was born. My Lamaze training was helpful. So was the fact that this was the third time. I knew what to expect, I breathed as instructed, and I didn't need stitches. "You have a beautiful baby boy," the midwife said as she held him up for me to see. His round face even at birth resembled Clem, his mother, and his brothers and sisters. She put him in my arms as Clem came into the room, looking a little sheepish.

"Are you all right?" Clem said, leaning over to kiss me. "He's so little."

I ignored his first question since he'd disappeared at the critical moment. "Actually, he's bigger than the others were." I held the baby close, trying to see into his dark eyes. Clem followed as I was moved to a spacious, well-lit room.

"Are you glad it's a boy?" I spoke softly so I wouldn't wake the other new mother who was sleeping across the room. Her baby was in a crib at her feet.

"I knew it would be a boy," he said. "It's my power!" He assumed a boxer's stance and demonstrated a couple of jabs. I had to laugh at his need to feel like he was the master of the universe.

The next day, he brought Chinaku and Beth to the hospital to meet their baby brother. They approached my bed gingerly. "Come see," I said, holding the baby where Chinaku could touch him. He put his hand out tentatively. Then he leaned closer and held the baby's hand. "He's your brother, and he'll want to be just like you," I said.

Beth held back, holding Clem's hand. "Come closer." I motioned to her. "He wants to meet you."

"He's very soft," she said, holding his tiny fingers in her small hand. "What's his name?"

"I don't know yet. We have to ask Papa."

"I want to call him Samuel, after my dad," Clem said, surprising me. It's not common to name a child for a living relative, or even a dead one. "But Papa will give him his Igbo name."

"Do you know you were this size once?" I said to the children.

"Did you born me here?" Chinaku asked.

"No, you were born in another, bigger hospital very near here. I'll show you one day soon." He was happy to know his hospital had been larger.

"Where did you born me?" Beth said.

"You were born in a very small hospital, in Enugu. It fit you better."

Three days later, I was home again. "Here's the name Papa chose," Clem said, reading from the telegram in his hand—Chukwugekwu." I treasured this custom of having Clem's father choose the name.

"'God will speak.' What's the significance?" I said. "Is it related to the end of the war and the Igbo loss?" Clem wasn't sure. It reminded me of his own middle name, Chukwukadibia, meaning 'God is greater than the Dibia,' or native doctor. But from the beginning we called him Sammy.

With Chinaku and Beth away during part of each day, Rosa was able to devote attention to the new baby. I didn't attempt breastfeeding; my past experiences had been too frustrating. I went back to teaching within a month so I could end the school year with my class.

In May, Reverend Payne christened Sammy. We held a party that afternoon to celebrate, with twelve adults and at least as many children. As soon as St. Saviour's and the American School were out in late June, we took Sammy to the East for his naming ceremony. Heavy rain fell as we started out early in the morning, making the drive treacherous. The roads were still in poor condition from the war. And Clem's car was getting old.

The Niger Bridge had been partially rebuilt and rattled ominously. Beth was frightened. "It's going to fall," she said as the planks rattled beneath the tires. She began to cry.

"Scaredy cat," Chinaku teased her. I pulled her into the front seat with me. I wasn't afraid, but I didn't like the noise either. I was happy to have her in my arms and assured her we'd make it safely to the other end. I glanced back at Chinaku, snuggled up against Rosa, who held the baby. He looked smug, and I guessed he was a little frightened too but not about to admit it.

We had a joyful reunion with Clem's parents. It was such a pleasant change to be reunited with relatives the children remembered, instead of strangers, like Clem had been and my parents would be the next time we saw them.

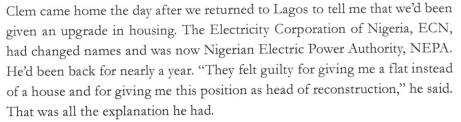

Clem came home the day after we returned to Lagos to tell me that we'd been given an upgrade in housing. The Electricity Corporation of Nigeria, ECN, had changed names and was now Nigerian Electric Power Authority, NEPA. He'd been back for nearly a year. "They felt guilty for giving me a flat instead of a house and for giving me this position as head of reconstruction," he said. That was all the explanation he had.

I dreaded another move—and again with a new baby. This would be our sixth change in three years. We had two different homes in Madeira. In the United States, we'd stayed first with my sister. We'd left there for the awful rooms with rodents in Covington, Kentucky, then moved to Fay Apartments in Cincinnati. We'd been in the flat for not quite a year. I wondered how long we'd stay at our new house.

Still, the two-story, stucco, duplex house, half a mile away, had more space inside and out, and I was grateful. We now had a walled yard with sparse grass and a few scraggly bushes, so the children could play outside.

Summer was over quickly with the visit to the East and then the move. In September 1971, it was Beth's turn to start St. Saviour's School. "Do I have to take her? Is she going to cry again?" Clem said.

"Yes, you have to take her. But you're already taking Chinaku, so it's now only one stop for you. And you'll find out how she reacts."

When Clem returned home the first evening, he smiled at my questioning look. "Not a peep! Chinaku took her by the hand and led her to the hall. I don't know what happened after that, but she didn't cry." I was sure Beth would love the structure and the discipline. Her year with Mrs. Vernon had prepared her well, and she was reading and counting without difficulty. Unlike Chinaku, she loved having assignments. She did her homework every day, writing out words and sentences and doing easy addition problems in her neat lettering.

It was my second year back at the American School. I was asked to attend the Sub-Saharan Africa Regional Conference of Overseas Schools, held in Kinshasa in December. The broad, tree lined boulevards of the capital of the Republic of Zaire reflected the French influence, so different from the utilitarian style of the British in Nigeria.

Not only was the setting intriguing, but so were the people from other African countries teaching in schools similar to mine. We faced the same challenge of wide variation in students' backgrounds and abilities, so the individualized instruction we learned about seemed ideal. I returned to Lagos a couple of days before my birthday, full of ideas. Over the next few months, I provided options in language arts assignments based on what I'd learned.

Chinaku, meanwhile, was reading avidly. He became intrigued with the pets in the stories he read and started asking for a pet of our own. I remembered how I'd disliked the dogs at my sister's just two years earlier. Clem was perplexed, not being accustomed to the practice. But on our visit to the East that Christmas of 1971, the children found a kitten. How this kitten happened to be wandering around Nanka was a mystery. It looked helpless and very sweet. The children begged and begged, and between their eagerness and my entreaties on their behalf, Clem consented. Chinaku suggested the name Tiger for the kitten's striped markings.

I regretted the decision to adopt Tiger before we even reached Lagos. He was carsick and vomited or mewed all the way on the drive—ten hours. Once we got to Lagos, all he seemed to enjoy was chasing us on the stairs and nipping our ankles. I tried to train him but couldn't break him of this habit. I was not sad when he disappeared a month later. I looked halfheartedly. "I drove all around the neighborhood for hours and didn't see any sign of him," I lied. "Maybe he'll come back on his own." We didn't see him again.

A few years later, we got a dog that turned out to be a much more satisfactory pet.

Clem had returned to the manuscript of his second book, *Men and Management in Nigeria*, which I had helped him start before the war. From the beginning of our relationship, we loved discussing cultural differences between the West and Nigeria. We talked about the problems of managers, often expatriates but also many Nigerians, who brought foreign practices to Africa and were puzzled when they ran into difficulties.

By the middle of 1972, the book was sent off to Longman's. It was published the next year as part of a series on management practices. In his acknowledgments, Clem said, "It is to my wife that I owe much of the inspiration in finishing this book. Much of this book would not be in its present form without her patient and loving interest." It was all true.

On Saturday evenings, Clem and I would often go to a movie, or cinema in Nigerian parlance, or visit friends. On Sunday mornings, when the courts at the Lagos public tennis site were nearly deserted, we frequently played tennis. In the evening, we attended the service at St. Saviour's.

Rosa had asked to return home, and we had gone to the other side of Clem's family for a replacement. Nebechi, the daughter of Papa's brother, came to stay with us. She was always smiling, a cheerful addition to our household.

I enjoyed teaching, my relations with Clem were happy, and the children were content and thriving. But no situation is static.

16

PROMOTION, ANOTHER HOME, DEMOTION

CHINAKU AND BETH were becoming ever more British in their speech, influenced by their teachers and classmates. When Beth started calling me Mummy, instead of Mommy, I drew the line.

"I'm not a mummy," I said. "Mummies are dead bodies. That's not me."

At the same time, I was becoming more American in my professional life. The first year back at the American School, I'd had an amazing class. I'd left them in March 1971 when Sam was born but had returned to finish the school year. The next year's class was not so exceptional, though still an interesting mix of children from several countries, and I knew I was improving my skills.

But I wondered if there would ever be an opportunity to be more than a teacher. In early April 1972, the principal called me to his office. "You know that the upper elementary coordinator is going back to Tacoma," he said. "Would you be interested in the job?" This was a combination of supervisor and support for fourth through sixth grades.

When he offered to send me to another conference on individualized instruction and team teaching to help me prepare, I thought it was an ideal opportunity and accepted. The conference would take place in Madrid in July.

The program, Individually Guided Education, IGE, was an extension of what I'd first encountered in Kinshasa seven months earlier. It was an ideal method to counteract children's boredom with subjects they already understood. I was convinced I could persuade teachers to implement IGE in our classrooms in Lagos.

Clem had agreed to join me with Chinaku and Beth at the end of the conference. We had arranged to leave Sammy and Nebechi with Jean Obi so we could be tourists without a baby along. Although Beth woke up the first morning in Madrid with swollen jaws, which I recognized as mumps, we swaddled her face and took her along on the bus tour I had booked. I worried that she might be contagious; Clem thought I was being too careful. She never felt ill, and we had a lovely week, even seeing a bullfight.

I took up my coordinator position at AIS, inspired by the training I'd received. But my few days at two different conferences didn't prepare me to impart the methods to other teachers, most of them senior to me in age and experience.

Still, I plowed ahead. When it came time to order textbooks for the next year, I wouldn't let teachers order a whole set of a single texts for social studies. I thought that was the best subject in which to implement the technique of letting students develop questions around a theme, then search in a variety of texts for answers. I annoyed one senior teacher in particular with my stance.

I was also responsible for audio-visuals. I found I had a knack for tinkering with the equipment and was often called to help teachers who weren't sure how to thread a film or adjust the projector. I surprised myself with this newfound ability.

I became even more aware than I had been of the disparities between those of us hired locally and those brought from Tacoma. "Doesn't it seem strange that we are paid about one-third the salaries of the Tacoma teachers, yet we do the same work?" we asked each other. "Why do they pay no fees for their children, when we have to pay 50 percent of the cost?"

"I think we need to draft a letter to the principal and the board," Eileen said at a meeting she and I organized. She looked round the room to see others nodding their heads in agreement. "You should be our representative, Cathy, since you're now in a position that a Tacoma person held before you." Eileen drafted the letter and got signatures. I took it to the principal.

He called me in. "I'll talk to you individually, but I can't recognize you as a representative of all the local-hire teachers." He said that arrangements for Tacoma staff were made through State Department. He knew, as I did, that other teaching jobs available to us paid even less.

I should have challenged him. He couldn't change Tacoma teachers' conditions, but he probably could have asked the board to consider changing ours. And I had to go back to the other teachers to say I'd failed in my mission.

Clem was facing his own professional issues. A couple of weeks before Christmas when the children were asleep and we were in our bedroom, Clem put down the manuscript he was working on and turned to me. "I can't stay in NEPA, reporting to a man I trained. It's humiliating. I'm fed up."

"What would you do? Is there somewhere else you can work?"

"I want to set up my own engineering company. I see so-called engineers getting contracts all the time. I know more than they do about how projects should be managed."

The idea of Clem's own business was exciting. But what would we do about housing? Without NEPA, we would have to buy or rent on our own, and prices seemed impossible.

The question was pushed aside when my parents came for Christmas. Clem hadn't seen them since our wedding in 1964, and the children probably wouldn't remember them from Christmas 1969 when we were together in Cincinnati. And they had never seen Sammy.

Even though I made a conscious effort to remind the children about them, I feared this would be another reunion, like bringing the children back to Nigeria, where they would feel they were seeing relatives for the first time. I didn't regret the choice I'd made to marry and stay in Nigeria, but I was seeing more of its downside.

Clem and I met them at Lagos Airport. The conversation on the ride to Ikoyi was lively. They seemed impressed with the new buildings, the new Mainland Bridge, and the vivacity of the city. I realized that on their previous visit, Nigeria still had the remnants and some of the feel of colonial times, but no longer.

"Tell me about your school," Mother said to Chinaku after the initial greetings. He ran off to get his notebooks. "You're already doing division like this?" she said as she looked at the lessons.

"You know it's the British education system," I said. "What he does now is what fourth graders, two years older, do at the American School." Chinaku's work was correct but messy. Beth brought her own notebooks, a contrast with their neat and careful printing.

I took them to the bank to change travelers' checks and on to Kingsway, where they bought bikes for Beth and Chinaku and blocks for Sammy. Christmas morning was exciting for me, and I warmed again to my parents in their grandparent roles.

The most fun was taking them to the Hausa traders. I proudly showed off my bargaining skills as they chose presents to take back to their friends in Madeira. Schools were closed for the holidays, but we drove to St. Saviour's so the children could show their grandparents where their classes were. Clem and Father had many deep conversations about economic development, world affairs, and electricity in Nigeria. They became fond of each other. And Clem told him about his hopes for his own company and the housing problem we faced.

After my parents had gone, we returned again to the question of housing. "Why don't you ask AIS to give you housing?" Clem said as we drove back home from church in January 1973. "After all, they provide accommodation for their Tacoma people."

"You know, I talked to the principal last year about the disparity between the Tacoma staff and those of us hired locally. He wasn't ready to give an inch," I said, but I agreed to try.

I gathered my courage and went to the principal. "I know that you have to provide accommodation for the Tacoma people," I said, pausing to review in my head how I wanted to present my case. "I understand that you cannot provide the same benefits to those of us hired here. But would you consider housing for me since I have replaced an administrator from Tacoma as the coordinator?"

"Don't you have housing through your husband's position?"

"We do, but he'd like to set up his own business. He can't do that unless we have another place to live." I handed him the letter I'd prepared.

"I'll have to take your request to the board," he said. I heard nothing.

"Why don't you go back to the principal? Maybe he's forgotten," Clem said after church on Easter Sunday. I was by now familiar with Clem's persistence.

It was an admirable trait that could be frustrating, especially when it was about something I had to do! But I was as eager as he was for him to become independent.

He had already consulted me about a company name. Onyemelukwe was too long to use as a business title, so we chose Freeman Engineering, totally fitting. He had also succeeded in getting one contract. He'd used the check that George Butler had sent us soon after the Biafran War, filling it out for one thousand dollars, which allowed him to get the supplies and staff he needed to start. He would get his first payment from the client soon. But it wouldn't come close to paying for housing, so he was doing the work on the side while still employed at NEPA.

Easter Monday was a holiday in Nigeria, so on Tuesday I went to the principal's office again. "I don't have an answer for you, but I wouldn't get my hopes up if I were you," he said. "I'll take it to the board at the next meeting."

"I don't think he'd even asked the board yet," I said that night when Clem had changed into his wrapper.

"Could you ask your parents?" he said. "I know they like me, and your father wants me to prosper."

"No, I can't do that. They took care of us for nearly a year, remember, and helped even when I was in the United States. It doesn't feel right," I said.

"I thought a wife was supposed to do anything she could to help her husband, but I guess you don't care." He didn't speak to me for the rest of the evening. I knew that if he had his own business, he would probably succeed. If the business grew, we'd be able to afford to live where we wanted. But the sulking was too much.

"You know I care, don't you?" I said as I got into bed beside him that night. "We will find a solution." I kissed him and felt his anger soften as he kissed me back.

In late June, the first Saturday after school let out, I was buying gas at the Mobil petrol station near Ikoyi Hotel. Rain was beginning to fall and threatening to get heavier as night approached. I was waiting in my VW while the attendant filled my car. A tall American got out of his embassy car, pulling his raincoat over his head. He walked over to me.

"You can have the duplex at Seven-A Macdonald if you want it," he said. It took me a moment to understand.

"Oh, yes, you're on the school board. Yes, I want it," I said as soon as I grasped who he was and what he was saying.

"Come to the embassy on Monday. You can sign the papers and get the key."

My hasty and heartfelt thank-you didn't seem adequate. It didn't matter. He was already gone. My mind swarmed. What if I hadn't stopped to buy gas? What if he hadn't seen me?

"You'll never guess what just happened." Clem was seated in front of the TV, reading the newspaper. I could hear the children upstairs laughing with Nebechi. They must have just come out of the bath. "We have a house!"

He dropped the paper. "What happened? How did you find out?"

"Mr. Bellinger from the embassy saw me at the petrol station and told me I can get the key at the embassy on Monday morning. I wonder when they planned to tell me."

I wasted no time on Monday morning. "You have to get your husband's signature, too, before you get the key," the embassy official told me. So I took the papers home. There had been no mention of any payment I had to make. Was it really free?

Before Clem came home that evening, I had read the contract. Indeed, I would not have to pay. And there was no end date to the contract. I couldn't have been happier. When I had told Clem that we would find a solution, I didn't know that I would be the one to provide it.

"You did it," Clem said with a hug and a kiss when he signed the contract that evening. "Let's toast to your success. You have taken a huge burden off my shoulders." I brought a bottle of red wine, Clem opened it, and we called Beth and Sam to witness. "To Freeman," I said.

"To being a free man and having a wonderful, loving wife," Clem said as we clinked our glasses.

The next morning, key in hand, I walked to the front door of the house.

"You must be the elementary coordinator." I turned to see a woman in front of the adjoining unit. She looked about thirty-five, with olive skin and a slight accent that I couldn't place. "I'm Jackie," she said. "I'm just leaving for the embassy. I heard you were coming. When are you moving in?"

"As soon as we can. Maybe this week."

"It will be good to have someone next door," she said. "Welcome. I'll see you later." She turned toward her car.

"How did you know I was coming?" I called after her.

"I typed the minutes from the school board meeting last week, so I saw that they authorized your request. The principal was to call you this week." She waved good-bye as she got into her car and drove away.

I unlocked the door, walked through the downstairs, and admired the neat American colonial look. Upstairs there were three bedrooms, each small, a bathroom with American fittings, and a hall closet. The rooms were smaller and more closed in than where we were, and the yard had less space. But I wasn't complaining.

Because this move was to housing I'd secured and had such an important purpose, I didn't even mind packing up again. One item was damaged—the painting of Venice that had been my grandmother's. I had to laugh. That painting had survived its travels from Danforth, Illinois, to Cincinnati, to Lagos. We had carried it with us when we fled Lagos for Enugu in 1967, from Enugu to the village after the bombing got too hot, and back to Lagos in 1970. Now we moved it less than a mile and cracked the glass. I took it as a symbol of the break from quasi-government service that Clem was making.

That house led to lifelong friendships with the Nigerian family that lived across Macdonald Road. Our children matched up well in age. It took only a few days before they had discovered each other.

We made plans to see my parents in the summer of 1973. I booked flights for Lisbon and on to Madeira for mid July. "Your husband will need a visa to get into Portugal," the travel agent said. "And don't forget that you need a reentry visa and current residence permit to get back into Nigeria."

Clem's visa was straightforward. We had both US and Nigerian passports for the children, so their entry and return were easy. But the ritual of getting the right papers for me was time-consuming and frustrating. At last, with the documents in hand and the move to our new home complete, we departed for Madeira, leaving behind the rains that had started two months earlier.

I was elated to see my parents waiting for us at the airport. They appeared genuinely happy to see us, and I was so glad we'd had the recent Christmas together. Mother hugged each of us with enthusiasm. Even Father looked happy and came as near hugging us as I could remember. The children were chatty as we waited for our luggage. Other passengers watched our family with interest.

Someone spoke to Clem in Portuguese, probably assuming he was Angolan, but he just shook his head to show he didn't understand.

When I walked into the house, I was flooded with memories of the nine months I'd spent there during the Biafran War. The maid, Theresa, the same one we'd had when I was there, dropped the potato she was peeling and shouted when we walked into the kitchen.

The children were at home quickly. Father played cards with Beth, sometimes giving her a chance to say "Pounce" first and win the stack in the middle. Sammy stayed at her side reaching for the cards. Chinaku was content with a book.

We fell into a pattern that continued for most of our visits for the next few years. We would have breakfast, swim, and eat lunch at the pool of the hotel where we stayed. Clem loved relaxing on a reclined beach chair while I swam and watched the children. Around four, we'd shower and take a taxi to the house, where we had dinner.

On more than one evening, I found myself irritated by Father's sarcastic comments. "Are you sure you're comfortable enough?" he said to Clem, who was dozing in an armchair. A little later, he turned to Chinaku, who was seated peacefully on the sofa reading. "I hope we're not disturbing you," he said.

I'd grown up with these remarks. The children were little when we'd spent the year with them. Maybe they couldn't do too much that he disapproved of. Then I remembered the fireworks during our first New Year's, when Chinaku at age three was frightened by the blasts that reminded him of bombs in Biafra. Father was annoyed and critical rather than sympathetic. Now I was tired of it. I didn't want to become used to it again, and I certainly didn't want to adopt the habit myself.

I came to realize that Father wouldn't say what he meant but instead would use a cutting remark or apparently humorous comment to convey his message. I didn't know there was a name for this until years later when my brother's wife, Mary, commented on his passive-aggressive behavior.

Beth was spared his criticism. Father had taken a fancy to her at Christmas and loved having her by his side at dinner or in the living room where we had drinks before, and conversation after, dinner. Sammy was too little to receive this kind of negative attention. But Chinaku, with his love of reading, was a target.

On our third night, Chinaku asked to be excused from the table when he had finished his dinner. Father looked at him across the table. "Go, we don't want to keep you from something important." He kept his tone light, as if it were all a joke. I gave Chinaku a hug as he stood up and went to the living room. Overall, though, I loved the week in Madeira and enjoyed my parents' company.

The 1973–74 school year was one of major change for AIS as we began the process of converting to team teaching and Individually Guided Education, or IGE, which I had learned in Madrid the summer of 1972. A year later, I was asked to be the team leader for one of the new units, made up of third and fourth grades.

I didn't mind leaving the coordinator position because I was excited to implement these new methods. Three other teachers were assigned to my team. We had two days of planning before the school year started. I thought we could develop a social studies curriculum that used our unique geography in a port city in West Africa to expand children's understanding of the world. But I was too ambitious and optimistic about what I could accomplish in a few hours of preparation with my team members.

When the students arrived, we were not well prepared. We had decided as part of team teaching that children did not need their own individual desks but could store belongings in cubbyholes on shelves in the center of the large open area. Whole-group meetings would have children sitting on the floor, and they would then use desks in the area of their own work groups.

There were parent complaints about team teaching in general. But some of the concern was related to the fact that the school had promised a Tacoma leader for each unit. Instead, the school had placed me in charge of Unit B.

At its January meeting, the board made the decision to remove me as team leader, and the principal informed me the next morning. I was stunned and insulted. The teachers on my team and others, including one from Tacoma, came to my defense immediately with letters to the board asking that I be reinstated. I also wrote, defending our team's practices.

The principal called me in to say that the board had been shocked to learn that I didn't have a teaching certificate. I wondered why they hadn't known that; I'd never made a secret of it. He also said he could persuade the board to let me stay as team leader if I would take the following year off to go to the United States to get a certificate. I agreed, knowing that with the courses I'd already taken, I could get the certificate and also get a master's in education. Then I surprised him by asking the school to pay my costs.

Two weeks later, I received a letter in my school mailbox from the principal. "It is with extreme good pleasure that I write to inform you of the AIS Board of Directors' decision to assist you in furthering your studies in education." The letter went on to say that the school would cover my airfare. They would pay one year's tuition, room, and board at the rate of a public institution so I could obtain a bachelor's degree or better in education. They would even pay half my salary.

Clem had been upset at the treatment I received. Now he was unhappy that I would go away for a year. As we talked, he realized he could focus on Freeman Engineering, and I would be sure of a job and salary when I came back. The children would have a year to remember that they were Americans.

But I didn't know where to go. The Tacoma teachers gave me literature from Pacific Lutheran University in Tacoma, but it seemed too parochial. So I contacted Alice and Fred Hedglin, who encouraged me to apply to California State University in Sacramento, not far from where they lived. Alice said that it had a good reputation for education courses, including its master's in elementary education program. She also told me that there was housing for married students. When I was accepted at CSUS, she made arrangements for my apartment in the large housing complex near the university.

Soon after we'd moved to Macdonald Road, Clem had resigned from NEPA to give his full attention to Freeman Engineering. He'd fulfilled the first contract and got others, hired staff, and opened an office. He was the happiest he had been since the war.

When I left him in September 1975 for another extended separation, he promised to visit at Christmas. I departed with a clear mission and a clear return date. I didn't know then that I would return with a new view of myself and how our marriage should work.

17

California, New Schools, and Change in the Air

Clem had been with me to assist, at least a little, in taking care of the children on our last flight, when we visited my parents for a second summer in 1974. Now, at the end of August 1975, I was on my own for the much longer trip to California, with Chinaku, age ten, Beth, eight, and Sammy, four.

"I'll miss you. Take care of yourself and write often," I said, hugging Clem.

"Take care of your mother," he said, holding Chinaku and then Beth. "Study hard." He kissed our two older children and then grabbed Sammy for an extra embrace before giving me a squeeze. We waved as we entered the boarding gate for the flight to London. There we changed for a direct flight to San Francisco.

Chinaku was deep in the Narnia Chronicles. Beth entertained Sammy, and once we persuaded him he couldn't kick the seat in front of him, the flights were uneventful. All three slept for several hours on each leg of the flight to California, and I nodded off now and then.

Fred and Alice called out to me when we walked into Arrivals. Fred's easy banter with the children made the time waiting for luggage pass quickly. I wondered again how much Alice had known about my earlier relationship with Fred when she arrived in Nigeria. But I hadn't dwelled on the thought then, and I didn't now, as she was so welcoming.

I brought them up-to-date on mutual friends and Nigeria, though they kept up with what little they could glean from US media and occasional correspondence. "It's still a military government and not popular," I said. "They talk about elections someday, but I don't see it happening soon."

In the morning, Alice drove me to College Town, the married student housing, near the campus of CSUS. "I asked for a three-bedroom, two-story apartment for you," she said. "It's not fancy, but I think you could make it comfortable."

"It's great. I love it," I said after we picked up the key and were walking up the stairs to the second floor. "But where will I get furniture?"

"I found a rental place. Let's take care of the lease, and I'll drive you there," she said. I was thankful to have her as a guide; I would have been lost on my own.

She accompanied me back to the office to sign the contract for the nine-month lease, and then drove me to the furniture rental outlet, where I ordered essential pieces. She said she'd bring me a TV, a couple of shelves, and kitchen equipment to keep my costs down.

Next, she took me and the children to Phoebe Hearst School. The administrator asked me about their prior school and suggested a placement test. "What if I don't do well?" Beth said, looking at me for support. Chinaku seemed unconcerned.

"You'll do fine," I assured her. "You'll be surprised." Both children finished quickly and gave their tests to the administrator.

"They're clearly very well prepared," she said after she'd reviewed the results. "I think they'd each be better off a grade ahead of their age." I agreed; Beth would start fourth grade and Chinaku, sixth. We were given the names of their teachers and shown their classrooms. She told me about the school bus schedule, and Alice added a warning. "You have to take the children to the bus at least the first day, and they have to be on time, or they'll be left."

With the two older children set, Alice drove us back to College Town, where I registered Sam for the on-site preschool. But I didn't know who would care for the children in the evenings when my classes took place. Alice was willing to have them come over, and I would take them until I found a better solution, but it was too far to be workable for the whole year.

My next step was to buy a car. I found another VW, a used, cream-colored beetle. "I'm only going to use it for nine months. Will you take it back then?" I said to the dealer.

"Of course, as long as it's still in good condition," he said. The children christened it Sunny Jim II.

The day after I moved in, and the day before Beth and Chinaku were to start school, I left the three children alone while I dashed over to CSUS to register for my own classes. The two older children were sensible and responsible, so although I didn't like leaving them, I wasn't worried. When I returned, my neighbor across the courtyard, a pleasant woman with two kids of her own, knocked on my door. When I opened, she said, "You can't leave your kids alone like that. I wouldn't report you, but someone else might." I was shocked. I had no idea it was a reportable offense.

"I won't do it again," I said, feeling very embarrassed and naïve, "but I have to find someone to take care of them." I hadn't realized how many details there were to living without household help.

"Try looking at notices in the Laundromat or at the university career office. Maybe you'll find someone," she suggested.

That evening, I went to the Laundromat. A carefully hand-printed notice leaped out at me: "Seeking babysitter. Need care for three-year-old daughter during day. Call Terry." I wrote down her number and raced back to my apartment, hoping no one had yet called.

I was in luck. She came over right away, bringing her daughter, Jennell, just a few months younger than Sam. Terry was fifteen years younger than I, slim, with long, straight, brown hair, no makeup, and the clothes of a California hippie. She lived just around the corner from us. She was taking college classes in elementary education, and all her classes were during the day, while my classes in the graduate program were all for working teachers, held during the evening.

She'd already registered Jennell in the same preschool as Sam. I'd found my savior! I had slightly more money and two more children than she, but she needed more hours of care for her daughter. It took only a few days for us to have a workable, happy solution. After Chinaku and Beth left for the school bus in the morning, she would drop off Jennell on her way to classes. I would take her and Sam to preschool and pick them up shortly before Chinaku and Beth came home. Terry would cook dinner after she arrived at five, when I would leave for my classes. This was more than workable—it was fantastic.

"You look very pretty," I said to Beth as she pirouetted to show off her dress on their first day. "Are you nervous?" I said on the way to the school bus stop.

"I won't know anyone," Beth said with her eyes knit together.

"You will soon. Look how many other children are here," I said, gesturing to the six or seven others waiting at the bus stop.

That was her only day of wearing anything but jeans to school. She adapted right away to Sacramento style, probably the school dress code all over the United States then. Chinaku didn't have to alter his wardrobe, but both he and Beth certainly had to change their understanding of proper school behavior. No more standing for the headmistress or reciting morning prayers.

Beth made friends with Gwen, a black girl in her class who lived close to us. They would spend afternoons at our house or Gwen's or outside on their roller skates. Chinaku played ball outside or went to the homes of classmates.

In November, the children brought home notices about teacher conferences. At St. Saviour's School in Ikoyi, there had been no teacher conferences. I had met with parents at the American School, but I was always on the other side of the table. I wasn't sure what to expect at my first ever teacher conference in the role of parent.

Both teachers reported that my children were extremely bright and advanced. Of course, I was thrilled to hear it. I wasn't surprised to be told that Chinaku didn't always have his homework done, and Beth was a model for others in how neat and well prepared she was. They both brought home excellent report cards and seemed happy. I knew they weren't learning anything new in math or science, but they were gaining an education in American living. And they would remember this experience, unlike their earlier time in the United States.

At the same time, I was making progress and soon confirmed that with the classes I'd taken before and the education credits from the Kinshasa and Madrid workshops, I would be able to complete a master's in education in a year and get my teaching certificate. Though I was occasionally a procrastinator like Chinaku, now I completed my assignments carefully, just like Beth. I was amazed at what there was to learn about how to teach reading and math. I was able to draw on my experience to participate well in discussions. And others in the class enjoyed hearing about Nigeria and the American School where I taught.

I loved the class in teaching reading. One evening, I made a comment displaying my stereotyped image of Southerners and racism. The professor called me on it. "I'm from Texas," she said, "and that's not what I believe." I was embarrassed, but I became more thoughtful about how easily we can hold stereotypes and how difficult it is to erase them from our minds.

Terry and I took the children out on weekends, and on some evenings, she would stay for a while when I came home from my classes. "How is it that you and Clem can stay apart for so long?" she said. "I know you told me about going away during the Biafran War, but wasn't that really unusual?"

"Separations from family, even from spouses, are more common in Nigeria than here," I said. "Of course, the war was an exception, but Clem had left his family and gone to England for nine years to study and work before returning to Nigeria. Lots of people did that."

"But he wasn't married then. Isn't that different?" she said.

I explained that even married men left for extended periods, leaving their wives and sometimes children behind. I said, "When I met Clem, his cousin Jonathan was already married, and he was in England in seminary. Another cousin had left his wife at home and was in the United States."

I was curious about her life too. I knew she grew up on a farm, was the first to attend college, and had seven siblings who were closely connected. I hardly thought about my siblings. We were so different.

I spoke to Alice often and took the children to see them and their children frequently. "What are you doing for Christmas?" Alice said one evening as we were cleaning up after dinner at their home.

"Clem is coming for two weeks. I haven't thought about what we'll do."

"Why don't you come with us to our cabin? It's beautiful in the mountains. We should have snow."

I shivered. Winter weather didn't have any appeal, and I knew Clem would also hate the cold, but a trip out of town with our good friends sounded appealing. The children were excited about the idea of seeing the mountains and the snow. Clem arrived in Sacramento a couple of days before we were due to leave. Letters traveled so much faster than during the Biafran War, and we'd talked on the phone a couple of times. There was no feeling of strangeness between us now.

He immediately noticed the children's American accents. "Don't worry. I'm sure they'll recover their British accents when we get back," I promised.

"Na wattin' you say?" Beth said in perfect Nigerian Pidgin English, making us roar with laughter. She switched to a proper British accent. "You think I can't speak like Mrs. Payne?" she said. "I can even talk like the queen."

Alice loaned us coats and mittens for our trip to the mountains. The children tobogganed and sledded, while Clem and I mostly stayed indoors. Alice and I cooked, and Fred entertained us all with his stories and jokes. He was especially fond of Beth, and I guessed that he may have wished for a daughter.

"What are we going to do about the school entrance exam for Chinaku?" Clem said the day before he left. "He should be starting secondary school when you get back. Maybe he should return earlier, when the exam is given."

"There must be a way he can take the exam here. Why don't you ask Jean Obi? She's still at WAEC?" The West African Exams Council was the coordinating body for all the standardized tests given to decide entrance to secondary school as well as the school certificate at the end of secondary school.

We needed an exam administrator; the principal at Phoebe Hearst agreed. On the assigned day, Chinaku was placed in a room by himself, while the principal unwrapped the test papers, came back periodically to observe him, then took the papers and shipped them back to Jean in Nigeria. Jean let Clem know when they arrived, and we waited to hear the results.

Meanwhile, I began my own self-improvement regime. I had always been around average or a little over in weight until Sam was born. In just a few years, I'd put on thirty pounds. I had started noticing ads for Weight Watchers and decided to take action. So in January, after Clem returned to Nigeria, I found a daytime meeting near me.

"Your weight is 180 pounds," said the assistant who manned the scales at the back of the room. She wrote it on my form and directed me to a seat in the church basement.

"You have to learn the points system and track what you eat every day," the instructor told me and other newcomers. "Here's where you'll record what you eat every day."

I went home with a yellow booklet that reminded me of my international vaccination card. I changed my shopping habits, and Terry accommodated me with her cooking. I tracked my points faithfully and lost steadily. It was like magic! By the eighth or ninth week, I was tired of the same enthusiastic pitch from the instructor. Still, sharing my weight loss with others was helpful, and I continued attending and getting weighed weekly. By the time I headed back to Nigeria, I'd lost twenty-eight pounds and was very near my goal.

I also made dental appointments for myself and the children. But it was the one day that Sacramento had snow, and the children missed being at school to enjoy it.

I made friends among classmates, began listening to talk of the second wave of feminism, now in full flow, and I bought *Our Bodies, Ourselves* to take back to Nigeria with me. I read the popular *Fear of Flying*, already out three years. I got my own credit card. I wasn't sure how relevant the women's movement was for me in Nigeria, but I knew I felt more in control of my life and my decisions.

"Sacramento Memorial Day Parade 1976 invites children to participate. The Brownie Troop of Phoebe Hearst will have a float." Beth brought home the notice in April. "Children are invited to wear costumes commemorating the two-hundredth anniversary of the United States Declaration of Independence."

"Can I be in the parade, Mommy?" she said.

I signed her up. We went back to the sewing store, where I'd already bought a portable Singer electric sewing machine that I would take back to Nigeria with me. We found the perfect pattern and cotton fabrics—one red and one blue with large white stars. I sewed for days. On parade day, I dropped her at the meeting point and dashed back to pick up Terry, Jennell, Chinaku, and Sammy. We stood shoulder-to-shoulder in the crowd lined up along Front Street. The three children were restless until we heard the band playing "Stars and Stripes Forever." Then we saw the Shriners in their tiny car.

The sun was intense, and I realized again how fortunate I was that the heat didn't bother me.

Soon the float with the Phoebe Hearst Brownies came into view. A few girls wore their uniforms, and others, like Beth, were in costumes created for the parade. Sam was the first to spot her.

"Beth, we're here," Terry, Chinaku, and I shouted as we all waved and yelled. Beth waved like the queen when she saw us. I had tears in my eyes as I waved back. I hadn't known the parade would be so emotional.

"She's so beautiful," Terry said. I had to agree.

The academic year was drawing to a close. I finished the major paper about individualized instruction I was writing for my master's degree in education and turned it in. I was notified that I qualified and would receive the degree. I had also completed the requirements to get my teaching certificate. Mission accomplished.

I had treated my car well. I went back to the dealer, who offered me half of what I'd paid. "I'd love to buy it," Terry said when I told her. "Let me call my mom to see if she can help me out." Her mom agreed. I was glad to let her have it, even though she paid even less than the dealer had offered.

As I prepared to depart, I felt more American than I had in years. The parade had awakened latent patriotism, and I was proud of our democratic traditions. Now I would return to a military government in Nigeria. I'd become accustomed to the ease of life in the United States, and I was more aware and less willing to live with some of the craziness of life in a developing country. Why shouldn't I have electricity all the time? Why not have a supermarket where I could find any food I wanted so that I could maintain my weight loss? The Weight Watchers guide didn't have point values for pounded yam, okra, or egusi soup, or any of the other Nigerian foods I ate regularly. There would be no Weight Watchers meeting to attend.

Spending time with Fred and Alice gave me a window into a marriage with a dynamic different than my own. They were a close couple and showed it openly. They collaborated on decisions. I began to think of myself as more independent. I knew Clem relied on my advice, but I had let him act like he could make decisions for both of us or for the whole family. I didn't want to cater to his ego in this way now.

Fred and Alice also shared their child rearing. Clem loved our children, but he didn't always let them know this. He thought he should demand their obedience and stressed the importance of listening to and adopting his opinions, rather than teaching them to reach their own conclusions. "They have to learn to be Nigerians," was his fallback position. I wanted them to be inquisitive and independent thinkers. I knew we would have some discussion about this when I returned home.

Terry also taught me about being independent. Though she received help from her mom to buy the car, she was determined to care for her daughter on her own and earn her degree. The women's movement and the books I'd read had also influenced me during the nine months.

And I could now envisage the day I might want to live in the United States again, especially if one, two, or all three children settled in America. I wasn't questioning my future in Nigeria in a serious way, but the first hint that I could choose to live in the United States had entered my mind. Of course, I was returning to Nigeria where Clem was the native and I the outsider. Although I didn't feel like an outsider there, and I loved the sense of belonging Clem and his family gave me, now I knew I could have the same sense of being at home in the United States.

Meanwhile, I had to plan for the next school year. Beth and Sam were already enrolled at St. Saviour's. But Clem had received no word about the secondary school exam results for Chinaku, so sorting out his school was a priority.

A month before I left, Clem had written that the embassy had asked him to vacate the house we had lived in for three years. I hadn't been in it for the last nine months, and I was no longer the American School's elementary coordinator. But I would return to teach at the school. We were comfortable there. I was surprised and a little angry, but he had already agreed.

He had to turn in the key before I got back and was looking for a house for us. Ten days later, he wrote to say that he'd found a place in Ikoyi he could afford. He'd paid the required year's rent in advance and would take us there when we returned. So again I was going back to a new house, one I'd had no hand in choosing.

We didn't want to be in a hotel for even one night, much less for weeks while we looked for housing. It made no sense for him to wait for me. There was nothing I could do but accept. So much for the shared decision making I was determined we would have!

18

RETURN TO NIGERIA TWO, CHINAKU STARTS BOARDING SCHOOL

"THERE'S DADDY." BETH pointed to Clem, standing under the sign announcing the new name, Murtala Muhammed International Airport. In his red-and-white, tie-dye shirt, and under the huge sign, he looked quite small.

This time, there was no doubt that the children were happy to see him. His stay at Christmas, six months earlier, had been too brief, and letters were no substitute for being together. I, too, was glad that we were returning to him and to Nigeria.

We were still in the queue, waiting for immigration to stamp our passports. I held my US passport, the children's Nigerian passports, and the completed immigration form and currency declaration forms. My hands were hot and sweaty. There was no air conditioning, and the fan standing nearby wasn't moving.

"Who's Murtala Muhammed?" Chinaku said.

"He was head of state when we left for the United States, but he was assassinated while we were away. People here liked him a lot."

Finally, we were through the immigration formalities. Beth ran to Clem, pulling Sam beside her. Chinaku followed in a more stately fashion, the big brother. By the time I reached him, they were all in his arms. He released them to hug me and ask about the flight.

"It wasn't too bad. You know Ann put us on the plane in New York. Chinaku was happy with a book, Sam charmed the stewardesses, and Beth organized a few school papers she carried with her. They all fell asleep after we had dinner and didn't wake up until we landed in Dakar this morning."

Baggage handlers were bringing in suitcases and dumping them on the immobile baggage carousel.

"Why are they doing that? Why don't they use the carousel to bring the luggage in?" Beth asked.

"Maybe they want to use people to do the work. That way more men have jobs, and they're not wasting electricity," Clem said. This was a regular theme for him, but I suspected lack of maintenance was a more likely reason.

By the time all our suitcases had appeared, my cream-colored, cotton blouse was stuck to my body, and sweat ran down my back. The children were wilting in the heat.

"The car is air-conditioned, isn't it?" I said to Clem, wiping perspiration from my eyes. He nodded.

There were no luggage trolleys, so Clem signaled to one of the disheveled-looking boys hovering nearby to help us get our belongings to the parking lot. When the baggage was stored in the trunk, Clem dug in his pocket and found a couple of naira bills. The boy grumbled but took the money and departed

"I see the traffic is no better," I said as we heard the horns from every side. Even the heavy rain that began to fall didn't shut out the sound of afternoon traffic.

Then, to confirm what his letter had said, I asked, "You found us a place to live?"

"I did, and it's in Ikoyi, very near our first house on Alexander Avenue. We got the contract to build the power generation and distribution for Ahoada military barracks, and I used the first payment."

"I hope you like it," he added as he waited for the watch-day to open the gate. I had accepted that he couldn't wait for me to return to find a house, though it didn't meet my new interest in making sure Clem acknowledged that we were sharing decisions equally. My American friends would find it strange that I was not involved in the choice. But they didn't know how few houses at reasonable prices were available in Lagos in this time of the oil boom or the necessity of acting quickly when one was.

The rain had nearly stopped as he pulled into the driveway, and I saw the pale yellow stucco house. The sweet smell of the frangipani tree in the front yard surrounded me. Ixora bushes, with their bright red flowers, lined the gravel driveway.

Chinaku was first through one of the wide-open doors. The matching French doors at the other end of the sitting room and large windows gave it a feeling of openness. "I just moved in a few days ago. I bought beds, but you will have to buy other furniture," Clem said.

The high ceiling and terrazzo black-and-white floor and almost no furniture made it look gigantic. "This is really spacious," I said, looking to my left at what would be our dining room. "We'll have plenty of room. You did well."

"Madam, you are back," Felix, our cook/steward, had come in so quietly I was surprised when he spoke. He had a smile for me and a broad grin for the children.

"Yes, Felix, we're back," I said. He had no idea how pleased I was to see him. I would not have to prepare meals, clean, or wash and iron clothes any longer. I was willing to give up a little privacy for this luxury.

The watch-day brought in our suitcases and took them upstairs. We followed, and Clem led us into the bedroom on the left. On the outer wall, there was a door leading onto a tiny balcony. "I didn't even see that," Clem said when I pointed it out. At the other side was a door into a dressing room and beyond that a generous, tiled bathroom.

"What's that?" Beth asked, spotting the bidet next to the toilet.

"It's for washing your bottom." I said. She dissolved in giggles and hurried out with her brothers to find their rooms.

Clem started to follow her, but I turned and put my arms around him. "How did you find this? I love it," I said.

"What else can I do? I have to give you a place to live."

Chinaku was already sitting on the lone bed in the room across from ours. "This is mine," he said. He'd already dragged his suitcase in.

Beth called from the other room. "Here's our room." She and Sam were bouncing on the beds, their suitcases on the floor.

And we were in our new house, though with little furniture. Apart from the beds, we had just the TV and piano, one card table, and a couple of folding chairs. With no dressers, we couldn't do a lot of unpacking.

"Chinaku, pull the piano bench over," I said when Felix announced an hour later that dinner was ready. The three children squeezed onto the wooden bench. We sat down for our first dinner together in our very own home.

I helped the children find their pajamas and toothbrushes and reminded them not to drink the tap water but to spit it out when they rinsed their mouths after brushing. Baths could wait. "Come say good-night to Daddy," I said. Clem had a pile of papers on his bed, but he pushed them aside and pulled all three children onto his bed.

"You are all talking like Americans. Do you remember any Igbo?"

"*Kachifo,*" Chinaku and Beth responded in unison. I laughed as Sam copied them. Chinaku corrected his pronunciation.

"I never thought about it before, but it means 'let the dawn come.' I like that," I said, as Clem tickled first one then another of his children. When I took Beth and Sam to their room a few minutes later, I heard her correcting him as he tried again to get the tones of "*Kachifo.*"

"Any news about Chinaku's school?" I said as I came back into our bedroom, where Clem and Chinaku were in deep conversation.

"I was just telling Chinaku," Clem said. "They've just posted the list of places, and his name isn't on it."

I was jerked out of my exhaustion. "How can that be? Didn't Jean say that they received his exam at WAEC?" I'd sent it off carefully, and Clem had confirmed with her that it had arrived. "He's so bright, and he scores so well on tests, just like I always did. It's impossible that he didn't get a place. He was in the ninety-ninth percentile on the US standardized tests."

The federal government colleges were the best secondary schools in the country, but the number of places was limited. We had made Federal Government College, or FGC, Enugu, our first choice for Chinaku. It was 350 miles away in the capital of the Eastern, and primarily Igbo, region.

The options other than federal government colleges were few. There were private and religious schools, but we wanted the top. And we wanted him in the East. "We will find a solution," Clem said as we wished Chinaku goodnight and sent him to bed.

"You should call Jean tomorrow morning," Clem said.

"No, you should call Jean," I said. "This is your country, with its senseless, restrictive, secondary school system." Clem would not pass on to me this task that rightly belonged to him.

I wouldn't have responded this way before my nine months in the United States. I'd seen *Time* magazine name American women as those who had most influenced events in the year 1975. The women's movement and feminism had caused me to change, and I was more assertive. Clem was taken aback.

The next morning, he made the call.

"Jean said she will check. I called Obelagu, too. I remembered he's at the Exams Council. They both said they will investigate," he said. There was nothing more I could do except worry.

In line with my new idea of shared responsibility, I persuaded Clem to come with me to choose furniture. I made selections, and he protested, trying to find items we could eliminate to save money. I said, "Would you like to have our good china—the plates Mr. Sun gave us—stacked on the floor?"

"Well, no," he said.

We went through the same process with the bureaus and dressing table. Finally, with a frown, he pulled out his checkbook and paid. I gave him a kiss and assured him he'd done the right thing, and he broke into a smile as we got into the car.

We returned home to find Chinaku lying on the floor, his face buried in a book. Beth and Sam played chopsticks on the piano, Beth's Sunshine Family set, with its dolls and bright orange plastic bus, spread around on the floor.

The next morning when the rain stopped, I took Beth and Sam to St. Saviour's School. Clem had already told Mrs. Payne, still the headmistress, that we were returning and confirmed their places. I wanted to know when the school year would start. She gave me the start date in late August, and Beth took Sam off to show him his classroom.

Later that day, I drove to the American School to find out about my own teaching position. I learned that I would be part of the fifth- and sixth-grade team, with a new man coming from Tacoma as the team leader. I felt little excitement about the new school year despite my new qualifications.

On my way to the parking lot, I was stopped by a hefty Nigerian man in a dark-blue uniform who looked familiar. "Do you remember me?" he said.

It took me a moment and a glance at his name embroidered on his uniform to register the round, smiling face. "Sunday?" He'd been George Butler's driver from before the time of our wedding. "What a surprise! I'm so happy to see you. I had no idea you were working here."

"I started here last year. They told me you were away."

"Whatever happened to George and his family? He wrote to us right after the war ended, and then we didn't hear from him again." George had not only written to us, he'd sent the blank check with a lovely letter telling Clem to use it as needed. "I heard they left Kaduna unexpectedly."

"Yes. You know he helped a couple of Igbo friends get back to the East early in the war, and when he had to renew his visa, the authorities refused to grant it." I realized Sunday had acquired a bit of an American accent and language pattern in his years with Ford Foundation and now the American School.

"Ford Foundation couldn't help?"

"They tried, but the immigration people refused. He didn't want to go, but he had no choice." Sunday shook his head in sympathy.

I relayed the story to Clem that evening. He was as shocked and sad as I was, and we remembered again with gratitude the check he'd sent, which had allowed Clem to start Freeman.

Each day, I waited for news about Chinaku's school. After a week of suspense, Obelagu called to say Chinaku had indeed been on the original list for Federal Government College Enugu. "He thought the name was removed to provide a place for the son of an army officer," Clem said. "It will take a couple of days to sort out."

"This means someone else will be taken off the list, right?" I said.

"Yes. They'll find someone who doesn't have friends at Exams Council or a relative in the army."

"It's a wonderful country! Is there any hope?" I loved my adopted home, but the nepotism that spread through every aspect of life disgusted me. Still, I was very relieved.

Chinaku would be a boarder at the school. He'd just turned eleven in June. There wouldn't be a phone available, and we knew no one on the staff. "You shouldn't worry," Clem said. But I hated the thought of him so distant and unreachable.

"Don't we know somebody in Enugu who could check on him?"

Clem called his friend Mkparu, who'd been part of our wedding planning committee and now lived in Enugu. He agreed to look after Chinaku and invited us to stay with them when we took him to school. His son was at the school and would also keep an eye on Chinaku. This gave me a little relief from the nagging worry about sending my eleven-year-old son away.

The drive to the East seemed even longer than usual. I kept thinking about Chinaku—I wouldn't know if he was getting enough to eat or if he got hurt. Clem talked about Freeman and his contracts, but I barely listened.

We stopped briefly in Onitsha to see Clem's parents and remind them that Chinaku would be only a couple of hours away in Enugu. With warm wishes for their first grandson, they sent us on our way. Two hours later, we pulled up at the Mkparus' house. Their son Afam, in his second year at FGC, took Chinaku in tow immediately. That was a good sign.

Mrs. Mkparu led us to the school on the outskirts of the city the next morning. It was dreary, but I didn't want to say that to Chinaku. There were two large dormitories, two classroom blocks, an administration and dining building, and a football pitch with goalposts. The whole compound was spread over several acres. Everything was a dusty, miserable-looking brown. There were almost no trees or shrubs and no grass.

An older student guided us to the section of one boardinghouse reserved for first years.

"Take this bed," Mrs. Mkparu said, pointing out the cot near a window and at the end of a row of twenty. "You'll have more privacy and a little more space." There was a cupboard beside the bed, big enough only for a few books.

"Where does he keep his clothes?" I said.

"In his suitcase under the bed," she said.

I thought of the new furniture in our house in Lagos and the big bedroom Chinaku had to himself. I could hardly bear the contrast and the separation to come. I reached into my bag for a tissue.

"Don't let him see you cry," Mrs. Mkparu said. "The other new boys are the same age. He'll be fine. We will visit him soon."

"You will write very soon, won't you? Don't forget your Daraprim."

"Study hard, and make us proud," Clem said. "Christmas holidays are not too far away."

"Yes, Mommy, I'll write." He turned to Clem. "I'll work hard too, Daddy."

"I'll miss you so much. But I know you'll be fine," I said. I hoped my doubts weren't apparent. Other boys were milling around. Chinaku seemed ready to join them, and I sensed he might not want to be singled out as the one with a white mother unwilling to leave. I could see other parents departing. With a final hug, I said good-bye to my little boy and followed Clem and Mrs. Mkparu out of the dorm.

When I married Clem, I accepted the whole package of life in Nigeria. We had agreed early on that we wanted the children to have a solid Nigerian education, which included boarding school.

But that conviction didn't make the reality any easier. Would he make friends quickly? Would there be any music program? I thought of my own junior high, with its rich choral program. I also recalled entering seventh grade after the school year had started, when I'd had a hard time getting accepted. Chinaku was starting at a good time—the beginning of the term with other new students. And I knew the education would be good in the British tradition. He was bright and personable. His football skills would come in handy.

Of course, I couldn't turn off the thoughts, but the American School and my own teaching started the next week and kept my mind occupied. Armed with my master's degree in education and teaching certificate, I was more confident than ever. However, I was frustrated. I felt sure I was a more natural teacher and leader than the man heading our team. I knew I had made mistakes when I was the team leader two years earlier, but now I was wiser.

In his letters, Chinaku told us about his classes and sports. He always asked about Beth and Sam, and most of his letters included a note for them, often with a drawing. In November, he said, "It's only nineteen days to the end of term, and everyone is excited," and I knew he missed us. He specifically asked to spend a few days in Lagos before going to Nanka for Christmas, so he could see his friends. He said he was happy, though he confessed years later that he was homesick at first.

Beth and Sam said they missed their big brother, but they were engaged at school. Beth had been enthralled with her Brownie troop at St. Saviour's since she had joined before going to the United States. She would lay out her uniform carefully the night before, with her sash and beret, and go to school looking very smart on Brownie day. She also continued the ballet and piano lessons she'd started before we went to the States. She had several good friends, with Ruth her closest companion.

Sam had school friends too and another friend, Keno, who lived on the nearby street but was at the French school, as his mother was French. He had the same light-brown complexion as our children, but he was leaner and taller than Sam. They were together many days after school and began a project that continued for years—digging a six-foot-wide, deep hole in our backyard.

On March 23, 1977, we had celebrated Sam's sixth birthday with a party in the afternoon. Clem and I were watching the 9:00 p.m. news in our sitting room, which now had two comfortable yellow recliner chairs in addition to the furniture I'd bought on our return. I listened halfheartedly to talk of the up-coming Constituent Assembly, which was to draft a new constitution, bringing the long-awaited end of military rule.

"Now I'm the one who's fed up," I said to Clem, looking up from the papers I was grading. "The Tacoma teachers are no smarter than I am. And they pamper the children."

"Why don't you quit?" he said. "You only promised them a year in return for their paying for your year in the States."

"True enough. But what would I do?"

By early 1977, Clem had hired several staff and had completed the Ahoada contract that had financed our home. He had a contract for improvements to Federal Palace Hotel, and other projects were in the works. Freeman Engineering was doing very well.

"You could come to work at Freeman."

"To do what? I'm not an engineer."

"You could help in the office." I knew this was a very bad idea. I loved him, but I had seen enough of how he treated his staff to know that his harshness would make me uncomfortable all the time. Nor did I have an interest in clerical or administrative work.

"I think I'll decline your generous offer," I said, getting up from my chair to give him a kiss. But I began to think seriously about leaving the school. There must be something else I could do besides teach at the American School.

Maybe I could make my hobbies pay. I loved the Nigerian trading beads, made in Italy or Holland and brought to Nigeria by traders in the nineteenth and early twentieth century. I bought them in Jankara Market, the huge central market in the heart of Lagos. The beads were strung on raffia, knotted at the end, the right length to go over the head. Chevrons—blue, red, and white—were the most expensive and rare. I had strung a few together to make a necklace.

And I had an added interest—I had started giving piano lessons to a couple of children.

When the rainy season started in April, I told the principal I would finish the school year but not return in the fall. He said he was sorry, but I think he understood my dissatisfaction. I would miss my fellow teachers, but I was ready to move on.

We decided on a couple of weeks' holiday in England, then a week in Madeira for the coming summer. I would celebrate the end of my teaching career, Clem would celebrate his business success, and Chinaku would have finished his first year away. Mother wrote to say my sister Beth was also coming to visit them with her daughter, Michelle, just a couple of months older than Sam, so we arranged our dates to coincide.

We stayed that summer of 1977 in the Bayswater area of London in a shabby, short-term, rental apartment. On our second morning, Clem surprised me. "Maybe we should buy a place of our own," he said.

"Are you serious? This isn't like you," I said. "I love the idea. And you wouldn't have to pay for hotels anymore." I could come more often too, now that I wasn't teaching, if we had our own place.

He was indeed serious, and I called estate agents that very day. I developed my criteria. It needed to be near a tube stop so I could get around London easily. I wanted easy shopping for groceries. Other than that, I didn't care what part of the city we'd be in.

Clem and I looked at a couple of places in our price range, but nothing was appealing. Then one of the estate agents we'd contacted asked us to meet him to Hampstead, a pleasant suburb north of London. We took the children with us on the tube. The estate agent took us to Trinity Close, just around the corner from Hampstead High Street, talking as we walked.

"This property was converted from Trinity Church when it was decommissioned," he said. "The middle of three semidetached houses has just been completed and is available." He led us across the cobbled courtyard. Over the entrance door to the middle house was a window that looked like it belonged in a church. I entered to find two rooms on the street level. The children were already on the stairs to the main floor, which had a large, open area with the high ceiling of what had been part of the sanctuary. The kitchen was new with modern fittings. I was intrigued.

"Look, there's even another room up above," Beth said. The balcony was built over part of the seating area and ladder-like steps led up to a small room with a gabled ceiling. The tube stop was a five-minute walk up the hill. There were restaurants and shops on the way.

"I love it," I whispered to Clem. "Could we actually buy this?"

We told the estate agent that we were interested. I negotiated for a couple of days, and we came to an agreement when I said we would pay cash. I could hardly believe we were doing this. Clem was justly proud of the success of his company and his ability to buy this property. And I was proud of him. We could move in as soon as the check cleared.

We only had a few days left in London, so I hastily bought beds and had them delivered. We spent just one night in our new London house before leaving for Madeira. But I knew I would be back soon to buy furniture and enjoy Hampstead.

Now, however, we were headed to Funchal, Madeira, and family time.

Mother met us by herself so we'd have room for everyone in the VW. My sister was waiting for us at the house with her daughter, Michelle, and Father. I hadn't seen Beth for several years, when she had asked me to move out of their house at her husband's request. Now she and Tom were divorced.

I was pleased that my children were meeting her and her daughter. They knew too little of their American relatives, while they were close to or knew well many members of their Nigerian extended family.

On our second day, we left Father at home, and Mother led the rest of us to the famous white church with dark trim, *Nossa Senhora do Monte*, on a hill above the city. I had visited Monte with Mother during the year I lived with them.

But there was a tourist attraction at Monte that I had not tried. The toboggan ride, often featured in pictures of Madeira, is done in a sled, a wicker basket seat for two mounted on wooden runners. The toboggan speeds down the narrow, winding streets from the church into Funchal. Two men, dressed in traditional white shirts, baggy black trousers, and straw hats, control it, using their rubber-soled boots as brakes.

"Come on, let's go down," my sister said to Clem and me. "The children will love it."

"It's too fast for me," I said to Beth. "You go."

She turned to my husband. "Clem, I know you'll go down with me," she said, and he agreed.

With that, I couldn't let her show me up with her bravery. "All right, I'll do it. We'll have two toboggans. Who wants to come with me?" I said to the children.

"I do," Sam said, jumping with excitement. The other children were also eager, so Clem and I took Beth and Sam with us while my sister took Michelle and Chinaku with her. I held Clem's hand, hoping he could impart his lack of fear to me.

We stood at the top of the hill waiting for our turn. I read the sign: "The downhill journey to Funchal is made in about ten minutes...reaching at times a speed of forty-eight km/hour."

"How many miles per hour is that?" I said to Chinaku.

"Just twenty-nine. It's not fast," he said. Maybe not for you, I thought.

Michelle and Chinaku waved to us as they got into their toboggan and started the downhill journey. Then it was our turn. We started slowly and then sped up past the houses that lined the route. I screamed as we approached the bottom. Sam and Beth were beaming.

"Why did I let you talk me into this?" I said to my sister Beth as I got out on shaky legs. "I hate roller coasters. I should have known better."

"Did you like it?" she said to Sam, looking down at him by my side.

"Can we go again?" he said.

My sister looked at me. "How come you're scared of coming down the hill in a sled, but you weren't afraid of a war and living in a primitive village?" I didn't have an easy answer, though I did suggest she not call the village "primitive," and I reminded her that she'd seemed to enjoy her time in the village with us when Chinaku was a baby.

"I could never just go to live in another country," she said, "especially in a village with no electricity. The two weeks we spent there were more than enough."

I was struck several times during our week together by how similar my sister was to my father in her speech, her appearance, and even how she walked.

Her teasing sarcasm, such as, "You haven't grown any taller, have you?" to Clem did not sit well. Still, we had lots of laughter together. I was sorry to say good-bye to her and Michelle when we put them on the plane. Then it was our turn to say good-bye to my parents and fly back to Lagos. I was sure we'd be back next summer with Clem's newfound sense of wealth.

Three weeks later, the children went back to school—Chinaku to Enugu, and Beth and Sam to St. Saviour's. I taught my piano pupils, made jewelry with my beads, and joined a women's morning tennis game. I wrote more often to my parents and kept letters going to Chinaku. In late November, I left Beth and Sam at home with Rosa and went to London for a week with Clem to buy furniture for the house.

But I knew these tasks and activities were not all I wanted to do. I had to decide what was next for me, and I had no idea.

19

BETH DEPARTS, PRESIDENT CARTER VISITS, CLEM STRAYS

UNLIKE HER OLDER brother, Beth fretted for weeks—months even—about the Common Entrance exam she would take in March 1978. I worried too—not about her ability, but about where she should go. Though I had temporarily regretted the decision to have Chinaku far away in Enugu, I was now sure it was right. I felt even more strongly that Beth shouldn't be in Lagos, even though Queens College was the top girls' secondary school. It would be just too hard to have her close and not visit often.

We had met Miss Gentle, the assistant principal of Queens College, who was British but had spent many years in Nigeria. Her name suited her. At the time we were debating, I learned that she was being transferred to Kaduna Federal Government College in the northern capital.

"Edwin and his wife are there too. We can tell them to keep an eye on her," was Clem's response to my suggestion. How like Clem to say "tell them" instead of "ask them" to a younger cousin. Edwin had stayed with us for two years before the war. We'd seen him in the village recently. He was now married and had two children. So we made Kaduna Beth's first choice. We would learn the exam results in April.

My teaching career at the American School was over, and I missed not the school but the teaching. I was enjoying my piano pupils, however, and I began practicing as I hadn't done since college. I had always played classical music; that year I discovered ragtime. The movie *Sting*, with Scott Joplin's *The Entertainer*, had won awards, and a movie biography of Scott Joplin had come out in 1977.

As Thanksgiving approached, I regretted not having the American connections the school had given me. How would I celebrate the holiday without any American connections? I remembered hearing mothers at AIS talk about the American Women's Club, AWC, and I had already been using their small lending library for children's books. I went to a meeting. I had little in common with the forty or fifty women, but I knew a few whose children I'd taught. And I enjoyed the conversation about Thanksgiving celebrations.

I heard women complain about cooks who didn't understand their directions and nannies who behaved in puzzling ways. I decided right then to adopt the role of interpreter of Nigerian customs that these women found baffling. The next month, I wrote an article for the newsletter. "Your cook has the same desire for a better life for his children that you do. He wants to please you. His difficulty in following your directions comes from his unwillingness to ask questions, a habit bred into him from early childhood," I said.

At the meeting after the newsletter came out, two women approached me. "That article was helpful," one said. "I'm trying to be more patient with my cook, though it's hard sometimes."

"I agree," said the other. "You explained some of my difficulty well. I told my husband about Nigerians who won't ask for an explanation when they're given directions, and he said it's the same at his job." I was proud to illuminate Nigeria and its customs for these women and their families.

In January 1978, I was asked to join the board. Philanthropy had been part of the mission of the club since its inception. But the discussion about the charitable cause at the time, the Motherless Babies Home, seemed paternalistic. I didn't want to be part of fundraising or events for "those poor Nigerian babies." My husband and so many other Nigerians were talented and educated, running their own businesses or running the government. Besides, Clem and I had enough to do to support people in our family and clan.

Then the president introduced the topic of governance. "Is there anyone who would volunteer to head a committee for bylaws revision?" The club's constitution and bylaws had been written in the 1960s. After a decade of feminism and a much larger membership, some changes in language and procedures were needed.

"I'd be interested in that." I looked around after I spoke and saw Mary, across the table, making a face as she said, "You like that stuff—rules and procedures?"

"I like creating procedures that work. And I like organizational structures that make sense." I also wanted to lead something, even a committee. Two other women from the board agreed, though without great enthusiasm, to help. I was good at the nitty-gritty details, and they knew the recent history of the organization. We worked well together. Two months later, I presented our recommended revisions, and the board approved. The changes would go to the whole membership for a vote in June, and the project was my stepping-stone to becoming president the following year.

I bought more trade beads, and on a trip to London with Clem, I found a shop that sold bits and pieces I could use in my jewelry making. These were the hooks, different sizes of nylon fishing line, and filler beads to use in jewelry making, called "findings," a new word for me. I bought tiny pliers to use in bending the hooks and tying the nylon. I had bought a heavy wooden bar with three leather-covered barstools, and I set these up as a room divider between the living and dining areas. I could now spread out my beads and implements and leave unfinished projects. I added books on African beads.

I sold a few necklaces and earrings at American Women's Club craft fairs. I'd never before thought of myself as artistic or creative, and this gave me a thrill.

In early spring of 1978, President Carter announced a visit to Nigeria. He was bringing Rosalyn and Amy. This was a major diplomatic event for the Nigerian government and a major social event for the American community in Nigeria. I was invited, with other American Women's Club board members, to the ambassador's residence for a Saturday evening reception for the Carters. "What can I give Mrs. Carter that shows her the beauty of Nigeria?" I said to Priscilla, the mother of my newest piano pupils.

"Your necklaces are lovely," she said. "Why don't you make one for her?" I loved the idea and worked hard over a necklace with several lovely chevrons—blue, white, and red beads of different sizes. I wrote a note to go with it to say that I wanted her to have something from the country that I, an American citizen and former Peace Corps volunteer, had made my home.

"Thank you very much. This is lovely," said the aide to whom I handed the package. "But the Carters have agreed not to accept personal gifts. Mrs. Carter will be told, but the necklace will go with all gifts into a vault at the White House. If you decide not to donate it, I'll understand." I kept it. A few weeks later, I displayed it at the American Women's Club craft fair, with a sign, "Necklace made for First Lady Rosalyn Carter, but declined, as are all personal gifts."

Before the Carters left, there was a swimming party at the ambassador's for ten-year-old Amy Carter. Beth was invited. I was excited for her to be swimming with the president's daughter at the residence of the ambassador. For her, it was just another fun afternoon.

I knew the exam results were due to be announced soon. One evening, Jean, still at Exams Council, came over with her husband, Johnson. "The results are completed," she said when I placed their drinks on the side tables.

"I didn't know," I said, pausing on my way to my chair. "Can you tell us?"

"They're not public, but I thought you'd like to know. Beth came first in the whole country," she said.

I could hardly believe what she said. Clem was visibly swelling with pride. "She clearly takes after me," he said with a huge grin.

"Don't tell her yet," Jean said as I started toward the stairs. "The official results will be published in the next couple of days."

Three days later, results were printed in the *Daily Times*, and there was Beth's name at the top! Mrs. Payne called her to the front at the next morning's assembly at St. Saviour's, and the whole school applauded her achievement.

In late April, Beth received a letter from Queens College inviting her to an interview, even though it hadn't been our first choice. Though we were still determined that she would go to Kaduna, five hundred miles away where Clem's cousin Edwin lived, I nevertheless took her to the interview. I waited in the hall while she went into the room with two staff members.

"There was a mouse in the corner, behind the women interviewing me," Beth said when she emerged twenty minutes later. "I kept looking at it, and I don't think I answered their questions. It was hard to concentrate."

"Did you tell them about it?" I said, embracing her.

"Yes, but every time they turned around to look, it disappeared. Maybe they thought I was making it up." Two years later, Beth and I laughed about the mouse when we were at Queens College for the Royal Academy piano exams.

Despite the mouse distracting her, Beth was asked to come to Queens. But Kaduna also invited her, and she agreed to follow our original choice and go away as her brother had done. So in September of 1978, I flew with her to Kaduna.

Edwin's wife, Evelyn, came with us to find Beth's dorm and choose a bed. The dormitory was as uninviting as Chinaku's; again I kept my opinion to myself. I knew she would make her own space organized and as comfortable as possible.

I took Beth with me to the principal's office to greet Miss Gentle, who assured me she would keep an eye on my daughter. Still, I was as torn as I'd been with Chinaku and could barely contain my tears as I said good-bye. She looked so young and vulnerable.

At home that evening, Sam was even sadder than I was. I didn't even want to think about how I would feel when he'd leave home in another few years. When Clem came home, we all three sat down to a miserable dinner together.

Chinaku, now starting his third year at Enugu, wasn't learning to speak Igbo, which had been one of our goals, but he continued to write regularly except when he ran out of stamps or aerograms. He frequently reported on basketball games and his achievements. Nearly every letter said he was studying hard.

Sometimes his letters were painful. "My money was stolen. Please can you send me ten naira, so I can buy provisions," he said in late October. Then in November, with still a month and a half before the Christmas holidays, he ended a letter with, "I can't wait to get home." I also couldn't wait to see him.

Beth's letters, too, came regularly. She didn't say she was homesick, but it was clear from her comments. One letter in October had a drawing on the back, which said, "I want to come home." But most of her news was cheerful.

Then came an upsetting note where she said, "If anyone is coming to see me, tell them it is extremely compulsory to come on Sunday between 4:00 p.m. and 6:00 p.m. Otherwise, I'll get punished." This seemed somewhat extreme. Beth had hardly ever been punished at home, and I hated to hear that she had to worry about it. I didn't suspect that worse was to come from her school.

I had more than my absent children to worry about at home. "I missed you," Clem said as he hugged me with more enthusiasm than usual on his evening return from a trip to London. It was early December 1978, so he wore his black winter coat. The wool felt scratchy against me. He was beginning to get a little chubby. The roundness of his face was more pronounced than when we'd met.

"You look happy. Was your trip useful?"

"Yes, very."

Before he could elaborate, Sam bounded down the stairs to grab him with seven-year-old enthusiasm. "Did you bring me something?" he said.

Clem pulled a bag of peanuts from the pocket of his coat and handed it to Sam, who tore it open and stuffed a handful of nuts into his mouth.

"I got a house point for my drawing," he said, chewing.

"What did you draw?" Clem asked. "Aren't you going to offer me any nuts?"

"I drew a leopard," Sam said, giving Clem a tiny amount of the nuts. "House points" were a concept I'd learned from the children's early days at St. Saviour's. The children were assigned randomly to one of four houses or clusters, all named for birds. Beth's had been hornbills. Sam's was egrets. The house with the most points was recognized at the end-of-term assembly, and the other children had to cheer for them.

Sam ran back upstairs; he'd had dinner earlier while I had waited for Clem. The steward, Damian—hired a year earlier—brought our meal of pounded yam and bitterleaf soup to the table while Clem began telling me about his conversations with Tom Wright and the London bankers for his Benue State project. We finished eating and took turns washing our hands in the basin Damian brought.

Clem moved back to the sitting area to watch the 9:00 p.m. news. I joined him. When the newscast ended, I went up to unpack Clem's suitcase. I always took care of packing for his trips—I was neat and organized, and he was the opposite. I unzipped the cover, lifted the top, and gasped. His clothes were as neatly folded as when I'd packed them. His favorite blue tie was on top next to the other three ties, the shirts that needed laundering were just below them, and his socks were all in pairs.

I was stunned; had he suddenly become orderly? What could have caused this change? Then it hit me. Someone had packed for him. Of course! He was having an affair.

The realization stunned me. So that's why he had been so warm in his embrace. He was feeling guilty. How could he? Tears of anger welled up. I left the suitcase as it was and started downstairs to confront him.

I paused on the landing halfway down. I recalled a conversation we'd had a week before our wedding. "You know that those affairs never mean anything," Clem had said when I asked him if he would behave as many other Nigerian men did. "Besides, I love you. Why would I take up with another woman?"

I had thought I was safe. Coming up on our fourteenth wedding anniversary, I was less naïve. Still, I had convinced myself that if Clem did stray, I would accept and know it was not a sign he didn't love me. It would be an affair for casual sex, meaningless in the context of our family life. But that was before the reality.

Now I was deeply hurt and humiliated. Maybe I just wasn't attractive to him anymore. Should I challenge him? I knew he would deny it and make up an explanation for the packing. At worst, he would admit it and give me some lame excuse—how it wasn't really his fault. I couldn't bear to hear him bluster with lies or self-defense.

I continued down the stairs. "Why don't you go to bed?" I said when I found him asleep in front of the TV. "I'll be up later." He didn't notice my flat tone. I gave him plenty of time to find the suitcase, pull out his wrapper, and get into bed before going up myself. I didn't want any chance of his attempting to make love. I was more relieved than ever at his ability to fall asleep in less than thirty seconds and sleep soundly through my tossing and turning.

The next morning, he called to me while I was getting out of the bath. "You didn't unpack my suitcase."

"No, I didn't. You can unpack it yourself." I said nothing more, and he didn't ask why. I guessed that he knew the answer. I didn't confront him, and we didn't discuss his suitcase or my discovery for a long time. But I never packed for him again.

Over the next few days, I reflected on what I'd uncovered. It wasn't a great surprise to learn that Clem was not so different from other Nigerian men. And I had imbibed enough of the Nigerian way of thinking to believe that infidelity didn't necessarily lead to divorce.

So I stayed quiet, got over my initial anger and embarrassment, and carried on. When Beth and Chinaku came home from their boarding schools for the holidays, I was busy with preparations for Christmas.

Clem had always made a big deal of his worries about presents when December rolled around. He had to find a birthday gift for me on December 13, then Christmas, and finally our anniversary on the day after Christmas. Because he had missed my birthday this year—he'd come back two days after—he made a point of saying that he had a special gift for me for Christmas.

Chinaku assumed his role of giving out the presents. He handed me a beautifully wrapped box from Clem.

"Who chose this?" I said when I opened it to see a delicate gold filigree necklace.

"Why do you ask?" Clem said with a look of surprise.

"Don't you like it, Mommy?" Beth said.

"It's beautiful. It's just not the sort of gift Daddy has usually given me."

"I'll take it back if you don't like it," Clem said.

"No, no, it's fine. Thank you," I said with a quick kiss. But I didn't put it on. After lunch, I took it upstairs and put it away in my jewelry box. I didn't look at it again for weeks.

The day passed peacefully, with a visit to Jean and Johnson and preparing for our trip to the East the next day. Clem and I wished each other a happy anniversary quietly the next morning before packing the car and driving off to Nanka. I'd seen a card he'd bought for me, but he didn't even give it to me, and I didn't have one for him.

We were confined together in the car, with the children in the backseat, and we relaxed a little with each other. Christmas holidays in Nanka had become an annual ritual. Some years we went before Christmas and some years, like this one, just after. The first night was for seeing the closest relatives or making any required condolence calls on families whose relatives had died during the last year. We made our usual visit to Agulu, ate the soup prepared by Nne Julie, and enjoyed the dancers and the masquerades, who were plentiful that year. We shared a double bed, and by the third night, without discussion about his affair, we made love again. When we returned to Lagos, we were almost normal with each other. I hadn't forgotten, but I was ready to move on.

A few days after our return to Lagos, Chinaku and Beth went back to their schools, Sam was again on his own at home, and I began another teaching assignment—Igbo lessons for other foreign wives of Igbo men. First Joanne, a fellow American who had taught with me at the American School, and then Joan, from the West Indies, asked me to help them learn. Soon Katia, an Italian woman, and Lorraine, another American, joined the lessons. We gathered weekly at my dining room table.

The levels, or tones, in Igbo were a challenge. "Listen to my name— Onyemelukwe. It has five syllables, and they are low, high, mid, mid, and high." They tried. I used easier words, but they couldn't remember the tones. When they got frustrated, I said, "Even if you can say just a few words, your husband and his family will be so appreciative. And when they laugh—and they will—they are expressing their joy. They are not attempting to embarrass you."

When I saw the husbands of my Igbo students, I explained to them that I had an ear for music, and they should commend their wives for trying but not be critical of mistakes. They were grateful for my efforts and usually patient with their wives' difficulties.

It was weeks before we got to simple sentences like, *"Anam eje afia.* I am going to the market." We sometimes ended in laughter. But I wasn't discouraged. Teaching, whether at the three schools where I had worked or now with my Igbo and piano students, came naturally to me.

20

JOINING, SINGING, ORGANIZING

WHEN I HAD gone to my first AWC meeting a year earlier, I wasn't sure I belonged. Now I knew that I did. The board members had appreciated my work on bylaws revisions and articles about Nigeria. I was rewarded in the spring of 1979 when I was nominated to be president, a first for a woman married to a Nigerian.

The recognition helped assuage my feelings of self-doubt that had arisen since I discovered Clem's affair. The election would take place at the annual meeting in June, and if elected, I would preside over the opening meeting in the fall of 1979 at the American ambassador's residence. My election was pretty certain since I was the only nominee—when I had revised the bylaws, I had confirmed the single slate of nominees.

Yet, I was still pondering my next career move. So I was ready for the suggestion that Clem made that spring. He returned from another trip to London. I didn't even look at his suitcase. But when he unpacked, he brought out three brightly patterned cotton skirts with a white ruffle extending below the hem, popular in London. "You like to sew," he said. "You could make skirts like these and sell them."

I stared at him. "I sew for myself and Beth, not for selling."

"But you could, or you could hire others to sew."

"Yes, I probably could. But what makes you think women here would buy these?" I said.

"Well, clothing from abroad is banned. The women in the UK are buying them, so wouldn't women in Nigeria?"

"I suppose they might," I said, beginning to see his point. "Most women want to be fashionable."

Certainly the economic situation offered an opportunity. Nigeria was faced with a shortage of foreign exchange because of a drop in demand for its oil. The Central Bank put restrictions on importation of many foreign goods, including clothing.

Like other women who traveled abroad, I bought clothing to bring back with me. Now, with the restriction on importation of garments, we cut off tags and packed our purchases so they didn't stand out as new. Clem had reason to think this might be a smart business.

"What would it take for you to set up a sewing business?" he said.

"I have no idea. But I'll investigate." I was getting interested and glad he'd thought of this. I was sure there was a market for well-made women's clothing, though I didn't believe we could sew skirts like these for more than one season.

The next day, I called Singer Sewing Machines. David, the general manager whom we knew, was away for a couple of weeks. By the time he returned, Beth and Chinaku were home, and Sam was out of school for the summer. I let the matter rest until September. I didn't know then that September would bring another crisis that would delay my business planning.

Clem and I had attended a performance two years earlier of *Kiss Me, Kate*. "I think I'll see if I can join this group. It looks like such fun," I had said to Clem during the intermission.

"No, you won't," he said.

"Since when do you decide what I will or won't do?"

"Well, I don't think you should be singing or dancing in front of an audience. What you do reflects on me," he said with a frown and a rueful smile. I knew he only half believed what he was saying.

"Don't worry. I won't embarrass you." But the intermission ended as I spoke, and the applause for the start of the next act drowned out my answer. After the performance, Clem and I spoke with a few of the performers. I asked about rehearsals and went to my first a month later, by chance when Clem was away. By late 1978, just weeks before I learned about his affair, I had performed with the group for the first time. Clem came, and he wasn't embarrassed at all.

I loved singing again. I had missed it. Teaching piano was fun, but making music with a group was a pleasure all its own. As I got to know people in the group, I joined the planning committee. Gradually, I became part of the decision-making process about what to perform.

While Nigeria's foreign exchange shortage was providing an impetus for me to think about the sewing business, it also led me to the creation of a new organization.

For years, the foreign wives of Nigerians had enjoyed a special status that allowed us to send half our salaries to an overseas account. Since returning to the American School after the Biafran War, I had regularly sent 50 percent of my salary to an account in Fort Thomas that I'd had since my teen years. It was a little security blanket.

But in early 1978, the Central Bank had decreed that remittances for foreign wives would be limited to 10 percent of our salaries.

"What are you doing about this change?" Jean had said to me when Clem and I were at their house on a May evening in 1978, after we'd learned about Beth's stunning performance in the Common Entrance Exam. "I have written a letter to the minister of finance."

"Do you really think he will pay attention to your letter?" her husband said, laughing.

"You don't know unless you try," she said.

A few days later, I was speaking to an American friend, Doris, about the cut in our remittances. "Jean wrote a letter to the minister. Maybe if you and I and a few others wrote, too, it would have an effect," I said.

"It's worth a try. I'll write today," she said. I sent a letter of my own.

A month later, I saw Jean again. None of us had a response.

"Maybe we need to think about a strategy together," she had said. I invited her and Doris to meet at my house. Jean suggested inviting her friend Josephine. Over tea, we talked about our dilemma.

"One by one, we're not going to get anywhere," Doris said. "Even if ten people write, it won't make a difference."

Our conversation progressed until someone said, "We need an organization behind our request."

"Yes, but what organization?" I said. "British Wives and the American Women's Club wouldn't be interested in this, would they? Most of their members aren't affected."

Between us, we gradually came up with a plan—an organization of foreign wives of Nigerians, the group directly affected. I agreed to draft bylaws. Jean knew how to get an organization registered.

"What do we call ourselves?" Jean said as the four of us sat at my dining room table a week later.

After several minutes of suggested names that did not ring true with us, we hit on it: Nigerwives. We also thought about our purpose. Our immediate goal was to restore the 50 percent foreign remittance, but we soon realized that we had a broader mission of helping foreign wives of Nigerians live satisfying lives in our adopted country.

By late 1978, we had registered our organization. Soon we had twenty members, and then thirty. We began to meet at St. Saviour's Church hall. I became the first president, with Josephine as vice president.

Clem thought this was all a pleasant diversion. When we talked more seriously about getting our 50 percent remittance restored, he paid attention. Though the amounts I had sent were never large, he liked knowing that I had money in the United States.

Josephine had the best connections with government officials, and she was able to get an appointment for us. We waited half an hour before being shown into the office of the deputy minister of finance. "Thank you for agreeing to meet with us," Josephine began when we were seated. "We are the officers of a new organization, Nigerwives, and we are here to make a request." She handed him the letter and explained what we wanted.

"We understand that you are concerned about finances for you and your families when you visit your homes," he said. "But we have to consider the position of foreign exchange for the country. We will give every consideration to your request." His sanctimonious comments gave us little hope. One of our husbands offered to help, and although we weren't happy to depend on a husband to pull strings, we were ecstatic when we were notified quietly that we could again send our 50 percent.

The summer of 1979 started calmly. Chinaku and Beth came home from their boarding schools about the same time Sam's term at St. Saviour's ended. We celebrated Beth's twelfth birthday on June 25 with her friends from St. Saviour's and a new friend from her Kaduna boarding school who lived nearby. They played the Jackson Five, danced, and sang along.

Friends from his St. Saviour's days came to Chinaku's fourteenth birthday on June 29. They retreated to Chinaku's room upstairs after they had their ice cream and cake.

On days it didn't rain, I took them all to Ikoyi Club to swim and play tennis. On other days, I drove them to Aigboje's, where they would spend hours with their friends. Clem and I took them with us on the weekends or evenings to Johnson's and Ben's homes and to church.

I was proud of everything about my children—their sporting ability, their pleasant behavior, their intelligence, and their good looks. Chinaku was now taller than Clem and close to me in height. His hair was cut close to his head as his school required. Beth and Sam had short hair, too, Beth's in tight curls and Sam's softer and looser.

In July 1979, I led my first board meeting as president of the American Women's Club, where we planned the calendar for the year and prepared for the opening meeting in September. I was excited about my role and the year ahead.

Clem and I took the children to Madeira for several days with my parents and then on to London in August. I had furnished our house on Trinity Close in the Hampstead area of London. I felt very sophisticated walking up the steep hill past the Mulberry store, which sold unusual women's clothing, to the tube station at the corner of Hampstead High Street and Heath Street, where we could get the Northern Line into the center of London.

When I had been in London in the spring, I'd found a summer camp for Chinaku. I thought he'd prefer that to hanging around with me and his siblings during all three weeks in London. So he went off to Olympia Sports Camp, while I dragged Beth and Sam around to museums and shopping. They complained, "Why can't we take a taxi?" But it was a badge of honor for me to figure out the underground and buses, so I rarely gave way to their wish.

I had grown in my self-awareness and sense of power in the years since leaving the American International School. Nigerwives, the American Women's Club, and Ikoyi Singers each provided me with a sense of my own influence, independence, and ability to lead. Having our own place in London added to my sense of self.

I had also picked up enough of the women's movement in the States and read enough to know that other women seemed to find more pleasure and excitement in lovemaking than I had recently with Clem. In fact, our love life had become somewhat boring since my return from the United States in June 1976. Or I had become more aware.

The discovery of Clem's affair was in the background but not forgotten. All of these forces led me in unexpected directions, including a final return to the United States.

21

PAPA'S DEATH AND THE DIBIA

We were due to return to Lagos in a few days. Chinaku was back from camp. The children had cleared the table and were watching TV. Clem and I were making plans for the next day when the phone rang.

"Good evening, Cathy. I'm sorry to call so late. I have sad news. Is Clem awake?"

I recognized the voice. "It's Jonathan. Something is wrong." I gave Clem the phone.

"No, no, it can't be true. Are you sure?" I watched his eyes tighten and fill with tears, his eyebrows drawn together.

"What is it?" I said, touching his arm.

"He wasn't even sick. How could this be?" Clem ignored me, gripping the phone tightly. Then he changed his mind. "Talk to Cathy," he said. Unable to listen further, he handed the phone back to me.

"What happened, Jonathan?"

"Papa had a stroke this afternoon. Before we could even get him to the hospital, he was dead."

"Oh, my God! I can't believe it. Poor Mama," I said. "We'll be there as soon as we can," I said. "Please tell her we are on our way."

I hung up and looked at Clem, his face twisted in pain. I held out my arms and pulled him to me. I had never seen him cry before, and his grief tore at me. I wanted to protect him, though I couldn't change what had happened.

I was the model of efficiency the next morning. Back in Lagos, I called the vice president of the Women's Club. "You may have to run the opening meeting on September 13," I said. "My husband's father died suddenly, and I need to go to the East. I'll come back if I can."

We all piled into the car and headed to Nanka. Our trips to Clem's hometown were usually happy occasions but not this time. I tried to lighten the atmosphere as Clem drove. "Do you remember when Papa was so frightened about Mama's going to Aguleri to buy fish during the war?" I said.

"Yes," he said, coming out of his misery for a moment. "And do you remember how Papa said the name 'Chinakueze' when he first held him? He was so proud to have a grandson." I looked around to see if Chinaku had heard. He was smiling broadly.

"I remember how he shook his stick at us when we skidded along the veranda in the rain," Beth said. Chinaku and Sam laughed and imitated Papa's gesture.

It was raining as we drove but let up when we reached Nanka around five in the afternoon. As we drove the two miles down the muddy road to our house, I wondered how Mama was feeling. What would she be doing? I knew there were traditions to be followed, but I wasn't sure what they were, and Clem was in no mood to provide explanations. When we pulled into the compound, he was caught up in his own grief.

Clem's mother was seated on a mat on the veranda at the front of the house. She was surrounded by women from Agulu, her hometown. She wore only a dark paisley wrapper tied over her breasts. I bent down to her. "Mama, I'm so sorry. We came as soon as we could." Clem leaned over and wiped her tears but couldn't keep his own back. They held each other, sobbing softly. The women around her started wailing just as I had seen at other condolence visits. I felt like I was watching a Greek chorus.

Papa's three remaining brothers, Clem's uncles, were seated in Ejike's hut in the next compound. They welcomed us with subdued greetings and offered us palm wine. I could see that they were in shock. They'd lost their sibling, the next to youngest, so suddenly and unexpectedly. All three of them had regarded Papa with some admiration and even deference because he'd left the village life. He'd gone to school briefly and had become a Christian. He'd run away when the other young men his age were undergoing scarification of their faces. He'd become successful enough in his work and business to pay for the education of his own children and even some of theirs.

We sat with them briefly but declined the palm wine Ejike offered and went back to sit with Mama until someone called us for supper. I had looked in the kitchen earlier and realized that it had been taken over by Mama's relatives. I wouldn't have to cook.

The next morning, Obi, the youngest uncle, told me that he was going to visit the dibia. I remembered the two times I knew when a dibia had been consulted. The first was to prevent rain for Chinaku's naming ceremony, and the second was to appease the ancestors after the snake was killed.

I guessed this visit was about the weather—it was the rainy season—and the wake and funeral would be outdoors. I was intrigued. The dibia couldn't prevent rain anytime, of course. Wouldn't he be discredited if he said he could? So what would he tell Obi when he heard the request?

"I would like to go with you," I said.

"You can come," he said, "but I will do the talking." That seemed reasonable.

Obi led me out of the compound and across the road. We passed Nnadi's compound, opposite ours, and walked for about fifteen minutes, entering a part of the village I'd never seen before. It was densely populated, similar to the area around our compound, with stone walls separating one family property from the next.

Obi turned into one of the compounds. "It's here," he said as he preceded me across an open area toward the hut in the center. I approached it with a little trepidation, wondering how the dibia would receive me, a foreigner.

I'd never met a dibia before. Although I was sure he could not influence the weather, I did believe he could exert psychological power. What would he be like?

"Remove your shoes," Obi whispered as we stooped to enter. I could barely make out the person inside in the dim light. Then the dibia spoke, and I saw him seated cross-legged on the floor. He welcomed us with the customary greetings. "*Nno unu*. Welcome."

"*Dalu*. Thank you."

I took my place on the floor, sitting in front of him as he indicated, with Obi beside me. Gradually, my eyes adjusted. "How is your family?" he said, continuing in Igbo. "They are fine. And yours?" I said after Obi had answered.

The dibia had a wrinkled face with penetrating eyes, gray hair, and slender limbs.

The woven raffia mat where he sat showed red and green edges, but with use had mostly faded to dull beige. On his right was a well-worn, black leather bag. A cracked clay pot with a narrow opening was on his left. Several small animal skulls, leaves, and feathers hung from the rafters. The thatch roof rose to a peak of sixteen feet or so and sloped down over the walls.

The dibia reached into the leather bag by his side and brought out two kola nuts, saying in Igbo, "Creator of the universe, I thank you for this kola. I honor our ancestors. He who brings kola brings life." He broke one nut into four pieces, took a piece for himself, and placed the other nut and the remaining pieces on a small enamel plate for us. Though I sometimes only palmed the bitter nut, this time I thought prudence required chewing and swallowing.

Obi explained the purpose of our visit. "You know that our papa, Clement's father, Samuel, will be buried in a few days." This was no surprise to the dibia, who already knew, as everyone in the village did, that Papa had died.

"When an important man dies, the earth trembles," the dibia said.

"We have come to ask you to intercede with the spirits who control the elements. The wake will take place on Oye in two weeks," Obi said. "The next day, Afor, will be the funeral. The chief will be there and many other important people. It is the rainy season, and only you can assure that there will be no rain for these events."

"Yes, you are correct that I am the one who can talk to the spirits," the dibia said. "I have practiced my craft for many years. I can ask the spirits to hold back the rain."

I was impressed by his calm manner and self-assurance, but they didn't make me a believer. He's hedging his bets, I thought, as he continued, "I cannot say if the spirits will comply. I know that Samuel's life was long and his children many. The whole village mourns him."

He reached again into his leather bag and retrieved a few dry seeds the size of lima beans and scattered them on the mat. He seemed to pray, explaining the need and calling on the gods to help him. He gathered and threw the seeds two more times. Then he announced in a confident voice that the prognosis was positive.

"With the correct offerings and the instructions I will give you, the rain will stay away," he said. He asked us to come back with five large yams, two chickens, five kola nuts, a jug of palm wine, a bottle of schnapps, and one thousand naira, about twenty-five dollars. He insisted that the chickens should be *okuko agric*, or agricultural chickens, from a farm that was operated by the district government to produce larger, more tender poultry than the chickens that fended for themselves.

Obi protested, "This is a very heavy offering that the spirits request. We have many expenses because of the funeral. We have to buy not just one but two cows, and we must also pay the butcher."

"You are asking me to halt the rain in the rainy season. You think that it is easy? The spirits need to be appeased if they are to comply," the dibia said.

"I know it is not easy, and I know that you are the expert," I said, despite Obi's instruction that he should do the talking. I was proud of my bargaining skills and Igbo language, and this was an ideal opportunity to put them to work. "That is why we are asking for your intervention. But we are only asking you to halt the rain for one night and one day, not for a week!"

I was using my learned negotiating power to bargain in a tribal language with a dibia to get him to halt the rain. Had I lost my mind? What if my family or American friends could see me now?

Eventually, we reached agreement on the offering: two large yams, one agricultural chicken, five hundred naira, and the other items. We thanked him, promised to return in two days, and took our leave. Obi and I divided up the tasks.

Early the next morning, I drove to the government farm in Ekwulobia, ten miles away on a paved, but much worn, road. Because this was a government agency and prices were fixed, I couldn't bargain for the chicken. So I handed over three hundred fifty naira and took the struggling hen by its legs, tied together with raffia, to the car. I bought the schnapps at one of the small supermarkets nearby.

While I was making my purchases, Obi was arranging for the other items. He sent a message to his favorite palm wine tapper to bring the fresh palm wine. He asked Ejike to provide the yams, and he bought the kola nuts. When I got home, I counted out five hundred naira in crisp new bills and put them in a small white envelope. Obi and I compared notes and decided we were prepared.

The following morning, we called two young boys to carry our gifts. Obi balanced a yam on each boy's head. Obi gave the jug of palm wine to the older boy, and I handed the struggling chicken to the younger. Obi himself carried the bottle of schnapps, the money, and the kola, all stored in his own ancient leather bag.

After the greetings, Obi said, "We have brought the gifts the spirits asked for." He motioned to the boys to bring in their loads while he took out the schnapps, kola nuts, and money and spread them on the dibia's mat.

"You have done well," the dibia said. "I will break kola for you again." The rituals of two days before were repeated. I ate the kola again. "Take this," he said, handing Obi a calabash. I couldn't imagine what magical properties it held. It was a ten-inch, dirty tan sphere, with a three-inch opening at the top. "Keep it with you, and if it looks like rain is starting to fall, you should rub it. Listen carefully to what you need to say." He spoke quickly in Igbo. I heard him say ancestors, rain, and Samuel but couldn't catch the rest.

I don't think the dibia believed a white woman would have the necessary power to convince the spirits. Given that I was still a doubter, he was right not to entrust the task to me. Maybe no woman would be entrusted with this role. I was happy to let Obi take responsibility. We thanked the dibia again and departed.

We had done what we could about the weather. Now we had another major issue to face. Igbo custom demanded that Mama shave her head when her husband died, and she refused. She and Papa had joined one of the evangelical churches in the village. "It's a pagan custom, and my church says I shouldn't do it," she said.

But the *umu ada*, the women of the Onyemelukwe family and the larger clan, insisted on keeping the tradition. "We will boycott the funeral, and we will block the compound so no one can enter unless she does what she should," they announced. "She is trying to shame us."

"She's doing no such thing," I said to Clem when we were upstairs, out of earshot of Mama or any of the *umu ada*. I thought the custom of a wife shaving her head was barbaric. I had little sympathy for the evangelical church either, but I did believe in women's rights. "She's standing up for her beliefs, as she should."

"No, she shouldn't. She really doesn't have a choice," he said. I wanted to defend her, but I couldn't persuade Clem that her opinion was more important than what seemed to me like a tradition that could be discarded. It was her head, after all.

The wake and funeral were still several days off. I had alerted my vice president of the American Women's Club that I might not make it for the opening meeting, but I badly wanted to be there for my debut as president.

"What do you think?" I said to Clem later that night. "I could make a quick trip to Lagos—it's only 350 miles, and the driver can take me. I'll be back in two days." He agreed, so early the next morning, I left him with the children in the village and departed for the American side of my life, the complete opposite to the village. I wondered if, and how, the contest between Mama and the *umu ada* would be resolved while I was away.

In Lagos the next day, I dressed and applied my makeup carefully before driving to the ambassador's residence, arriving a few minutes before the meeting was due to start. Ambassador Easum met me. I had last seen him at the reception for President and Mrs. Carter. I asked about his son, whom I'd known at the American School.

"John is fine. My wife has already taken him back to the United States so he can start the school year. You know, I'm leaving next month," he said.

"I didn't know; I'm sorry to hear that. You'll leave a gap. Where will the music community find another trumpeter like you?" I knew he was well liked by Nigerian leaders and would be missed for his diplomatic skills as well.

I called the meeting to order. "Thank you for hosting us," I said to the ambassador, "and for your service to our country and our relations with Nigeria." I turned to the audience. "Thank you for the honor you've given me to serve as your president." I announced upcoming events, introduced the other officers, and asked them to give their reports.

As I looked out at the one hundred well-dressed American women seated comfortably on white chairs on the lawn of the spacious embassy residence, I couldn't help comparing them with the group of mourning Igbo women seated on the floor of the veranda in Nanka that I had left twenty-four hours earlier.

My two worlds were such a contrast. I was the confident and capable president of the American Women's Club, easily conversing with the American ambassador and addressing a crowd of one hundred women. I was also the daughter-in-law of a woman who had to deal with the heartrending decision of whether to shave her head to honor her dead husband, as custom dictated, or remain true to her principles. And I had asked the dibia to hold back the rain.

In an hour, the meeting was over. I visited with several women before getting back in the car. By evening, I was in the village again. Mama still sat on the veranda. Her head was bare, and the dried blood of razor cuts was evident. Her face was streaked with traces of tears. She seemed more forlorn than she had when we first arrived a few days earlier.

I bent over her again as I had then. "You tried, Mama," I said in Igbo. "I was hoping you would succeed, but I can see you couldn't." My heart hurt for her. She was a strong-willed woman. Yet she'd had to give in. The pressure of the *umu ada* and Igbo custom had defeated even her spunky character. The funeral would proceed.

What would happen to me if Clem died, indeed when, not if? We were still young, so I didn't fear his imminent demise. But what if he died unexpectedly and the *umu ada* insisted I shave my head? Would I get a pass for being a foreigner? Customs give way as people change, and I didn't have to face the question now. Maybe I never would.

The next afternoon, I went with Clem and Jonathan to accompany the hearse that would bring Papa's body back from the morgue in Onitsha, thirty miles away. Because Jonathan was the Anglican bishop of Onitsha, we were given a police escort for our trip back to Nanka. The police car, siren blaring, led the way. Next was the hearse, then the three of us with the bishop's driver. Keeping up with the police car on the bad roads was extremely trying for the poor driver, a timid soul at best.

A heavy downpour started, making the already harrowing drive even more treacherous. Somehow we made it to Nanka without leaving any casualties along the road. Perhaps the dibia was intervening here as well to get the body back safely to the village.

The rain let up as Papa's body was taken into the house. He was laid on the bed that had been prepared in the living room, fully decorated with white lace and satin ribbons. The family gathered around. The bishop said a prayer. Clem simply bent over the body crying quietly for several minutes. His siblings likewise made their final farewells. Clem's mother, in keeping with Igbo custom, was not permitted to see her husband. She remained on her mat on the veranda with her female relatives surrounding and consoling her.

As the sun set, the wake began. Guests sat on folding metal chairs or benches borrowed from the church. The *umu ada*, having achieved what they wanted, had positions of honor to the right. The *ndi anutara di*, my group of women married into the family, was seated behind them. Papa's brothers, including Obi, sat in front of the veranda. I sat with my husband next to the brothers. As the compound filled, I watched ominous clouds gathering. I glanced at Obi. He pointed to the ground below his chair, where I saw the calabash.

I was torn. Part of me hoped the rain would cascade in buckets, everyone would have to disperse, and we would all see that the dibia couldn't prevent the rain. But the other part hoped that rain would actually start and Obi would stop it with the calabash, using the words the dibia had told him to say.

There were prayers, hymns, and songs, including a moving solo by Clem's sister Grace. After forty-five minutes, a light rain started to fall. "Oh, no," Clem said to me, "the wake will be ruined. There is no cover for all the people."

I turned to watch Obi pull the calabash from under his chair. He began rubbing it while muttering softly. I nudged Clem and pointed toward Obi.

"What's he doing?" Clem said.

"What does it look like?" I said. And as if on command, the rain stopped. "I guess I didn't tell you that I went with Obi to the dibia a few days ago," I said.

"I can't believe it! How did he agree to take you?"

"I just asked. The dibia didn't mind. We had to go back with offerings. That's when he gave Obi the calabash. And look at the result," I said, looking up at the night sky, cloudy and humid but free of rain. Obi kept the calabash beside him for the rest of the night and used it again when a few threatening drops fell.

I retreated to our bedroom around two in the morning. The recorded gospel music and occasional hymns from the people outside continued until four, when people dispersed, so I slept little.

As I hauled myself out of bed in the morning, I was surprised to see that there were fewer clouds. "Look," I said to Clem, "the dibia must have driven the clouds away." I laughed nervously at hearing myself. I sounded as if I believed in the power of the dibia. Whether or not, I was relieved as I dressed for the day.

Several young men had been at work early in the morning to dig the hole near the wall that divided our compound from Ejike's. Later that morning, we took our seats again as the crowd reassembled. Ejike, Obi, and Ebueme, the three remaining brothers, carried the coffin from the house. With barely a cloud in sight, Papa's body was laid in the simple grave in our compound.

Mama remained on the veranda surrounded by her cohort of relatives. How sad that she couldn't say good-bye to the man she had married nearly fifty years earlier. But she had bowed to other traditions before, as she had in the last week. Her church people sang a hymn while the coffin was lowered.

Then Jonathan led the Anglican funeral litany. "Dust to dust," he said, as the grave was covered with dirt.

Obi did not need the calabash again. He kept it, but it had no more power. The dibia had done his work. The summer that had started in a normal fashion had come to a sudden and unexpected end.

Mama stayed on her mat with her cohort around her, slipping away occasionally to take care of basic needs. She even slept on the mat. She would remain there for the traditional twenty-eight days, or the equivalent of seven Igbo market weeks, before taking up her new life as a widow.

The morning after the funeral, Edwin and his wife left for Kaduna, and we sent Beth with them. I gave her an especially warm hug and covered her with kisses when she was ready to get into the car. I didn't want to let her go.

The next day, Clem and I, with Sam in tow, drove Chinaku back to his school in Enugu. He took us in to show Sam his dorm room. Again I hated leaving him, even though he was now fourteen and entering his fourth year away. He made it clear that he didn't want an emotional display from me, so I kept my feelings to myself. I had been so happy having him and Beth with us for the summer, and now it would be Christmas before we'd see them again.

Our car felt empty as we headed back to Lagos. Sam seemed small and alone in the backseat. Clem was morose. I tried a couple of times to revitalize him with more of the "Do you remember?" conversation we'd had on our way to the East, but he was intent on mourning.

Sam was asleep by the time we reached Benin, roughly halfway to Lagos, and I felt the absence of the other children even more. I lamented their being far away where I couldn't share in their daily routines. I regretted the lack of music and other extracurricular activities in their schools. Their experience was so different from what mine had been. But I'd made this choice. Had I been wrong?

At the next American Women's Club meeting, I was standing on the veranda of our meeting location when a woman I'd spoken with frequently came over. "I met a friend of yours during the summer," she said. "I was in the Hamptons. He asked if I knew you."

"Who was it?" But I already suspected.

"His name is Art, and he owns a bookstore. He knew you in the Peace Corps. He implied that you were close."

"Yes, we were very close. I was fond of him," I said. "In fact, if I were ever to have an affair, it would be with Art." I surprised myself with the comment; perhaps it had snuck out from my subconscious mind.

I had been reflecting on my marriage and Clem's affair. The anger I had felt at first had changed to an attitude of release and permission. I didn't want a change in husband, but I did want a little more excitement. Maybe it was time for me to explore. Other women had affairs. Could I?

22

MY COMPANY AND MY FIRST AFFAIR

THE FUNERAL WAS over, the children were back at school, and the American Women's Club year had started. I was ready to move forward with planning my business. The thought of an affair stayed at the back of my mind, not an active pursuit but an awareness that I was open. I didn't have doubts about my marriage. I loved Clem, and I knew he loved me despite straying. But I felt I was a less important part of his life now that he was completely dedicated to his company.

I finally met with the Singer Sewing Machines representative and asked his advice on what machines and what staff I would need to start production. He gave me a detailed list—one hemmer, one buttonhole maker, and four basic, heavy-duty industrial machines. He drew a floor plan of the recommended layout. He told me delivery would take six weeks, once I placed a firm order and paid a deposit. Clem had agreed to fund the business start-up and operations for six months. I hoped I'd be able to break even after that and even make a profit. He'd done it with his business in a few months, after all. I told him the estimated cost for the first few machines, and he didn't complain. We discussed what I might have to pay for rent.

Charles, who had become a personal assistant for Clem during the Biafran War, now lived in our boys' quarters. He worked at Clem's company, Freeman Engineering, but he also performed personal tasks for Clem and me. I asked him to begin looking for a suitable space. In addition to three large rooms— for sewing, cutting, and office—I had other requirements: running water, reliable electricity, and good light for the sewers. I wanted to be near Ikoyi, where we lived.

I thought about dozens of other issues. Who would cut and supervise the sewing? I put an ad in the *Daily Times* for a production manager. Where would I find tailors? What would we sew? How would I get patterns and fabric? Where would I sell the clothes? What prices? The questions were almost overwhelming, but again, I assumed I would answer each of them when the time came.

"How about the name Freewoman? It matches Freeman, your company name," I said to Clem as I was preparing the business registration forms. "It's not too risqué, is it?"

"I don't think so," Clem said. "I like it; it fits you as long as you don't get too free." He reached over, smiling, to take my hand, while he shook a warning finger with his other hand.

"You mean I shouldn't behave like you?" I said.

"I don't know what you mean," he said, pulling back.

"I think you do," I said. His reaction was to bury his head in the company documents he was reading and sulk. I wrote Freewoman on the form. The next morning, I handed him the papers to mail, along with a smile and a hug. He left for his office looking more cheerful. At least he knew better than to ask me to apologize for upsetting him, as he would have done before his affair was uncovered.

A month later, I got a reply from the company registration office. "Freewoman is unacceptable. The name is not decent. It cannot be used," was scrawled in big red letters across my form.

"Wow. I guess we were wrong. The women's movement clearly hasn't reached Nigeria yet," I said when I showed Clem the rejection letter that evening.

I rethought the company name. What had a foreign sound that would give the business cachet and had meaning in my life? After tossing and turning for a good part of one night, I had it. Our house in Hampstead was one of three townhouses converted from Trinity Church, with the address Two Trinity Close. Trinity would also encompass the fact that I had three children. I resubmitted the registration papers with the name Trinity House of Fashion. It was accepted.

A few people responded to my ad for a production manager. I asked the likeliest candidate, Mr. Ogunade, to come to our house for an interview. I opened the door to a tall, lanky Yoruba man, dressed in trousers and open shirt.

"I was a tailor and then overseer for six years at Austin Reed in London," he said in his easy-to-understand, slightly accented English. He pulled out a letter of reference from a supervisor at the British men's clothing company to show me.

"Why did you leave?" I said.

"My wife didn't like London. She wanted to be near her family."

"What work did you do at Austin Reed?"

"I started there as a lead tailor, and before I left, I was supervising four other tailors. We made high quality menswear. In my last two years, we started a line of women's wear that I supervised," he said.

"If I give you a dress pattern in a size twelve, can you cut the fabric and then adjust and cut other sizes too? And do you know how to find tailors or seamstresses?"

"Of course," he said. "I can do sizing, and I know several tailors. Men would be better than women—they always have female problems or sick children." Despite his comment, I hired him to start as soon as we had a location.

While one part of my life was coming into shape, another was in trouble. I was worried about Beth. Her letter in mid-November 1979 had said, "I've been taking my vitamin pills every day. But I'm still often tired." I wondered if she was getting enough protein in the school meals. She didn't complain, though her notes to Sam indicated that she wasn't happy.

She'd also told us about her tomato plants, which she was growing as part of the school's emphasis on practical subjects. She'd been bothered when they didn't grow, but in late November they recovered. "My plants are getting fuller, and I have seven tomatoes." But when she came home at Christmas, her first words were, "My plants died. I will get a bad mark for agriculture, and I was punished." I was devastated.

"What? How could that be?" I hugged her and pulled her down beside me on the sofa. I knew she wouldn't have forgotten to water or tend her plants, so the failure was surely not her fault. "Don't worry," I said, as she started to cry. "I'm sure you did your best."

"I did, but they died anyway. I had to cut grass every afternoon when the others were harvesting their tomatoes," she said between her sobs.

Miss Gentle, the English headmistress, had retired at the end of Beth's first year as part of the Nigerianization of posts in education and the civil service. The idea of asking foreign employees to retire when there were Nigerians who could take the posts made sense, but I wondered about the quality of leadership at Beth's school. Had some relative of an official in the Ministry of Education become the headmaster, when he wasn't suited for the position? Did anyone supervise the agriculture teacher?

Chinaku came home a day later, and soon we were on our way to Nanka. It would be Clem's mother's first Christmas after Papa's death, and I hadn't hesitated when Clem said we should go early. Trinity House and Beth's school would wait until the holidays were over.

In January, I urged Clem to come with me to take Beth back to Kaduna and see the headmaster to ask why Beth was punished when her plants died. He agreed; his daughter's tears had upset him.

Beth accompanied us. We found the headmaster seated on the floor with a couple of teachers, eating rice and stew. His desk was piled with messy stacks of papers.

"Good afternoon," he said, from his position on the floor. "What can I do for you?"

"We are bringing our daughter back for the second term, and we were curious about the agriculture program," I said. He didn't stop eating or stand up.

"Is this your daughter?" He nodded toward Beth but clearly did not know her.

"Yes, she's a second-year student," Clem said. "She was unhappy when she came home for the holidays. Her tomato plants had died. She was punished but learned nothing about the cause."

"Yes, well, if her plants died, she must have done something wrong," he said, shoveling another spoonful of rice and stew into his mouth. Beth was near tears.

"Is that what you call teaching?" Clem said, looking ready to explode.

"Let's go," I said. "We're not getting anywhere here." I didn't want Clem to get into an argument that might make Beth's life more difficult.

Walking with her to her dorm, I felt like I was exiling her to months of misery. I cheered up a little when she ran into her friend Rakia, but I was determined she wouldn't be in this school any longer than necessary. I left her with a heavier heart than when I had first brought her. I was so glad Clem had been with me and concurred that a move would be good.

I had never before seriously considered Hillcrest, the American mission school in Jos, about one hundred miles further from Lagos than Kaduna, but suddenly it seemed like a viable alternative. I called my friend Joanne, who'd moved to Jos two years earlier. She reported that her children were happy, with many friends and good teachers. But would we be wasting Beth's excellent preparation at St. Saviour's, with its British style, by moving her to an American curriculum?

I decided her happiness and well-being were more important than academics, so I called the school. The principal encouraged me to bring her for placement tests and an interview. He recommended she join the second semester of seventh grade with students her own age.

Then we were almost stymied because Hillcrest didn't provide boarding at the school. Instead, there were hostels run by the Baptists, the Lutherans, and a couple of other denominations, and there was a nondenominational hostel. I called every one of them, but they were all full.

I called Joanne again. "Could you possibly let Beth stay with you? We could pay you for her board," I said. She agreed. Beth was soon feeling at home both at Joanne's and at school, where there was a healthy mix of Nigerians and children from other countries.

As soon as I returned to Lagos after getting Beth settled, Charles reported that he'd found a suitable location at a decent price. I asked Mr. Ogunade to meet me there.

The building at Ninety-Nine Lewis Street was in a busy area, a mix of business, retail, and residences. Charles led us down a narrow walkway at the side of the building to the unpainted stairwell and up to the second floor.

"It's not an impressive entrance with all that cement, but I think this space would work," I said over my shoulder to Mr. Ogunade. "Do you agree?"

He paced the length of the center room. "I would put my table here, under the windows." He spread his arms, index fingers pointing to the walls at each end, to indicate how long it would be. "Ten or twelve tailors can work in here," he said in the third room, which had windows on three sides. "The light is good."

I asked Charles to negotiate with the landlord while I raced home to call David at Singer to order the sewing machines. He promised rapid delivery of the first three. I could hardly wait until Clem was out of his car that evening to tell him. "I love the space. Mr. Ogunade says it will work. Charles is negotiating with the landlord."

I met Mr. Ogunade there on a sunny morning in February as soon as the lease was signed. He'd brought along a carpenter who would build his table. He had already put out the word in the immigrant community for tailors. Ghanaians, Togolese, and Beninoise came to apply. I asked him to hire one person to start, and he chose a Ghanaian named Maurice. We asked the others to come back in a few weeks.

"Why don't you want Nigerian tailors?" I said.

"They're not as reliable, and they may steal. These people are honest. They know they dare not misbehave, or I'll report them, and they'll be deported."

Clem sent Charles over in the Freeman van with spare desks and office chairs for us. Singer delivered the first three machines. I brought in a pattern for a shirtwaist dress. Mr. Ogunade brought his cutting scissors. I took him with me to buy fabric for our first production line of eight dresses.

"I thought fabrics were supposed to be banned," I said, laughing as we bought dozens of yards of clearly imported, lightweight, pale-blue poplin from one of the hundreds of cloth vendors near Tinubu, across the street from the Central Bank, the authority that had issued the ban.

"The ban is stupid. It just means that the government doesn't collect any import tax," he said. "Even when fabric wasn't banned, people smuggled a lot of it in to avoid the tax." How sad that in Nigeria, laws seemed to be made to be broken. "Anyway, no one would buy dresses made from Nigerian fabrics." He was right. The locally produced cloth was rough and would not drape. The colors were too sharp. It even smelled bad, like starch that had spoiled.

In our first month in the office, I applied for a telephone line, but Posts and Telegraphs, the phone utility, said there were no lines available in the neighborhood. Mr. Ogunade went to a lawyer he knew in the next building.

He came back to say, "The line can be installed next week. We will need to pay one thousand naira to the lawyer and then pay the workers from P&T." I asked, but Mr. Ogunade wouldn't reveal how his friend had procured a phone for us. It remained one of the mysteries of running a business in Nigeria.

I wore my first Trinity House dresses proudly. Whenever a woman complimented me on my clothing, I invited her in to see and buy. I set up a curtain in the corner of my office where women could try on their choices. A few women did come. But selling one or two dresses at a time was not going to make a business. I needed another plan.

While I was waiting for and seeking inspiration for my fledgling business, I took on a new role in the Lagos music world, one that would lead me to unexpected pleasure.

I'd shared in planning the next joint production of Ikoyi Singers and Festival Players. Andrew, one of the committee members, suggested South Pacific. "It's perfect for Lagos," he said. "I'm just sorry that I won't be here to direct the music. But the British Foreign Service doesn't respect our extracurricular obligations as valid reasons to remain in a post, so I'll be moving on." He turned to me. "But you can direct this, Cathy." He showed more confidence than I felt.

"You know, we don't have a bass for the lead, the role Ezio Pinza played on Broadway," Alec Travers, who usually produced the Festival Players' works, said.

Richard, another planning committee member, said, "Someone will turn up in time. Someone always does." Then he turned to me. "But we need you to direct the music." I liked the sense of confidence in the meeting, and I loved being surrounded by all the British accents.

With the encouragement from Richard and the others, I agreed. I'd never been shy about undertaking a task that stretched my abilities. This was no different.

Andrew told me how to order and pay for the rented music scores. I recruited orchestra members. Two instrumentalists who had played for *Kiss Me, Kate* were eager to perform again. And Alec said that a new British musician had arrived in the country. He worked for an insurance company and was an avid golfer, but his second love was playing the bass. He would be a great addition. The music teachers from the German School and the American School completed the orchestra.

The scores arrived while I was in Jos with Beth. As soon as I came back, I gathered the orchestra for a run-through. Carl, the bassist, had sandy hair, a broad smile, and a good sense of humor. He also played well. He was indeed a great addition and an attractive man.

I joined Alec to hold tryouts for the key singing roles. A Frenchman Alec knew had been persuaded to audition. He was perfect to play the French plantation owner, Emile, who falls in love with the American nurse, played by Alec's wife, Helen. A Latin American woman was a ringer for Bloody Mary, the native Tahitian woman. TJ, an American working for Ashland Oil, got the role of Lt. Cable, who sings one of the signature numbers from South Pacific, "You've Got to be Carefully Taught."

> You've got to be taught to hate and fear,
> You've got to be taught from year to year,
> It's got to be drummed in your dear little ear,
> You've got to be carefully taught.
>
> You've got to be taught to be afraid
> Of people whose eyes are oddly made,
> And people whose skin is a diff'rent shade,
> You've got to be carefully taught.
>
> You've got to be taught before it's too late,
> Before you are six or seven or eight,
> To hate all the people your relatives hate,
> You've got to be carefully taught!

This song and the whole show were indeed perfect for Lagos. I loved its explicit denunciation of racism and its embrace of intercultural and interracial romance.

I spent each day at Trinity House, getting the business going. In the evenings, twice a week, I was at rehearsal. As conductor of our little orchestra, I learned quickly how to set the tempo and cue the singers. Our wonderful pianist, Dave, was able to transpose "Some Enchanted Evening" for our Emile, who was a tenor, not the bass called for in the role. Dave also filled in whenever others faltered or I forgot to cue people properly.

The love scenes in the play made me more aware that my love life with Clem had become less exciting now that I knew about his affair. Surely there were possibilities. Why shouldn't I explore? I began looking with fresh eyes at the orchestra and cast members. But I really didn't know where or how to start.

After eight weeks of rehearsal, we presented the show at St. Saviour's. The auditorium sat 150, and we filled it on all four nights in March 1980. The male lead won everyone's heart with his authentic French accent and earnest portrayal of the sophisticated Emile. The duet, "Some Enchanted Evening," sung by him and Helen, was a showstopper. The only hitch was the curtain call on the first Friday night, which we had not rehearsed. It was ragged and confused, with the singers and orchestra completely uncoordinated. By the second night, we had it corrected.

Clem came on that Saturday night. "Why didn't you tell me you were the leader of the orchestra?" he said when I joined him in the hall at the end of the show.

"I did tell you. I said 'I'm conducting the orchestra.' What did you think I meant?"

"I just thought you were singing. Anyway, it was very good," he said. He'd forgotten that he was ever opposed to my being part of the music world in Lagos. Had he only known where it was leading, he would have worried. But he didn't know, nor did I yet. He left for England before the second weekend of performances.

The British ambassador Mervyn Brown had invited the cast for the traditional end-of-run party. His residence was, appropriately, on Queen's Drive. It had a pool, a large garden, and a covered patio.

The compound was spacious enough to host gatherings for hundreds of government officials, diplomats, and business leaders when royalty or British government officials visited. So our cast party of about seventy, made up of the actors, the orchestra, the support crew, and families, fit easily.

My excitement grew as I drove to the residence. This was my chance. Clem was away. I hadn't identified anyone specific, and I had no idea how one starts an affair, but I had a vague desire for sexual excitement and the even more vague thought that I could attract someone.

I'd dressed for the last performance in a red, silk like, sleeveless nylon dress with a draped neckline, from Trinity House, of course. With Clem away, I wore high heels instead of the flat shoes I wore with him to minimize my height advantage.

The party was primarily outside. After the buffet supper and several conversations with others, I approached the ambassador on the patio, where he sat chatting with a few other guests. "I hope you enjoyed the show," I said with a bright smile. "Thanks for hosting us tonight."

"You're welcome. I did enjoy the performance," he said before turning back to the others. I hesitated for a moment. Then I realized he wasn't going to ask me to sit down. I began to edge away, hoping to appear nonchalant, while blushing deeply. That clearly got me nowhere.

To my relief, Helen came up behind me. "Come to the pool with me," she said. "Did you bring your bathing costume?" I was by now familiar with this British phrase.

She led me to the bedroom set aside for the women to change. I pulled on my one-piece blue swimsuit, thinking my moment might have passed now that I was no longer wearing my red dress. We walked to the pool together and slid into the slightly chlorinated water.

A moment later, I found myself next to Carl, the bass player. He was about five ten, solidly built, with a proper British accent.

"We pulled off a good show, don't you think?" he said.

"Yes, I'm very happy. I had a wonderful time, though there were a few moments of worry!"

"You mean like whether Emile would come in on time and on the right pitch?"

"Yes, like that," I laughed. "But you were excellent. You're quite a player."

"I've played for a long time," he said. "I try to stay in shape."

I purposely mistook his meaning, as words I never expected came out of my mouth. "You look like you're in great shape."

"So do you," he said. "Do you swim often?"

"Sometimes but not usually in private pools. I play tennis. What about you?"

"I play golf," he said.

In the gentle motion of the water as other people moved around, our bodies were suddenly touching. "Is your husband here?" he said.

"No, he's away."

"I'm glad to hear it," he said. The pool area was dark, and suddenly he was stroking me in a way I hadn't experienced before. But we were at the ambassador's house, at a party with dozens of others. I had no idea what we would do.

But he did. "Would you like to come home with me?" he said.

"Yes, I would." I could hardly believe I'd said these words. I must have turned a brilliant red. "Do you mean now?"

"Yes. Let's get dressed and leave. The party's far enough along. We won't be missed."

He gave me his address and directions to his house, but I was too excited to make sense of them. "Let me follow you," I said. "Wait for me outside."

Ten minutes later, we met in the parking area. I was glad no other guests were around as I walked past the drivers gathered under the coconut palms at the entrance. "Don't drive too fast," I said, as I got into my car and watched him climb into his.

He sped out of the ambassador's residence and onto Queen's Drive, then up Kingsway. He nearly lost me at the bend at the end of Kingsway when he made a sudden right turn. I sped up, and a minute later he pulled into his driveway.

He escorted me first into the kitchen. He poured himself a glass of red wine and handed me one. "Shall we take these upstairs?" he said.

In the bedroom, he kissed me while unzipping my dress. I finished removing my clothes while he undressed. Although he took the lead as we made love, I felt myself responding actively in ways I hadn't with Clem in the last few months.

"Do you have to go home?" he said later when we were lying quietly.

"No, my son is spending the night with a friend. The other two children are away at school. No one will miss me."

We made love again and fell asleep together.

When I woke up, I was beside myself with joy. We made love a third time. I could hardly believe I was really there, in his bed. I'd done it! I felt like I was walking on air knowing that I was attractive to another man besides Clem, a man I found appealing too.

We went downstairs and into the kitchen for breakfast. "Mrs. Onyemelukwe will have coffee," he said.

"No last names," I said softly and too late, realizing that the Igbo stewards in Ikoyi probably had connections.

"I had a lovely time," he said as he walked me to my car.

"Me too." As I drove home, I wondered if I should have suggested another meeting time. Why hadn't he? Had I been a disappointment to him after all? I'll just take my chances, I thought.

All through the next week, I wondered if I should go to his house. I knew he was married, but we hadn't talked about his wife or when she was coming. Clem was away for another two weeks. Sam was accustomed to my being out often in the evening. He would draw, do his homework, or watch TV. Damian would stay in the house until I returned home.

I drove by two days later just to be sure I could find his house again. I didn't consider phoning; somehow that seemed too forward. I also couldn't imagine connecting with him from my own house, where I felt Clem's presence even when he was away.

I had no regrets, and I didn't feel guilty, but I was aware that a woman's right to an affair was distinctly not the same as a man's in the context of Nigeria and the time. Yet, by the end of the week, I could resist no longer. When I left my office on the Friday after the cast party, I drove to his house. I was in a haze of remembering the pleasure. I rang the doorbell with no plans for what to say. I imagined that he would sweep me into his arms and take me to his bedroom.

Instead, his wife came to the door. Why hadn't I considered this possibility? I recovered quickly.

"I wanted to let Carl know that Ikoyi Singers' rehearsals start again in a week," I said.

She opened the door wider, motioned for me to come into the hallway, and called into the sitting room. "Carl, you have a message."

"Hello. How nice to see you," he said, approaching me. "Won't you come in?"

"No, thanks," I mumbled. "I just wanted to make sure you knew about the rehearsals."

"I'll be there," he said. "See you then."

The next Thursday as I was leaving rehearsal, he walked up beside me. "I'll let you know when my wife is away," he said softly. It was two months before he told me she was in England, and he hoped I could come over. After that, on the rare occasions when her absences coincided with Clem's, we would get together at his house. If Sam was at a friend's house, I would stay for the night.

My life didn't change substantially now that I had started an affair. But I felt ever so much more worldly and more self-confident.

23

Business and School Strains, Second Affair, a Visit

Beth was thriving in Jos. She became ever more adept at accents and had no trouble toggling from the proper English to Nigerian Pidgin to the American accent she'd picked up in the States in 1975–76. In her second year, she took up piano lessons again, started playing the flute, and sang. A year later, she began to accompany chorus rehearsals.

Chinaku went back to Enugu for his final year. I regretted that he didn't have the same chance for music, but basketball and his role as prefect kept him busy. He seemed fine and was getting ready for the university entrance exams that he would take in the last semester. He had to decide where to apply and was leaning toward the University of Benin, where friends had gone.

Meanwhile, I was enjoying music along with my affair.

Six months after we'd finished South Pacific, an American embassy cast member held a musical soiree. Carl and I prepared a piano–bass duet. He didn't have a piano, so we practiced at my house. Both our spouses were in town, so our rehearsals were chaste.

We performed for the audience of friends, including his wife and my husband, at the soiree. I was nervous, not about my affair with Carl, but about playing for an audience, which I hadn't done for years. I barely got through the piece. When I sat down beside Clem again, he squeezed my hand and said, "You were good." If he only knew, I thought.

That December, I turned forty. Clem was away, so I didn't plan a major party. But I invited Carl—his wife was also away—and a few other friends over after the rehearsal for the Ikoyi Singers' Christmas concert. He stepped right into the role of host, serving drinks as people arrived.

For a few minutes, I imagined what life with him would have been like. We would hold musical evenings where we would perform together for our guests. Our children would be at school in the United Kingdom. We would spend vacations in the UK with occasional visits to other places in Europe.

I was thoroughly immersed in Nigeria, extended family, children, and the start of Trinity House. I loved Clem, and I didn't want a change, but I did enjoy the fantasy while the party lasted.

In January of 1981, I was determined to make Trinity House a success. I considered my options for increasing sales. Each of the three department stores had small sections of European women's clothing. I took samples to all three, and one, Leventis, ordered forty-eight dresses. It was a start. The first time I saw a woman I didn't know wearing one of our dresses, I raced back to tell Mr. Ogunade. Leventis placed a repeat order.

We continued selling to women who came into our factory shop. Mr. Ogunade was filling orders for a few women he knew. But these were still not paths to business success. What else could I do? I'd known and admired Betty Okuboyejo, a Scots woman married to a Yoruba man. She held frequent fashion shows and sales where I bought her attractive tops and caftans, all made from Nigerian fabrics.

I had taken dresses to friends' homes to sell, but now I decided to hold a fashion show in the home of a friend. I recruited her and several others from the American Women's Club to be models. Clem loaned me the Freeman Engineering van. With Maurice's help, I loaded it with dresses and racks. I prepared a script for a friend to read as the models paraded across the front of the room. The people who attended were enthusiastic, but the sales were discouraging. We sold only fifteen dresses; we had lugged over one hundred items to the site. "Is it worth it to bring all these dresses and sell so few?" I said to Maurice, who was sweating alongside me as we loaded the clothes back into the van.

Even though sales were few, the show helped women know about our clothes. More customers came into the shop to look and buy. Leventis kept ordering. But we still had too many dresses hanging on the rack.

I thought of the thousands of children who wore school uniforms. I contacted the headmistress of Corona Schools, and she agreed that she would tell parents that I could make their uniforms. When mothers brought their children in to be measured and then came back to collect the uniforms, they sometimes bought clothing for themselves as well.

Then Mr. Ogunade got us an order for factory uniforms, and we hired more tailors. Soon we had two Togolese and two Beninoise, both of whom spoke French, and one more Ghanaian who spoke English. Mr. Ogunade would give directions to the tailors from Benin who spoke Yoruba as he did, and they would translate into French for the Togolese.

But I still operated at a loss for the first two years, and I was getting discouraged. I had to ask Clem repeatedly for cash infusions when I couldn't meet payroll. Even though I held several more fashion shows and the word spread that our clothes were fashionable and well made, I didn't have the retail outlets I needed.

As I puzzled over my business, I had the pleasure of seeing Chinaku finish his five years at Enugu and start university. He'd followed through on his choice of the University of Benin and done well on the exams. I liked his decision. Benin had a good reputation, and it was around the halfway point on the main road from Lagos to the East, so we'd driven by many times. But in September 1981, it was our destination for the first time.

"This is really pleasant," I said when we'd parked inside the campus on a well-paved road. "Look at all the trees and shrubs. What a contrast to Enugu's bare ground."

We walked around for an hour, and I got a look at the cafeteria, the classroom blocks, and the stadium. Too fast—the children grow up too fast, I thought. I was proud but sorry that, at sixteen, he was already making his own plans. With hugs and reminders to take his malaria prophylaxis and to write often, we left him.

Chinaku's letters from university were less frequent than they'd been from his secondary school, but he reported being pleased with his classes. He began his entrepreneurial activities in his second year with the creation of a dance club called Ebony. He would find a location on the campus, buy drinks, hire a DJ or a band, and charge admission.

He repeated the format during the Christmas holidays in Lagos before we went to the East and when we returned, enlisting Aigboje and another friend to help out. He advertised with a few mimeographed signs posted around Victoria Island and Ikoyi. Word-of-mouth was his best vehicle for attracting young people. At the start of his second semester in his second year, we bought him a car so he could go back and forth by himself.

As I struggled with the business and Chinaku entered the University of Benin, Sam started his final year at St. Saviour's. He had loved to draw since he was little and showed a lot of talent. The school was expanding and announced a contest for a mosaic to go on one wall of the new building. Sam entered with a drawing of children of many colors at play, cleverly entwined with the school's name. "I won the contest, Mommy," he said as soon as I walked in the door one late afternoon in early December. "But the builders said the design was too complicated, and they can't use it." He gave me the illustration. I could see he was near tears. He began to cry as I hugged him.

"I love your drawing. Let's put it up here." I took masking tape from the desk drawer and hung it over the piano.

He took the Common Entrance exam in March, just as Chinaku and Beth had done. We listed Enugu as his first choice. In May, we received his letter. He hadn't been admitted to Enugu; instead, he was given a place at Federal Government College Wukari.

"Where?" Clem and I said together. I grabbed a map of Nigeria. Wukari was in the far eastern corner of the country, beyond Makurdi, a town we knew of. Accompanying the letter of admission were two more pages.

"Read this," I said to Clem, handing him the second page.

"Go by lorry to Gboko. From the lorry park, take a taxi or lorry to Katsina Ala," he read.

I shook my head as I looked at Clem. "My Peace Corps friend was in Katsina Ala," I said. "He called it the end of the earth."

"I haven't finished," Clem said. "Take the ferry to cross the river. Find transport to Zaki Biam, and from there, get a taxi to Wukari." I dissolved in a mix of laughter and tears at the thought of taking Sam to this desolate place.

Then I read the final page. "The school is under construction. You will be notified when you should send your child."

"Sam is not going to Wukari," I said. "This is too ridiculous."

"Do you think he can join Beth at Hillcrest?" Clem said. "It's late to get him into Enugu. It would take too much."

"You mean we'd have to pay too heavy a bribe?" I said. He nodded.

I called Hillcrest the next morning. "I am sure we can take Sam. We love having Beth here, and he would be a welcome addition," the principal told me.

Again there was the question of boarding. Joanne had no more space. I finally found a place for him at a private hostel. In September of 1982, as Beth entered tenth grade, Sam started sixth grade. It was wonderful for them to be in the same place even though they couldn't live together.

I continued to have challenges at Trinity House. Mr. Ogunade lived on the other side of Lagos and had to drop his daughter at school. Try as I might, I could not get him to come in before nine thirty or so, while we had the tailors coming at eight. I was unwilling to give up my morning tennis games, so I came about the same time. Even if I had been in the office earlier, I didn't know how to instruct the tailors. I was frustrated when I did arrive earlier, and they had no work to do.

"Why don't we tell the tailors to come at nine or nine thirty, instead of eight, and stay until six?" I said in one of our regular conversations about his late arrival.

"That won't work. They won't agree. They need to leave by five to get to their homes at a reasonable hour," he said.

"Then you have to leave work for them every afternoon, so they know what to do in the morning before you come. It is unacceptable that they arrive and have no work." He did, for a while, but he was inconsistent. He knew, and I knew, that he would be difficult, if not impossible, to replace, so I lived with the frustration.

I was running out of ideas. Fashion shows gave me great exposure and sales of a few dozen items at best, but they were difficult to pull off. The frequent electricity failures were also a limitation. All work on the machines would halt while I sent a tailor to the nearby electricity office to find out when power would be restored. As often as not, the prediction was unreliable. Finally, I bought a generator, negotiated with the landlord to allow me to install it below the stairs on the ground level, and then built a fence around it so it wouldn't be stolen. We had to buy and store diesel fuel. One of the tailors became adept at starting the generator.

I needed help. At a Nigerwives meeting in early 1983, I met Caroline, a young Belgian woman married to a Yoruba man, the son of an old friend of Clem's. She had some ideas for marketing that I hadn't thought of, and I hired her as my assistant.

She visited embassies with samples and contacted other European women she knew, who invited their friends. She brought some additional sales and a few new clients to our showroom and to the fashion shows.

I followed up on a suggestion from my friend and inspiration, Betty O, who'd been selling her clothes at Quintessence, an upscale boutique in Ikoyi, owned by a Swedish woman married to a Nigerian. It was in the fairly new Falomo Shopping Center on Awolowo Road, not far from the Ikoyi Hotel and Ikoyi Club. There were several other attractive shops, the location was excellent, and there was parking. The owner took several dozen dresses, skirts, blouses, and trousers on consignment.

The American Women's Club held a fashion show during the Easter holidays to raise money for charity, and I was invited to participate. Even though we weren't producing children's clothes, I decided to have Sam model. He was so appealing with his long eyelashes, black curls, and winning smile, I knew the audience would love him. He wore a Nigerian outfit matched to a dress worn by my friend Priscilla, a tall, slender, black American with similar coloring to Sam's honey shade. They were a hit, and several women asked for copies. Sales in our showroom and at Quintessence picked up, and we continued to sew school and factory uniforms.

Just as I thought we were turning a corner, a new crisis erupted. The economic collapse in the late 1970s and early 1980s had contributed to substantial discontent and conflict between ethnic communities and nationalities. By 1983, the government announced a search for the two million illegal workers from neighboring African countries. All but one of the tailors disappeared overnight.

"The men will be back. You'll see," Mr. Ogunade told me. And in three weeks, they began drifting back. In three months, they had all returned.

The next crisis was a shortage of currency. Banks were told to close, then to limit withdrawals to small amounts. I asked the Quintessence owner for an advance. She gave it to me. Then I asked again a month later, and she again brought out the cash. But the next time I went into the store, she asked me to remove my clothing. She wouldn't say why. I think she didn't like the idea that I had cash-flow problems. Perhaps my clothes were competition for Betty O's, or the standard of our sewing wasn't perfect. I was very disappointed.

But the Quintessence sales were replaced by a new contract.

"My wife's cousin is the assistant police commissioner," Mr. Ogunade had told me. "They have to order uniforms. Can we sew those?"

"It's worth a try," I said.

"You know it won't be easy. I'll talk to him, but I know he will have to give something to his boss." With the help of a small bribe, we got the business. But even then, Trinity House was barely showing a profit. I didn't know how to improve our bottom line or how to run a business efficiently. I wasn't advertising, and I should have been. I should have had a marketing plan in place before we ever started. I didn't even price well, not building in enough to cover overhead and provide a profit.

By 1983, Carl's wife was spending more time in Nigeria, so he and I weren't able to get together. As part of the planning committee for the next Festival Players' production, I spent time at Richard's house. He lived where Beth had attended nursery school so many years earlier. The pegs I'd admired were still there in the hallway.

Richard had encouraged me to take on the music direction for *South Pacific*, leading to my deeper involvement in Festival Players three years earlier, and we'd been to many committee meetings together. He was always a voice of reason.

Sam was now away at school, so when Clem was in the UK, there was little to keep me at home. In March 1983, I stayed at Richard's when the meeting ended. "It's my son's birthday today, and I called him earlier, but it makes me unhappy that I'm not with him." I said. "He's only twelve."

"Where is he?" Richard said.

I explained where all three children were, and why, and how sad I felt that they were far away.

Richard said, "My wife doesn't like it here, so she's usually away, too—in England." The way he said it made me think that he didn't mind this arrangement and wanted me to know that.

I followed his cue. "Are you very lonely?" I said.

"You could make me less lonely," he said, patting the space beside him on the sofa. He had soft gray hair, balding in the center, and warm blue eyes. I moved to sit next to him. Conversation about Nigeria and music led to embraces and then to his bedroom. He told me he had wanted me for the past three years but had never spoken for fear of offending me.

I was overwhelmed by his comment. I knew that Clem loved me, and we had a satisfying love life. But Clem wasn't in the habit of telling me he found me alluring. And Clem was heavily wrapped up in his business. The thought that I'd been desired for years by another man was so flattering to me that I couldn't put it out of my mind for the next couple of days.

I started going to Richard's house often when Clem was away, sometimes straight from Trinity House and other times after going home for dinner. I still saw Carl occasionally. I felt like the heroine of a romance novel. Imagine me with not just one but two lovers! I was more than making up for my lack of boyfriends in high school and college. The need for secrecy added to my pleasure.

Also in 1983, I was delighted with a visit from my high school friend Ann. She'd always said she would come to Nigeria one day. "I thought New York was hectic and hurried," she said, as the driver negotiated through the throngs of vehicles and people on our way home from the airport.

"And this is the evening. Wait until you see it in daytime."

"You have to be careful in the bathroom," I said as I took her upstairs. "I've had a shock from the faucets a couple of times, and so far we haven't found the problem."

"That doesn't sound very safe," she said gamely.

"Well, just keep your rubber sandals on when you touch the handles. The landlord has promised to send someone soon to look at it."

Fortunately, she didn't turn around and head right back to the airport. Instead, she accepted it as a Nigerian challenge to tell her friends about—the shocking bathroom! We didn't find the cause until a couple of months after she'd left. There was a fault in the wiring of the house at the other side of the duplex. Only when we persuaded the landlord to bring in an electrician to investigate both houses thoroughly was the problem solved.

I took Ann to Jos to see Beth and Sam. While we were waiting for our luggage at the airport in Jos, I saw a man in army uniform pick up my suitcase and walk toward the exit. "Wait," I shouted as I ran after him. He didn't hesitate. He simply dropped the suitcase and continued out the door. I grabbed the bag and walked back to Ann.

"Does this happen often?" she said.

"No, I've never seen someone so daring." We were still shaking our heads in wonder as she retrieved her own suitcase.

Beth and Sam were delighted to see her and show her around their school. "How do you like having them so far from home?" she asked me as we flew back to Lagos the next day.

"I don't like it at all," I said. "But I've become comfortable with it. And I don't think it's harmful. We don't face the stress you hear about teenagers and their parents in the United States. With the children only home for holidays, the time is too precious for arguments."

Back in Lagos, I held a tea to introduce Ann to my friends. I served cucumber sandwiches with mayonnaise on the tasty whole wheat bread I bought at Nassar's Supermarket, and crackers and cheddar cheese, shortbread, and chocolate chip cookies I made. Carol, Jean, Anne, and a few others came. "What do you think of our country?" Carol said.

"Well, I've been to many countries but never one like this," Ann replied. "It's certainly exciting, with shocks in the bathroom and thieves at the airport. And Cathy took me to Sangrouse Market. I have to admit I prefer the supermarket where I shop."

Her last revelation about Nigeria was at the airport when I was seeing her off after her two weeks with me. "Only passengers can enter," said the guard at the entrance to the boarding gates. She held out her boarding pass, but of course I didn't have one.

"Good-bye, Cathy. I'll see you on your next visit to the States. I don't think I'm coming back here," Ann said, reaching out to hug me.

"Wait, I'll come with you to your gate," I said, turning to the guard. "My friend is leaving. I'd like to accompany her."

"You don't have boarding pass. Only people with boarding pass can enter," he said.

"I won't see her for a long time. I want to say good-bye," I said, using my best beseeching tone.

"What can you do for me?" he said, holding his hand out.

I pulled a five-naira note from my purse and gave it to him. "Go in," he said. Ann started laughing as we walked down the long corridor.

"I've certainly seen a lot. I have stories to last a lifetime!"

24

HMS Pinafore, Third Affair, the Olympics

FESTIVAL PLAYERS DECIDED to perform *HMS Pinafore* in the spring of 1984. I helped with planning and played Cousin Hebe, so I had a couple of lines to sing by myself.

After the final performance, I went to the cast party just around the corner from our house on Shaw Road. I looked around the room, got a drink from the bar, and walked over to Bruce, who'd been the captain in *Pinafore*, with his magnificent bass voice.

"That was a wonderful performance. Do you sing a lot?"

"No," he said, shaking his head. "I had to be practically tied down to do this."

I knew he was married, with the embassy, and often had to travel. "Is your wife here?" I said, thinking I could meet her and tell her about Trinity House. As soon as the words were spoken, I knew I didn't ask because of Trinity; I asked because I hoped she wasn't there.

"I'm a geographical bachelor," he said. He was attractive, black, five nine, with heavy eyebrows and strong features. He seemed very interesting and appeared interested in me.

"I guess that makes me a geographical bachelorette," I said.

After a few more moments of conversation, he said, "Would you like to come over next weekend to watch a film? I can ask another couple."

"I'd like to come," I said, "but I'd rather come alone." How had I become so bold, even brazen? We set a date. He promised dinner and a movie. At six thirty on the appointed evening, I drove over, parked in the driveway, and rang the doorbell. He answered within seconds.

"Dinner is ready," he said, showing me into the dining room. We ate quickly. Upstairs in the TV room, he had the video of *Casablanca* cued up and pillows arranged on the carpeted floor where we sat. Fifteen minutes into the film, our feet were touching. Soon we were entwined. I saw Humphrey Bogart on a balcony, and that was the last I recalled of the film before being in David's bed with him.

I drove home three hours later, looking forward to seeing him again soon, as we'd agreed. The second time I went to his house, he had chips and dip for us to eat but no dinner. The third time, we just had drinks. I didn't care. The more time we had for making love, the better. I visited now and then; again I had to fit it in when his family and Clem were away at the same time.

But Clem was spending more time in the UK or in Makurdi, where Freeman Engineering was working on three major projects for the government of Benue State. Even when we were together, he seemed so engrossed in his business that I wondered if we would ever be really close again. With the children growing up and each of us having a separate life, the frustrations of life in Nigeria were more apparent too. Was this how I planned to spend the rest of my life?

I relished the attention from other men, but the affairs were just that—affairs. They were not permanent. There were a few moments when I wondered if I was going too far. I didn't feel motivated by revenge or a need to get even; I was seeking enjoyment and diversion. And I didn't feel any guilt toward my husband. I was sure that he was still seeing other women when he was in London.

Then Richard went back to England. I was going to London every two or three months, sometimes alone and sometimes with Clem, to buy patterns and notions for Trinity House and to get my hair cut. I began to see Richard there occasionally. Carl was still in Lagos but not available often. Bruce would finally leave Lagos just a month before I did.

But that was still two years away. In the summer of 1984, the Olympics were in Los Angeles, and we were going! Clem had surprised and thrilled me by agreeing to my suggestion of the trip. I even planned to see my cousin Louise.

Way at the back of my mind, barely conscious, was the thought that I could see what it might be like to live in the United States again. When I had spent the 1975–76 academic year in Sacramento, I'd been busy with school and children. I also had been totally committed to my marriage, and although I'd been introduced to the women's movement, I hadn't given a lot of thought to how it applied to me. And of course, that was before I knew about Clem's affairs or had my own.

I ordered event tickets, found a three-bedroom house to rent, booked flights, and wrote to Louise. Clem took a minor interest in which events to see. But he took a major interest in the car we would rent; he insisted on a Lincoln Continental. "It's too big. We'll pay a fortune for gas," I said. "Besides, it's too ostentatious."

"We're going to America. We should have a big car," he said, "and I'll drive it."

So in late July, I left Mr. Ogunade in charge of Trinity House, and we flew to Los Angeles. We arrived on the Saturday morning of the Olympics opening ceremony, picked up the car, and drove into Beverly Hills. The children were excited about the huge car, so I didn't complain once we were in it.

We found the house, a yellow, one-story stucco structure with a modern kitchen, spacious bedrooms, and central air conditioning. Overall, it was about the same size as our house in Lagos. The children loved the yard and the air conditioning, and I loved the kitchen appliances.

I'd been too late to get tickets for the opening ceremony, so we watched it on TV. I thrilled to the parade of athletes and was as disappointed as Clem and the children when a commercial came on just as the Nigerian flag came into view. "Nigeria is near the middle of the parade, so it's a natural spot to pause for an ad," I said. "We shouldn't take it personally."

A few days later, we were all in the front row near the starting line at the track-and-field events. "Look, here comes Carl Lewis." I knew he was expected to win or place in the 200 meters. "He's going to walk right past us," I said, pointing down the track.

I pulled my camera from my bag so quickly that coins spilled all over the cement floor. "Give me a pen," Sam, age thirteen, said as he ran past me and onto the track, grabbing the ballpoint I held out.

He held out his baseball cap with the Olympics logo and the pen. Lewis stopped and signed, then looked into the stand to see Beth, now seventeen, and Chinaku at nineteen, standing between Clem and me. He waved to us before joining the other runners to warm up.

A few minutes later, we cheered and shouted as we watched him win. I was proud as he stood on the podium with the gold medal draped around his neck, and the "Star-Spangled Banner" played. I felt again the upsurge of patriotism I'd experienced on seeing the 1976 Memorial Day parade in Sacramento eight years earlier. My emotion then had been more than seeing Beth in her costume. It was the realization that I really was an American despite living far away.

We were again near the front of the stadium to watch Ed Moses win the gold, and again the "Star-Spangled Banner" brought tears to my eyes. Beth dashed onto the track as Moses came past, and she held out her hat and a pen. After he signed, he put his arm around her while I took their picture.

"You Americans win too many medals. No one else has a chance," Clem said to me, half laughing and half reproaching.

"Who's stopping the Nigerians?" I said. "There are some amazing Nigerian sports people."

"Why don't the Nigerians win medals?" Sam said.

"Nigeria has other, more important things to spend money on," Clem said. "Training athletes for the Olympics is hardly a priority."

"But the American government doesn't pay for our athletes' training," I said. "It's funded privately. Couldn't some wealthy Nigerians sponsor the training?"

"They would train their own relatives, whether they were any good or not," Chinaku said. That was sad but probably true. Still, we learned that Nigeria got the bronze in the men's 4x400 meters, and a day later, Clem and Chinaku attended the featherweight boxing event, where a Nigerian was contending. They came back to report the first silver for Nigeria.

I had called my cousin Louise on our first night in Los Angeles, and she invited us for dinner at their home in nearby Fountain Valley. Louise and I embraced a little awkwardly. It had been over two decades since we'd been together. As children, we saw each other for a week or two during the summer, and not even every year. She was nearer my sister's age than mine.

Their attractive daughters, Heather, dark-haired, with olive skin like her mother, was nearly Sam's age. Ashley, blond like Ken, was three years younger. They took our three children into the living room and over to the stereo. The adults followed and sat across the room. Ken served Clem wine and handed me the gin and tonic I requested.

I heard Heather say, "Do you like Wham?"

"Yes, and Lionel Richie too," Beth said, while they looked through albums. Soon I heard "When Doves Cry," as conversation flowed between the three girls and Sam, while Chinaku appeared more interested in the book he'd brought with him than the talk of his younger siblings and cousins.

"What events have you seen?" Ken asked.

"Basketball, gymnastics, soccer, and swimming," I said. "We don't have five tickets to very many events, so we split up."

"The Americans are really taking over and dominating the games," Clem said.

"But there are Nigerians competing, aren't there?" Louise asked.

"Yes, we have a boxer who has taken the silver and a couple of runners in contention," Chinaku said from across the room.

Ken took Clem outside to the patio to grill steaks, leaving Louise and me to get the rest of the dinner ready.

"Your children are so attractive," she said. "Beth is a beauty. She looks like you, except for her Afro and darker color. And your boys are so handsome." Chinaku was now at his full height of five ten. He had an oval face, evenly balanced features, dark brown eyes, and closely cropped hair. Sam's face was a little rounder, more like Clem's, and his hair a little looser, but his eyes were the same color.

As Louise put together the salad, we reminisced about our grandparents' house in Danforth, Illinois, and August and Evalina, tenants on the farm our grandparents owned. She recalled driving his tractor, and I remembered milking cows.

"When were you last in Danforth?" I said.

"For Grandmother's funeral in 1959. I think that's the last time I saw you," Louise said, looking up from the tomatoes she was cutting.

"That was before I went to Nigeria. It was even before there was a Peace Corps. It feels like a lifetime ago," I said.

Ken brought in the steaks. Louise called the children. I looked around the table, wondering how different my life would be if I'd never joined the Peace Corps or if I'd returned to the United States after my two years of service. Perhaps I would have attended graduate school in education, and now I would be a principal or senior administrator.

What would it be like to be married to an American, someone like Ken, and have American children, even white children? I couldn't imagine. But the question lingered. What if I did live in the States, on my own? What if I started over here, maybe in California? What would I do?

I snapped back to reality. Clem was enjoying himself, despite a few moments of pique about American sports superiority. Maybe he could get acquainted with other relatives of mine. Now that we had more money to spend, we could visit the States more often. Clem's business gave us the ability to take a trip like this.

Meanwhile, I had my business to go back to, friends I was close to, Nigerwives, American Women's Club, Festival Players and Ikoyi Singers, and piano pupils. How could I even imagine leaving all that? And Beth had her final year of secondary school and Chinaku his last year of university coming up.

Toward the end of the second week of the Olympics, I told Clem and the children that I had a special place to show them. I found UCLA and signs that led us to Mira Hershey Hall. I made Clem park.

"This is where I spent my two months of Peace Corps training," I said with a grand gesture encompassing the hall and nearby walks and buildings.

"It's the place where I learned the word 'prophylaxis,'" I said with a smile at Clem. "I read *Things Fall Apart* and learned what kola nuts were."

"How old were you, Mommy?" Beth said.

"Can you believe I was twenty-one, just three years older than Chinaku is now? I'd just graduated from Mount Holyoke. I came from my all-girls' college in New England to California. It was amazing and so much fun." I was flooded with warm memories of the time at UCLA and the intense preparation for going to Nigeria. The sight of the dormitory reminded me of Art, the two Bobs, and Dave—all good friends from Peace Corps days.

"I thought you were studying Nigerian history and culture," Clem said, frowning. I assured him I had studied and had fun too.

With the Olympics nearly at the end, we went back to the stadium to watch Sebastian Coe run the 1500 meters. Clem was thrilled for his beloved Great Britain when Coe took the gold, and we all rose for "God Save the Queen."

I was glad that Clem could boast now about the Nigerian boxer and the British runner. I wanted him to be proud of his own country and the UK, his second home. We returned to Nigeria with wonderful memories. I mailed photos to Louise, and we stayed in touch after that.

Chinaku went back to his final year at the University of Benin, while Beth and Sam returned to Hillcrest in Jos, she for her senior year and Sam to eighth grade. With the children away again and Clem traveling often, I was free to continue my relationship with David, improve my business, sing, teach piano, and participate in the American Women's Club and Nigerwives.

Beth began considering colleges during that fall of 1984. Hillcrest had arrangements for their students to take the SATs, and she was in advanced placement classes in French and music.

Would she consider my alma mater, Mount Holyoke? Since she'd shown her first interest in medicine, I'd been careful to leave out the *Alumnae Magazine*, turned to a page with an article or notice about a graduate in medicine, and subtly made sure she saw it. I'd mentioned my classmate and friend Joan with her degree from Harvard Medical School.

She decided to apply there and to Harvard as well. When she was accepted at both, Clem assumed she'd choose Harvard. In fact, he insisted that she should. After all, who in Nigeria had ever heard of Mount Holyoke?

She was in Lagos with us the weekend in April when she had to decide. "Mother, please don't be disappointed," she said as we sat at the dining room table. I was sipping a glass of wine, while she and Clem were drinking Ovaltine. It was time to say good-night. "I think I'm going to say yes to Harvard." She looked closely at me. "You're not mad, are you?"

"Of course not, dear. I'm excited for you. A tad disappointed, but I just want you to be happy with your choice." I gave her an enthusiastic hug, while Clem looked on a little too smugly.

"Wise decision," was all he said.

But what a difference a night made! She bounded down the stairs the next morning and into the kitchen, where I was making pancakes. "Mother, I've changed my mind. I'm going to Mount Holyoke!"

"What happened? Did you have a vision?"

"No, I thought about all the good things you've said and how you still have friends from college. Harvard is so big! I might be lost."

"Yahoo!" I shouted and gave her an even bigger hug than the one of the night before. "I'm sure you won't regret your choice."

Clem wasn't awake yet. "Tell Daddy gently," I said. "He's been counting on Harvard."

When he came downstairs, she was full of tact. "Daddy, I'm going to Mount Holyoke. But I'll go to Harvard for medical school, so don't worry! I'll still have a Harvard degree." And indeed that's what she would do.

25

THE UNITED STATES BECKONS

"MOTHER, I NEED a suit for graduation next month," Chinaku said over dinner of pounded yam and okra soup when he was home in April 1985 for spring break. He wasn't yet twenty, and he was about to graduate from university. Hadn't he just been eleven and heading off to boarding school for the first time?

I looked at my first son, so grown up. He had the well-spaced, dark eyes I'd admired since he was a baby, tight, curly, black hair with a tiny widow's peak in the center of his forehead, and a frizz of hair on his upper lip, which he sometimes shaved off and sometimes kept. He was lean and confident. "Can you really be at the end of your university days? How is this possible?" I said.

Husky, our black Labrador, stirred on the floor beside Chinaku. I remembered getting the dog that Chinaku had wanted the summer he turned fourteen. He'd spent hours that July and August playing with him, tossing a ball, and trying to train him to sit.

Chinaku came with me the next morning to Trinity House to get measured so we could make his suit. But Mr. Ogunade, who was sure he knew how the suit should look, was actually not up-to-date on the latest fashion. I should have made him follow Chinaku's guidance, but instead I let him have his way. In the end, Chinaku said he didn't want to attend graduation anyway.

"It's not because of the suit, Mother," he said. "It's not worth the petrol and the time to drive there to sit in the heat and listen to speeches." I was sorry not to see him graduate, but he was ready to move on to his next endeavor, Youth Service.

Since 1973, Nigeria has had a National Youth Service Corps requirement. Everyone graduating from university has to register for a year of low-paid work in a position assigned by the government. The goal was twofold. First was to help unify the country by sending graduates to regions other than their own with the expectation that they would become comfortable with people from another tribe. The second goal was to provide service to underserved areas of the country. There were camps set up all over the country for the three weeks of preliminary training.

"I am not going off to some godforsaken part of the country," Chinaku had announced during Christmas vacation of his final year at the University of Benin. "I had my years in Enugu. That was wilderness enough. I want to do my Youth Service at a bank in Lagos."

"You should ask your professors. I'm sure one of them can help you," Clem said. "And I'll talk to my DMGS friend who is a banker to see if he has an opening."

Now, in April, Chinaku still had not heard about a place. "Doesn't the Youth Service requirement allow you to do graduate school first? Maybe you should think about that," I said. "Let's at least go to the United States Information Service library and look." I knew he wanted to pursue a master's in business at some point, and the library had catalogs from all the major universities.

"Look at this." I held out the catalog from Harvard Business School the next morning. "Did you know you could take courses in marketing? It says you'll learn about product positioning and pricing. Here's a course in financial management. My God, did you know there were courses like these?"

"Of course I do, Mother. Did you forget my degree is in business administration?"

"Sorry. Naturally, you know. I remember now seeing names like these in your list of classes. But I didn't fully understand what they were about. Imagine learning about sales and marketing. I didn't even know they were different topics."

He gave me a quick synopsis of the difference between those and also between accounting and finance. He was so much more conversant than I was with business terminology, even though I'd been running a business for five years.

I was captivated by what I read and what Chinaku was telling me. I loved the words: market segments, price structures, and product placement. Would I have a more successful company now if I'd known all this?

I did know we had the school uniform market, and industrial and police uniforms, and women's wear. But I'd never thought about which was most profitable or where I could charge more because of high demand or lack of competition. At forty-five, was I too old? Could I go to graduate school? Was I crazy to want it?

I knew Clem would accept it, though he would bluster at first. He'd start with his objections—money, another long separation, not necessary—and then sum them up with his favorite phrase, "Let me put it this way." He would ask if I really thought I could succeed. Then he'd say that if I really wanted it, he'd support it. I knew we could afford it, and I knew he would be proud of that.

Then I thought about Sam. He was thoroughly enjoying his time at Hillcrest. What would he do if I went to the United States for a year or two? Could I leave him in Nigeria with Clem, who traveled often, or with Chinaku, who was living at home?

That night, I gently broached the topic with Clem. "Chinaku and I went to look at graduate school information today," I said when we were getting into bed.

"Is he interested?"

"Yes, but he'd rather do his Youth Service first. And I'm interested too. I think it would be fascinating."

"Why would you want to? You already have a business."

"Yes, I do," I said, "but think how often I've had to ask you for help with paying salaries or buying fabric. I'd like to understand it better."

"We'll talk about it tomorrow," he said, as he turned off his light. I was awake for another hour imagining myself as a student in a classroom again. Would this be my route out of Nigeria? Would it give me the chance to evaluate my marriage? Was that even what I wanted?

The next evening, he raised the topic himself. "So where do you think you could do a graduate degree? What degree would you do?"

"I'd go for an MBA. And I don't know if anyone would accept me," I said. "I'd have to take the entrance exam." I turned to Chinaku, who was reading, his usual evening pastime if he wasn't out with friends. "What's the exam?"

"It's the GMAT. You have to register to take it. You can't just walk in."

I went back to the embassy library a couple of days later, after Chinaku had returned to Benin. I found out where to write for GMAT instructions and sent a letter off the next day.

Yale had a fairly new management program, which I found in their catalog. They accepted students with unusual backgrounds, including those significantly older than the average age of twenty-six or twenty-seven. I wrote. And why not go all out? I wrote to Harvard, Northwestern, and a couple of others too. By the time the children were all home for the summer, I had received a few brochures and was reading them carefully, trying to assess where I might fit.

With a little string-pulling by one of his professors, aided by Clem, Chinaku got a position at a major bank near our house for his Youth Service assignment. He attended a few days of his training and then started working. He'd already had a car for his final two years in Benin, so he lived at home and drove to the bank every day.

One Sunday morning in August, we sat at the breakfast table. "What will you do after this year, do you think?" I said, as he poured maple syrup on his pancakes. He'd been at the job for a couple of months. "Do you think you'll go for the MBA?"

"I think I'll stay at the bank. They've said they want to hire me," he said.

"You'll be the head of the bank before I finish college," Beth said, taking another pancake from the platter.

"No, Chinaku will be head of the country," Sam said, reaching down to give Husky a bite of bacon.

A week before I left to take Beth to Mount Holyoke, I broached with Sam the idea of going to the United States. We were at the dining table finishing dinner of boiled yam and beef stew. "I could go with you," he said. "I wouldn't mind." Tears came to my eyes as he said this; it seemed incredibly generous for him to offer to give up the school he loved.

Sam accompanied Beth to their bedroom, where she was packing. I stayed downstairs to study. I'd ordered practice books for the GMAT when I registered, cleared space on the dining room table, and devoted nearly every free evening to study. As I did the practice questions, I felt some of my ability to excel at standardized tests returning. Maybe I'd be all right. After all, I had been a National Merit finalist in 1958!

The next day, Sam bid a tearful farewell to his sister and the rest of us and returned to Jos. I boarded the plane for New York with Beth. We stayed with Ann for a night, and then headed to Beth's destination, South Hadley, Massachusetts.

"I'm scared," Beth said to me as we drove through Connecticut. "The other girls at Mount Holyoke will be so much better prepared. How will I keep up?"

I hadn't felt this way when I was starting college so many years earlier. Maybe I should have, but I'd gone off to Mount Holyoke oblivious to the fact that other girls knew more than I did, had studied harder at more rigorous high schools, and were perhaps even smarter than I was.

"You have experiences that no other girls have, Beth. And you're so intelligent." I reached over and patted her arm. "Look at what your teachers said about you at Hillcrest. Weren't you valedictorian? And don't forget coming first in the country in the Common Entrance, not to mention getting the merit scholarship for black women."

I had last seen the college three years earlier when I came for my twentieth reunion. Now I was delighted to point out the sights to Beth. Before turning in to park, I showed her the observatory where I'd been a lab assistant during junior year. I found a place to park near Mary Woolley Hall, where a sign directed new students to get their room assignments.

"That's the auditorium where I heard Robert Frost read his poetry my freshman year," I said, pointing into the darkened hall. "And I heard Crick or Watson—I can't remember which—talk about their discovery of DNA, right there."

I wanted to share more details about my time at Mount Holyoke, but I knew Beth was more focused on finding her dorm and her roommate. A blond, blue-eyed student assisting with incoming freshmen gave Beth an envelope with a key to her room. "Welcome to Mount Holyoke," she said with a bright smile. "You're in Porter. Here's the map."

We headed out to the car, drove through the campus, and parked near Porter. On the main floor, I showed Beth the room that had been mine for a year. More memories came back—bridge games in the smoker, waitressing in the dining room, and coffee in the parlor. I remembered friends from that year.

We found her room and her roommate. The two girls seemed to connect right away. After an hour of helping her unpack and store her belongings, I knew that it was time for me to leave.

"I hope you're happy here, dear," I said, holding her close. "I don't like being so far away, in another country. Jos was one thing, but this is too much."

"I'll be fine, Mother, and I'll write often," she said. "And tell Sam to write."

"I'll miss you a lot," was all I could say as I walked out with tears clouding my eyes. I got in the car and drove off of the campus, leaving my memories and my daughter behind.

When I walked into the exam room at MIT for the GMAT the next morning, I understood Beth's fear at feeling unprepared. The room was packed with at least 150 young men. How could I possibly compete against these twenty-one- and twenty-two-year-olds, at one of the most selective colleges in the United States? I calmed down as I started the exam, but I was rattled again when a few men finished the first part before the time was up and left the room. Well, nothing ventured, nothing gained. I'd decided to try, and I would do my best.

A week later, I was back in Lagos and working to make Trinity House profitable. I also began wondering what I'd do with the company if I did go the United States. Caroline, my assistant, and Mr. Ogunade had a hard time working together. She would suggest a style change on a garment or something new to sew, and he would immediately say why it couldn't be done. She did bring in some customers and was an invaluable help for our fashion shows. But the tension between these two was trying, and I couldn't see how they would work together.

Ikoyi Singers started rehearsals for a Christmas concert. I had said goodbye to Richard a year earlier when he returned to the UK. Carl had also gone home. Only Bruce was left.

And then it was holiday time. Sam came home nearly as tall as Chinaku, who was clearly happy to see him and showed big-brother pride. When Beth arrived from the United States a day later, her brothers greeted her as if she'd been gone a year!

"American girl!" Chinaku said. "Do you even remember how to speak Pidgin?"

"Na wattin' you say," she said, getting a laugh from all of us. I couldn't get enough of watching her and her brothers.

With the smell of the palm oil that Mathias used to fry the plantain drawing us, we gathered at the table for a dinner of rice and chicken stew with the plantain.

"There's nothing better than this," Beth said, as she helped herself to more. I watched her cut the slightly blackened edges from her slices and move them to the edge of her plate.

"Do you mean us or the plantain?" I said.

"I think she means the plantain." Chinaku turned from me to her. "You and your burnt pieces. Will you ever change?" He pointed to her collection of her favorite bits.

"You're right! I meant the food!" she said. "Every time I thought about plantain in the last three months, I could remember the taste. It reminds me of caramel and sweet potato mixed together. At least that's what I told my roommate when I was trying to describe it to her."

Sam, next to her, reached out and tried to sneak a couple of her burnt pieces.

"Don't you dare," she said as she pushed his hand away. "I'm saving them for last."

I'd suggested to Clem that we stay in Lagos instead of going to the village for the holidays. His mother had died a few months earlier, and with both his parents gone, I thought it would feel too lonely for him. And I knew Beth and Sam would want time to connect with friends they hadn't seen for the past few months. He had agreed.

So I made a big deal of the traditions. Tired of droopy caserina trees that were poor imitations of evergreens, I'd bought a four-foot artificial tree from departing Americans the year before. Mathias had brought it out and placed it on a side table near the front door. The children helped me decorate it.

We went to the Christmas Eve carol service at St. Saviour's. At home afterward, I brought out the stockings the children had used when they were little. Clem and I went to bed before the children did, but I came down early the next morning and filled their stockings with trinkets, Cadbury chocolates, and oranges.

After a breakfast of pancakes and bacon, Chinaku took up his post near the tree to distribute presents. I loved watching him in his role as first son and big brother. Beth and Sam settled on the piano bench, and Clem and I took our seats on the couch. I was delighted to have the three of them together, with Clem at my side.

But I was also wondering when, or even if, this scene would be repeated. While we celebrated the holidays and family togetherness, I was also filling out my applications. I aimed high—Harvard Business School and Yale School of Management were my first choices, with Northwestern as an alternative. If I got accepted, what would happen after?

We had ordered catalogs from several prep schools for Sam. He pored over them, with Beth and sometimes me, too, at his side. He filled out his applications with her help or mine. I wasn't sure what we'd do when one of us had decisions before the other.

Too soon the holidays were over, and Beth left for the United States, not to return until summer. Sam left for Jos the next day but would come home for spring vacation in April. With a combined sense of dread—what if I wasn't accepted anywhere or Sam wasn't?—and excitement, I mailed our applications and settled to wait for the results.

But I wasn't idle. Trinity House still took most of my attention. Then Festival Players started rehearsals for our next production, *Guys and Dolls*, in late January. Bruce had the male lead, playing the gambler Sky Masterson. Helen was the female lead as Sarah of the Save-A-Soul Mission. I joined the dance troupe of Hot Box Girls that served as backup for Miss Adelaide, played by Sharon, who also directed the dancers.

We practiced the music and dance steps for "A Bushel and a Peck" and "Take Back Your Mink." During rehearsals for the first song, I kept having a feeling of déjà vu. As I drove home one night, I remembered. I had sung "A Bushel and a Peck" for our Minstrel Show at Highlands High School in 1957! It was so long ago and such a different time. Surely students at Highlands no longer wore blackface for the Minstrel Show.

In the years since, I had gained new awareness. Being the only white person in my husband's village made me stand out, and I knew people were looking at me. But it was completely different from being one of a small minority on a white college campus, as Beth was experiencing, or in a prep school where Sam might go. I could see that all the schools made an effort to showcase a racially diverse student body in their catalogs. But I wondered how true the diversity was.

While Sam was home for spring vacation in April, he heard from Lawrence Academy. "What do you think?" I said to him as we reread his acceptance letter. "It says we have to give them an answer and pay a deposit within two weeks to secure your place."

He pulled out the catalog again. "Maybe you'll meet her," I said, pointing to the photo I knew he'd liked of a girl holding her French horn. "Even if I don't get into Harvard, I'm sure I won't be too far away. And Beth will be nearby in Massachusetts." He wanted to accept.

A few days after mailing the check for his deposit, I heard from Harvard—rejected. I wasn't even on the waiting list, as I'd been for Radcliffe several decades earlier. Then Northwestern—rejected.

And finally from Yale—accepted!

"I can hardly believe I'm going," I said to Clem over dinner. "You can't imagine what it means to me that you can afford to pay for all three of us at high-priced schools in the United States."

He raised his arms beside his head. "It's nothing," he said, clearly enjoying his hard-earned affluence.

"It feels a little like Peace Corps. I remember the day I received that acceptance letter twenty-four years ago," I said. "I didn't know then what I was getting into, just that I was leaving the known for the unknown."

"You were a trailblazer, Mother," Chinaku said. I didn't realize he'd been listening.

"Now your mother is doing it again, going off to do an advanced degree at her age," Clem said as he settled into his chair in front of the TV.

Did he have any clue that I was leaving for more than the degree? I didn't think so. I knew I needed to be away from Clem for a while to evaluate my marriage. Did I want to spend the rest of my life with him? We hadn't been separated for an extended period since I'd learned of his first affair in 1979 or had my own affairs. Another continental separation seemed like the right step.

And I wanted a break from the country. I knew Nigeria was not going to develop overnight, or even over decades. I was tired of all the trivial inconveniences that come with living in a developing country. I was tired of the corruption that even I had to engage in to get things accomplished.

At the same time, I knew I could never separate myself from Nigeria completely, and I didn't want to. After all, my children were half Nigerian, and Nigeria's rich culture had been part of me for twenty-four years.

Sharon, who had played Miss Adelaide and taught us the dances in *Guys and Dolls*, and her husband held a Fourth of July party at their house, around the corner from ours. I remembered again, as I had the first time I'd been in their house two years ago, that the location was nearly the same as the Peace Corps Rest House where I'd stayed for my first month and a half in Lagos in 1962. The more I thought about leaving, the more the connections between those early days and today meant to me.

"Remember when you told me you were a geographical bachelor?" I said to Bruce. "We were standing just about here." I gestured to the spot in the living room where we had first connected. His wife and Clem were both away again now, as they had been on that night two years earlier.

"I do seem to recall that," he said. He laughed. "And you threw yourself at me."

"How could I resist such a handsome captain of the Queen's navy?" I pulled a line from *HMS Pinafore.*

I had already told him I would be leaving for Yale in September. Now he told me that he would be departing for Paris.

"Wow. That's smart of our government to send a French speaker to Paris. Are you pleased?"

"As long as I'm serving our government, it's not a bad place to be," he said with a chuckle. "Will you come to visit?"

"I'd be delighted. Just give the word when you're settled."

The day he was leaving, I came home early from Trinity House in case he stopped by. I made sure Beth, home for the summer, and Sam had gone to Ikoyi Club with friends to swim.

At 4:00 p.m., the embassy Land Rover pulled into the driveway, and Bruce jumped out. With a quick kiss and a hug, he said good-bye. "You can write to me care of the embassy in Paris. And give me your address in the United States."

I gave him what I had—the PO box of the Yale School of Management, and he put it in his pocket as the driver pulled out. Would I see him again? I hoped so. I knew the relationship would never be serious, but he was appealing, sexy, and fun to be with.

As it got closer to my departure time, I talked separately to Mr. Ogunade and Caroline about Trinity House. Both were eager to take the company over, but neither had the cash to buy me out. In late August, Clem and I agreed that I'd leave it with Mr. Ogunade. "If you can make a success of it, you can pay over time for the machines and the name. If not, my husband will sell the machines," I said to him.

I spoke to Caroline, telling her my decision. I was sure she would not stay, but I encouraged her to consider it.

Clem came back from his most recent trip to the UK just two weeks before I was due to leave. I concentrated on packing, leaving instructions with the cook, and making sure the house was in order. I didn't want any deep conversation about the pending separation.

I didn't take away family mementos. Maybe I would be back in two years and take up where we'd left off. If not, that would be time enough to consider how to get any possessions I wanted. Somehow, staying away forever seemed unlikely.

Clem and Chinaku took Beth, Sam, and me to the airport on the last day of August 1986. Chinaku had another couple of months of Youth Service Corps work at the bank. Beth, no longer frightened of Mount Holyoke, was eager to be back at school, and Sam was excited to start tenth grade in the United States.

Clem hugged the children. "Be good, and work hard. We'll see you at Christmas." I wasn't so sure, but this was certainly not the time to say so. Beth and Sam turned to Chinaku. As they embraced, exchanged jokes, and laughed together, I turned to Clem. "Thank you for making this possible," I said. Was I being a traitor, not revealing all my inner thoughts as we embraced? No, he had his secrets, and I'd keep mine for now.

The memory of getting on the plane in New York twenty-four years earlier, almost to the day, nearly overwhelmed me. I'd flown to Nigeria with no idea what was awaiting me. I thought I was going for two years and had ended up, two dozen years later, part of an extended family, married to a Nigerian man whom I had loved deeply and probably still loved—I'd find that out over the next two years.

I had three wonderful, biracial children. I had gone through a war. I had learned the Igbo language and customs. I had accepted my husband's affairs and engaged in my own.

Now I was boarding a plane in the other direction, and with no idea of the future, I set out again for the unknown.

EPILOGUE

TODAY CLEM AND I live together happily in Westport, Connecticut. In 2007, he became a US citizen. Boxing Day 2014 marks our fiftieth wedding anniversary. We travel to Nigeria often.

I received my Master's in Public and Private Management, MPPM, degree from Yale's School of Management in May 1988. I have worked for years as a fundraiser for nonprofits in Connecticut and New York.

Both sons live in Nigeria. Our older son Chinaku completed his National Youth Service in Nigeria and has worked in finance for the multi-national institutions Merrill Lynch and Goldman Sachs. He earned a Master's degree from the London School of Economics and an MBA from Harvard. For several years he headed the capital assets division at Zenith Bank – Nigeria's largest. He now has his own financial consulting firm.

Our younger son Sam earned a degree in Fine Arts from the University of Southern California. He ran a clothing company for several years. He returned to graduate school and earned his MBA from Boston University. He is now runs a French TV music channel breaking into Anglophone Africa. He married in 2006, and he and Onome have two children. His older child attends St. Saviour's School in Ikoyi, the same school Sam and his siblings attended to age 11.

Our daughter Beth graduated from Mount Holyoke in 1989 and went to medical school at Harvard as she had promised her dad she would. She became a gynecologic oncologist, combining clinical practice and research with being an assistant professor at Harvard. Today she works for a biotech company as Chief Medical Officer and VP of Medical Affairs. She married in 1993. She and her husband Kelvin have three children. In 2013 Clem and I took the umbilical cord of their youngest, a son named Ikem, to Nanka to bury.

FOOTNOTES

1   http://query.nytimes.com/mem/archive/pdf?res=FA0D13FC3F5F107A93
    C5AB1789D95F408685F9

2   Op.cit.

3   Author's personal archives

4   http://tinyurl.com/kaarrvj, Jet, January 14, 1965, p. 33

5   http://peacecorpsworldwide.org/babbles/2011/04/21/the-famous/

6   http://en.wikipedia.org/wiki/The_Common_Sense_Book_of_Baby_
    and_Child_Care

7   http://en.wikipedia.org/wiki/Northeast_blackout_of_1965

8   http://www.motherlandmusic.com/shakers-rattles.htm

9   Nigeria's Military Coup Culture (1966-1976), Max Siollun, Algora
    Publishing, 2009, New York, p. 59

10 Words: Henry Francis Lyte, 1847, Music: Eventide, http://www.oremus.
    org/hymnal/a/a062.html

11 Government Notice, No. 147/1966, Max Siollun op. cit. p. 63

12 Federal Ministry of Information Release and Government Notice No. 148/1966 as found in Siollun op. cit. p. 63.

13 op. cit. p. 229–230.

14 http://www.kwenu.com/biafra/on_aburi_we_stand.htm, Culled from Biafra: Selected Speeches and Random Thoughts; C. Odumegwu Ojukwu, General of the People's Army, Biafra Lodge, May 30, 1969; published by Harper & Row.

15 http://en.wikipedia.org/wiki/Chukwuemeka_Odumegwu_Ojukwu

16 http://en.wikipedia.org/wiki/Nigerian_Civil_War

17 http://en.wikipedia.org/wiki/Abagana

SUGGESTED QUESTIONS FOR BOOK CLUBS:

1. In 1962 when Catherine joined the Peace Corps, the position of America's engagement in humanitarian endeavors in the world and the beginnings of feminism informed her decision. How did these movements affect her actions and choices? Those of her American friends and family? The Nigerian community?

2. What did you expect the reaction of Catherine's parents to her news about her marriage to be? What about Clem's parents' reaction?

3. All marriages require compromise and accommodation. How much did the difference in cultures add to the need for compromises between Catherine and Clem? Within the extended family? How should we view the affairs?

4. How does race factor into Catherine's position in Nigeria? In America? How is it different for Clem? Their children?

5. How does Catherine feel about her visit to the dibia? Is her skepticism apparent in other encounters? How does the conflict between belief systems play out? When does wishing for a positive outcome become belief?

6. How did Catherine's children benefit from growing up in Nigeria? What did they miss?

7. Catherine found Nigerian life to be completely different, in some ways, opposite, from her life in the U.S. Did these differences make Nigeria more or less appealing to Catherine? How did her opinion change through the course of her years there?

About the Author

Catherine Onyemelukwe grew up in Midwestern United States, where she gained an international perspective from her German immigrant father and a sense of compassion from her American mother. After college she joined the newly formed Peace Corps, which assigned her to teach German at the Nigerian capital's Federal Emergency Science School and English and African history at a secondary school in a rural village near the capital. This began a lifelong relationship and deep connection with the country, its culture, and its people.

Catherine is the cofounder of Nigerwives, an organization of foreign wives of Nigerians; a former board member of the National Association of Returned Peace Corps Volunteers; and a founding member of Friends of Nigeria. She is past president of the Unitarian Universalist United Nations Office. She is a member of TEAMWestport, the town's official committee encouraging multiculturalism.

She holds a bachelor's degree from Mount Holyoke College, a master's degree in elementary education from California State University Sacramento, and an MBA from the Yale School of Management.

Made in the USA
Lexington, KY
15 April 2015